The Madisons at Montpelier

Ralph Ketcham

The Madisons at Montpelier

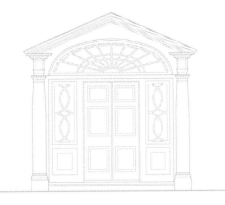

REFLECTIONS ON THE FOUNDING COUPLE

University of Virginia Press

Charlottesville and London

University of Virginia

© 2009 by the Rector and Visitors of the University of Virginia

All rights reserved

Printed in the United States of America on acid-free paper

First published 2009

First paperback edition published 2011

ISBN 978-0-8139-3104-3 (paper)

1 3 5 7 9 8 6 4 2

The Library of Congress has cataloged the hardcover edition as follows:

LIBRARY OF CONGRESS CATALOGING-IN-PUBLICATION DATA

Ketcham, Ralph Louis, 1927–

The Madisons at Montpelier : reflections on the founding couple / Ralph Ketcham.

p.   cm.

Includes bibliographical references and index.

ISBN 978-0-8139-2811-1 (cloth : alk. paper)

1. Madison, James, 1751–1836—Last years. 2. Presidents—United States—Biography.
3. Madison, Dolley, 1768–1849. 4. Orange County (Va.)—Biography.
5. Montpelier (Va. : Dwelling) I. Title.

E342.K47 2009

973.5′1092—dc22

[B]

2008050769

For Kayleigh Moon Ketcham and
Madison Ruth Yohanan

Contents

Illustrations

Preface

THE IMMEDIATE OPPORTUNITY AND IMPULSE FOR WRITING THIS BOOK come from the spectacular restoration of the Montpelier mansion to its appearance as it was during the years of the Madisons' retirement there, 1817–36. In the hands of several owners from the time of Dolley Madison's sale of Montpelier in 1844 through the long DuPont ownership of 1901–84, the mansion underwent drastic remodeling and substantial enlargement. The Madison house, though, remained essentially there under the changes and enlargement, so it was possible to remove the additions and restore the mansion as it had been in the 1820s. Originally built by President Madison's father in the early 1760s and enlarged by his son in two stages in 1797 and 1809, it was, by the time of Madison's retirement from the presidency, an elegant home for the nation's most famous and respected couple. James Madison was revered as the preeminent founder of the nation's political institutions and its fourth president, while Dolley was the widely beloved creator of the "office" of First Lady, suited to the republican political culture her husband had helped found. The completed restoration of their home was celebrated on Constitution Day 2008.

Irving Brant, Drew McCoy, Catherine Allgor, and others have written fully and with insight about this before, and I have depended as well in this account on the last chapter of my biography of Madison, first published thirty-seven years ago and republished by the University of Virginia Press in 1990. I hope now, though, that what we have learned about the Madisons and their era in the meantime and the vivid setting now furnished by the restored mansion and the enlarged understanding we have of its free and enslaved occupants will make possible a fuller and more compelling account of those retirement years.

I am grateful for the help and support of many people at Montpelier: John Jeannes for his knowledge of the mansion itself, Matt Reeves for his archaeological discoveries in the house and on the grounds, Tom Chapman for his genealogical research, and Beth Taylor, the educational director, for her historical understanding of the house and its occupants. I am especially grateful for her careful and exceedingly helpful reading of an early draft of the manuscript. Many others on the Montpelier staff and board of directors—Mike Quinn, Joe Grills, Bill Lewis, Bill Remington, Peggy Boeker, Hunter Rawlings, Lee Langston-Harrison, Pat Mahanes, Allison Deeds, Susan Borchardt, Will Harris, Andy Washburn, Michael Taylor, and others—have helped and supported in many ways. Ann Miller was an invaluable source of information about Orange County history, as she has been for decades. Penny Kaiserlain, Dick Holway, Ellen Satrom, and Raennah Mitchell at the University of Virginia Press have been expertly and congenially helpful. Fran Bockus has, as usual, provided efficient and cordial word-processing help. Erik Chaput's work in producing the index has been prompt, skillful, learned, and cheerful. My wife Julia has been a highly skilled editor and virtual coauthor for the entire project; in fact, it would not exist without her deep and loving participation. I record in the dedication the joy and stimulus that comes from my two grandchildren (and twins to come, probably before this book arrives!).

The Madisons at Montpelier

Return to "Books and Farm, to Tranquility and Independence"

JAMES MADISON, WITH DOLLEY AT HIS SIDE, LEFT WASHINGTON FOR THE last time on April 17, 1817. He was sixty-six; she was forty-nine, and they had been married twenty-three years. Their retirement began when, with all their trunks of belongings, they stepped on board an early version of a steamboat docked at Potomac Wharf. As the boat pulled away from the Federal City and made the forty-nine-mile voyage down Chesapeake Bay, one passenger said that James "was as playful as a child, talking and jesting with everyone on board." He was like "a School Boy on a long vacation." His old friend Thomas Jefferson would, as usual, capture the moment best, congratulating Madison on his "release from incessant labors, corroding anxieties, active enemies, and interested friends." The ship docked at Aquia Creek where the Madisons transferred to a carriage for the rest of the ninety-mile trip home to Montpelier. Now, said Jefferson, would come "return to your books and farm, to tranquility and independence."

Acclaim had accompanied the Madisons' last days in Washington, continued the whole way to Montpelier, and lingered long after. In the parties and tributes celebrating Madison's public service, the semiofficial *National Intelligencer* had pronounced that no statesman could have "a more honorable, a more grateful termination of his public life than that which crowned the administration of James Madison." The city of Washington was thankful for his "wisdom and firmness" that had rescued it from "the tempest of war . . . without the sacrifice of civil or political liberty." Another Washington orator proclaimed that during the War of 1812 under Madison's leadership "our Republic had taken her stand among the nations. Her character established—her power respected, and her institu-

James Madison, by Joseph Wood, 1817. (Virginia Historical Society, Richmond)

Dolley Madison, by Joseph Wood, 1817. (Virginia Historical Society, Richmond)

tions revered. . . . His name will descend to posterity with that of the illustrious Washington. One achieved our independence, and the other sustained it."

Dolley's lifelong friend Eliza Collins Lee wrote of "the gratitude and thanks of the community bestowed on her for having so splendidly filled the highest station our country can bestow" on a woman. "Talents such as yours," Eliza added, "were never intended to remain inactive on retiring from public life. . . . You will [display and] cherish them . . . in a more native soil, that will constitute the chief felicity of your dear and venerated husband." Supreme Court justice William Johnson wrote Dolley that "all who have ever enjoyed the honor of your acquaintance, will long remember, the polite condescension which never failed to encourage the diffident, that suavity of manners which tempted the morose or thoughtful to be cheerful, or that benevolence of aspect which suffered no one to turn from you without an emotion of gratitude." John Adams, not given to unearned praise, told Jefferson that "notwithstanding a thousand Faults and blunders," Madison's presidency "acquired more glory, and established more Union, than all his three Predecessors, Washington, Adams, and Jefferson put together." One can imagine the contentment and eager anticipation of James and Dolley as, between Fredericksburg and Orange Court House, the Blue Ridge Mountains came into view.

Montpelier: The Mansion in 1817

Montpelier in 1817 was very different from the house to which James Madison as a ten-year-old boy had carried small furnishings. First built by his father in 1760–64, this two-story, brick Georgian house of 3,600 square feet, four rooms down and five rooms up, was where James and his three sisters and three brothers grew up (at least four other children died in infancy), and where James lived until the 1790s. After his marriage to Dolley Payne Todd in 1794 and his retirement from Congress in 1797, he built a two-story, 2,000-square-foot addition on the north end of the mansion and, with design suggestions from Jefferson, added a four-column portico in front. James and Dolley, with her sister Anna and son Payne Todd, had separate quarters in this addition, while the senior Madisons (and only James's mother Nelly Madison after she was widowed in 1801) occupied the first floor of the original house. Finally, after Madison became presi-

Montpelier, restored as it was ca. 1820. (The Montpelier Foundation)

dent in 1809, one-story wings were added to each end of the mansion, and the central portion was remodeled to afford a main entrance and drawing room for the whole house.

The space and graciousness of the building were complemented by what twenty years of care, prosperity, and understanding of Age of Reason landscaping could do for the surrounding grounds. A telescope on the west-facing front portico was used to "explore" the Blue Ridge and to "spy the road where carriages and large parties were seen almost daily" coming to Montpelier. To the north stood a columned icehouse, "the Temple," a frequent conversation piece as well as a place to store ice for making ice cream and cold drinks in the summer months. Nearby was an immense mulberry tree, and beyond, silver poplars and weeping willows, which hid a mill and other farm buildings along a stream running down to the Rapidan River. In front, at a gate in a semicircular picket fence, where a gravel path led toward the mansion, was a large tin cup used to measure the amount of rainfall at every shower. On one side of the house was a well of pure, cool water, in use since Madison's grandfather first developed the land nearly a century before. Oak, cedars of Lebanon, boxwood, and willows completed the foreground of the scene across the downward-sloping lawn. Beyond that, rolling fields of grain and tobacco reached toward the Rapidan River and the Blue Ridge twenty miles

Montpelier, 1764, 1797, and 1812. (The Montpelier Foundation and Mesick Cohen Wilson Baker Architects, Albany, NY)

beyond. Behind the house a columned porch, entwined with roses and white jasmine, faced on a leveled, sunny yard with two large tulip trees in the center, surrounded by groves of oak, walnut, and pine shielding a ravine and farm buildings. The steep slope of the Southwest Mountains behind enclosed the scene. To the south were clustered slave cabins, an outside kitchen, smokehouses, the kitchen garden, and orchards of pears, figs, grapes, and other fruit. To the southeast was a formal garden laid out by the French gardener, M. Bizet, in which some visitors saw the horseshoe pattern of the seats in the House of Representatives. The Madisons strolled there with their guests, and we may imagine the always plentiful young people at Montpelier using it for courting, as Jefferson had the formal gardens of the Governor's Palace in Williamsburg a half century before.

Inside, from the vestibule with its semicircular window, visitors entered a large central drawing room. This was sometimes called "the hall of notables," for the many portraits and busts of the Madisons' friends, including Washington, Franklin, Jefferson, John Adams, Monroe, Lafayette, Baron von Humboldt, and others. Portraits of James and Dolley Madison hung among the likenesses. Two other large paintings were *Supper at Emmaus* and *Pan-Youths and Nymphs*. A Persian rug, sofas covered with crimson damask, and bright drapes lent color. Tall, triple-tiered French windows opened on the back lawn, which brought sunlight during the morning and early afternoon into the cheerful, elegant room.

To the right of this central room and a hallway, also hung with works of art, were the rooms of Madison's eighty-five-year-old mother, Nelly Conway Madison. Still alert and active, she lived there separately, attended by her own enslaved servants. One was the octogenarian Sawney, who had accompanied James Madison on his first trip to Princeton nearly fifty years earlier. To the left of the drawing room was a front-to-back passage with stairways and entrance into the dining room. In this hallway, apparently, was the perch for Dolley's pet macaw, Polly, brought from Washington. This "splendid bird seemed happy and proud when it spread its wings and screamed out French phrases," but it frightened the children of the household when it sometimes swooped down on them. The hallway was also the entrance to what came to be called "Mr. Madison's room." At first, after the 1809 renovation, it was a study and visiting room; but as he grew more feeble, it also became his "sitting" room and bedroom. It con-

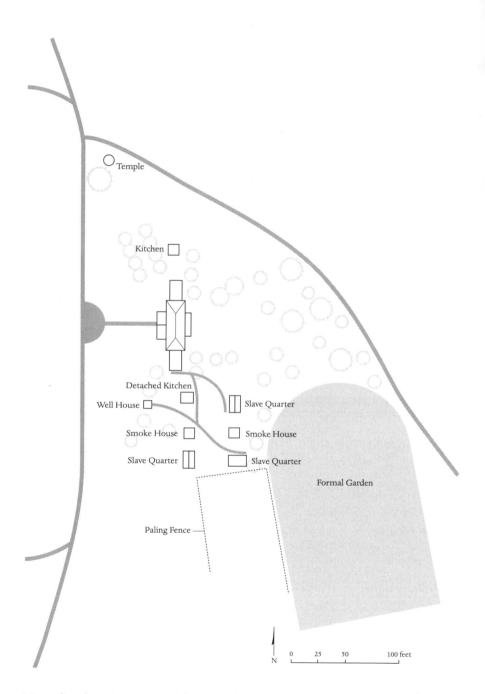

Montpelier plantation, ca. 1820. (The Montpelier Foundation)

tained an iron-posted bed covered with a heavy canopy of crimson damask, brought by Monroe "from the dismantled palace of the Tuileries,"
easy chairs, and a study table piled high with books and papers.

In the dining room next door hung portraits of Napoleon in ermine
robes, Louis XIV, Confucius, and others gathered by Payne Todd in
Europe in 1816. Looking at the portrait of Napoleon with Dolley nearby,
a British visitor once observed that they both had black hair and blue eyes
but the eyes of "the Corsican bespeak the ferocity of his heart; the look
of the American indicates the tenderness, generosity, and sensibility of
her noble mind." He observed further that it was not enough that Americans "elect a Brutus for their chief [James Madison], they must also be
convinced that his partner possesses the soul of a sister of Cato [Portia]—
the sentiments of the wife of a Brutus." Family portraits and a watercolor
of Jefferson looked down on a large mahogany table and two sideboards
covered with family silver. The new one-story wing on the north end of
the house contained Dolley's chamber, a smaller chamber, and a scullery,
while a similar wing on the south end added to the separate quarters of
"Mother Madison."

Upstairs Madison's library of four thousand or more volumes was
shelved around the sides and on stacks filling the large central room looking out over the portico toward the Blue Ridge. Books and pamphlets,
some gathered by Madison and others sent unsolicited to him in a steady
stream, were heaped on every chair and table. Six other rooms housed
transient guests, longer-term residents such as Payne Todd and the Cutts
family, and perhaps play and study space for children. The low-ceiling cellar under the whole house contained a kitchen for Dolley under the new
north wing and another for Nelly Madison under the south wing. A wine
cellar, other storage and work rooms, and probably some living space for
slave servants filled the rest of the bottom floor. Many windows, grade
entries, a hard floor, and perhaps five fireplaces or kitchen hearths contributed to the livability of the cellar.

John Payne Todd

Though by 1817 this large, comfortable house had only three permanent
residents, the former president, his wife, and his aged mother, others lived
there for months at a time, and multitudes, it sometimes seemed to Dol-

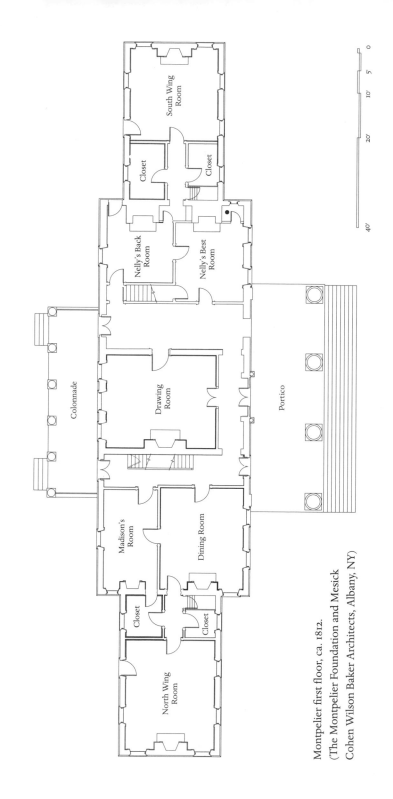

Montpelier first floor, ca. 1812.
(The Montpelier Foundation and Mesick
Cohen Wilson Baker Architects, Albany, NY)

ley, came to stay for weeks or days. One member of the next generation often came and went through the ups and downs of his troubled life. Payne Todd was Dolley's son by her first marriage, to John Todd, a Philadelphia Quaker lawyer. Todd himself, his father and mother, and Dolley's infant second son all died in the yellow fever epidemic of 1793. Of the young family only Dolley and her one-year-old child survived. This son, Payne Todd, twenty-six-years old when the Madisons retired, tried fitfully for a few months now and then to learn the life of a Virginia planter at Montpelier, but he seemed never to feel at ease or at home there, perhaps because it was so uniquely and utterly his stepfather's house. In his youth he had not really been a Virginian but had been popular and attended to over most of the Western world by his parents' well-placed friends.

He had been no more than an ordinary student at the Roman Catholic boarding school in Baltimore to which he had been sent while his stepfather was secretary of state and living mostly in Washington. Dolley had written proudly to her sister that he was "much-admired and respected" and "invited to all the great houses," including that of the famed and beautiful Betsy Patterson Bonaparte, the former wife of Napoleon's brother Jerome, made king of Westphalia. Payne's other excitement was two visits to the Baltimore "palace" of the Spanish diplomat the marquis de Casa Yrujo and his wife, Sally McKean Yrujo, the close friend of Dolley, Anna, and Lucy Payne from their days as dazzling belles in Philadelphia in the 1790s. Payne was already becoming dazzled himself by titled Europeans, courtly society, and wealthy American connections. He failed to fulfill his parents' plan to enter his stepfather's alma mater, Princeton, and instead spent social seasons during the War of 1812 in Washington enjoying Dolley's parties and meeting the important people there. His mother played Cupid ceaselessly but unsuccessfully; her letters to her sisters remained full of hints of hoped-for connections. He then spent two years as secretary to Albert Gallatin while he was traveling about Europe seeking a peace treaty with Great Britain. John Quincy Adams recorded that treated as the "American Prince," he spent more time carousing and playing cards all night with Henry Clay and collecting works of art for Montpelier than attending to business. He returned to Washington at the end of the war uneducated, unwed, and unemployed, but much impressed with his own social standing.

After that, Todd went through the years when he ordinarily would

John Payne Todd, attributed to Joseph Wood, miniature, watercolor on ivory. (The Metropolitan Museum of Art, Gift of Miss Mary Madison McGuire, 1936 [36.73]; Image © The Metropolitan Museum of Art)

have married and found an occupation without doing either. Instead he drifted restlessly from Boston to New York to Philadelphia to Washington to Richmond and back to Montpelier. He sometimes showed his old charm that caused happy reports of him to reach Montpelier, but more often he was making drinking, card-playing, and gambling rounds of hotels and taverns, always professing support and goodwill toward his parents but always troubling and failing them.

During one spree in 1824 and 1825, while his mother sent him money as fast as she could and also cleared $200 of his local debts, his stepfather paid a $500 debt at a Washington lottery house and received "unforeseen" board bills from Philadelphia. Postmaster Richard Bache, out of friendship for the former president who had got him his office, covered a worthless $300 draft of Todd's to keep him out of prison. This proved to be a small part of over $20,000 in debts Madison struggled to pay—without his wife's knowledge—to save her grief and embarrassment. Madison wrote

painfully to the thirty-three-year-old adolescent: "What shall I say to you?
. . . Weeks have passed without even a line . . . soothing the anxieties of
the tenderest of mothers, wound up to the highest pitch. . . . Whatever
the causes of [your long absence and debts,] you owe it to yourself as well
as to us, to withhold them no longer. Let the worst be known that the best
may be made of it. . . . You cannot be too quick in affording relief to [your
mother's] present feelings."

Two years later, again only heroic, sacrificial efforts by Madison and
his friends kept Todd out of prison. James reimbursed John Jacob Astor
$600 loaned to Todd during a New York binge. Madison covered $1,600 in
Georgetown and Philadelphia debts, but calamity threatened when Todd
diverted $1,300 sent him to pay old debts to make another round of the
gambling tables. The defaulted obligation of $1,300 reached Richmond
providentially just as tobacco prices rose for one of the few times during
these years, and Madison's agent there was able to pay the bill. Sales of
Kentucky lands and mortgaging of nearly half of Madison's Orange
County estate met other heavy drafts, while in another emergency Edward Coles loaned Madison $2,000 on Todd's behalf. "His career," Madi-
son wrote the loyal Coles, "must soon be fatal to everything dear to him
in life. . . . With all the concealments and alleviations I have been able to
effect, his mother has known enough to make her wretched the whole
time of his strange absence and mysterious silence." In 1829 Dolley Madison, longing for news "from or of my dear child," heard the worst: he
was "boarding within prison bounds!" He was soon released, but a year
later Dolley's faithful friend Anthony Morris wrote that Todd was again
in prison and that his creditors would release him for $600, which James
promptly furnished. Characteristically, when Todd was in Virginia for a
few months in 1832, he searched for gold unsuccessfully and talked of getting rich quarrying marble. He began to build an eccentric residence,
Toddsberth, over the Southwest Mountains from Montpelier and to take
all-night drunken rambles with his kinsman Colonel John Willis, long
legendary in Orange County. Todd resolved repeatedly to reform himself,
and his mother maintained her faith in him, writing, "Love shown to my
son would be the highest gratification the world could bestow upon me."
Yet he remained, as he confessed on his deathbed in 1852, "my own worst
enemy."

Shortly before his own death, Madison bundled vouchers for $20,000 and gave them to Dolley's brother John C. Payne, suggesting that he might give them eventually to his sister "as an evidence of the sacrifice he [Madison] had made to insure her tranquility by concealing from her the ruinous extravagance of her son." Payne apparently never did this, because he wrote after his sister's death, in passing the vouchers on to his nephew, that "Mr. Madison assured me these payments were exclusive of those he made with her knowledge and of the remittances he had made and furnished her the means of making. The sum thus appropriated probably equaled the same amount." Madison spent, then, at least $40,000 between 1813 and 1836 on gambling debts and other expenses of his wayward stepson, a huge amount under any circumstances but ruinous to a farmer during years of agricultural depression. This financial drain, together with the psychic pain inflicted on Dolley by her son's dissipation, caused Edward Coles, reflecting on the wasted life of his handsome cousin, to declare Payne Todd at Montpelier a veritable "serpent in the Garden of Eden." Another cousin, Mary Cutts, who was very close to her Aunt Dolley, summarized her relationship with her son: "Mrs. Madison's life was not exempt from trials. Her son, J. P. Todd, whom she loved so devotedly—and who returned her affection with the same ardor was frequently a drawback to her happiness. . . . On his return to America [in 1815] his mother continued her indulgences; he had no profession, was a favorite in society and with foreign tastes—he lost the power of applying himself to any pursuit, became a bonvivant, never married—outlived his mother nearly two years, and died from the effects of typhoid fever taken in Boston."

Madison Family Visitors

Most of the visitors to Montpelier, of course, brought more joy and less grief than did Payne Todd. Many of Madison's own relatives, especially the abundant crop of nieces and nephews, came often and stayed long at what was for them still the family home. Madison's sister Nelly Conway Hite (1760–1802) lived in northern Virginia. His sister Frances Taylor Rose (Fanny, 1774–1823) and her husband, Dr. Robert H. Rose, married at Montpelier in 1801 and lived at Litchfield in Orange County raising a large family of seven boys and four girls before they moved south to Huntsville, Alabama, in 1819. Fanny's youngest child, James Madison Rose, born in

Orange about the time of the Madisons' retirement and sixty-five years his uncle's junior, died in the Alamo three months before his uncle's death. The Madisons therefore saw little of these families during retirement.

The children of his deceased brothers Francis (1753–1800) and Ambrose (1755–1793), though, had largely remained in Orange and Madison counties and looked to their uncle for guidance and sometimes support. Francis, sometimes called Frankey in the family, had married Susannah Bell (ca. 1755–1834) in 1772 and lived on a large farm, Prospect Hill, in Madison County. Of his nine known children, four girls and five boys, most lived in Madison or Orange counties, and all but one would have been alive in 1817. The eldest, James Francis Madison, born in 1776, at the beginning of James Madison's public life, was forty years older than James Madison Rose, born near the end of his uncle's career. Married and raising families of their own by then, they seem to have had little to do with life at Montpelier.

The most congenial of James's relatives was Ambrose's daughter Nelly (1780–1862). Her husband, Dr. John Willis, had died in 1812, leaving her to raise her two children at Woodley, the plantation she inherited from her father, a short drive through the woods over the Southwest Mountains (past Toddsberth) from Montpelier. Nelly Willis, a good-natured, sensible, outgoing, unaffected woman of the kind that has always made the Virginia countryside proud, was at Montpelier for every family occasion. She was with her uncle, having breakfast, when he died in 1836. Her own home was so congenial to her uncle that the large tree in her front yard was called "the President's oak," because his horse was so often tied there while he visited inside.

The most numerous and closest other connections in Orange were the children and grandchildren of Madison's sister Sarah (1764–1843) and his brother General William Madison (who earned his militia title during the War of 1812), both of whom outlived the former president. Sarah married Thomas Macon (1765–1838) at Montpelier in 1790. He was the substantial proprietor of the neighboring plantation, Somerset, just south of Montpelier on the road to Charlottesville. Sarah, generally referred to as "Mrs. Macon," is often mentioned in Dolley's accounts of those present at Montpelier dinners and celebrations. Her family of at least nine children were doubtless among those who often visited their grandmother and uncle at Montpelier. One of them, daughter Lucie (1794–1871), married in

1811 Reuben Conway, the son of James Madison's cousin, childhood play-mate, and longtime congenial friend Catlett Conway (1751–1827), whose large plantation, Greenwood, was nearby in Orange County. By 1782 it contained 2,540 acres and was worked by twenty-five slaves. This double connection of the Madison and Conway families—Lucie Macon and Reuben Conway were second cousins—united young people each close in multiple ways to the squire of Montpelier. The Madisons' relations with Sarah and her family seem always to have been warm and congenial.

The same congenial closeness was not always the case with the equally large family of brother William Madison (1764–1843). Enervating efforts during the War of 1812 went unrecognized, frustrating William's last chance to gain the fame and fortune he had hoped for and his brother had helped him pursue in his youth. (Perhaps William blamed his lack of success in part on his brother in the White House.) By the time of his first wife's death of tuberculosis in 1832, nine of his children had also died, mostly of tuberculosis: four between 1809 and 1813 at ages thirteen, twenty, twenty-two, and twenty-three, and five more from 1821 to 1833, all less than thirty years of age. Only one son, Ambrose (1796–1855), and one daughter, Rebecca Madison Chapman (1785–1861), survived their father. Furthermore, his plantation, Woodberry Forest (several miles north of Montpelier on the road to Culpeper), suffered severely in the agricultural depression. He became dissatisfied with the settlement of his father's and mother's estates and presented unwarranted pension claims for his Revolutionary War service, which his brother apparently refused to endorse. In a further complication, after his first wife's death William married Nancy Jarrell, the mother, apparently, of William's illegitimate son, Jack Madison, who had been born about two decades earlier. Though William was mentioned occasionally as among the guests at Montpelier and seems not to have come into open conflict with the rest of the family before James Madison's death, an unmistakable uneasiness existed.

The former president nonetheless continued his special attentions to William's son Robert, whom he had put through Dickinson College during the War of 1812. There Robert, a serious and promising student, between stints of military service when British forces operated in upper Chesapeake Bay, took sophisticated legal instruction under his uncle's radical-thinking friend Thomas Cooper. In 1816, in a wedding celebrated at Montpelier, Robert married a beautiful Petersburg girl, Eliza Strachan.

They had three sons (one named for Cooper), and Robert served in the Virginia Assembly. He succumbed to the dreaded consumption in 1828, however. Madison provided in his will for the education of the three boys, the last of whom, another Robert, born the year of his father's death, went to the University of Virginia medical school, served as a Confederate army surgeon, and became the personal physician of General Robert E. Lee after the Civil War. Robert had married a granddaughter of Madison's favorite niece, Nelly Conway Willis, at Woodley in 1853.

Payne and Cutts Family Visitors

Dolley Madison had three sisters and three brothers who survived with her the terrible yellow fever epidemic in Philadelphia in 1793. Little is known of the two older brothers, but Dolley remained close to and anxiously concerned about her other siblings and their children the rest of her life. The four renowned Payne sisters—Dolley, Lucy, Anna, and Mary—adorned and enlivened Philadelphia society in the 1790s and Washington society during the Jefferson and Madison administrations. At age sixteen Lucy (1777–1846), ten years younger than Dolley, married eighteen-year-old George Steptoe Washington (1775–1808), the wealthy nephew and ward of the president. At their Harewood estate near what is now Charles Town, West Virginia, Dolley Payne Todd and James Madison were married the next year. Belle Grove, the home of Madison's sister Nelly and her husband, Isaac Hite, long a business and political colleague of his brother-in-law, was also in the vicinity, giving the region a strong connection with Montpelier residents. Lucy lived at Harewood, raising her family of four boys, until her husband died, when she largely moved to Washington with her children, age twelve, ten, nine, and three in 1809, to live at the White House with the Madisons. She remarried in the White House in 1812, to Supreme Court justice Thomas Todd of Kentucky (1765–1826; not related to Dolley's first husband John Todd). Lucy was wise to choose him, Dolley wrote Anna, "in preference to the gay flirts who courted her." Fatigued from tense and frustrated efforts to avoid war in 1812, the president found that laughing with Lucy, as she played "a bit of a fool," was "as refreshing as a long walk." Lucy did not see the Madisons much during the first years of their retirement, for she was in Kentucky raising another family, this time of two boys and one girl. When Justice Todd died in 1826,

Lucy resumed her visits to Montpelier, often with some of her children or grandchildren. Lucy Payne Washington Todd, perhaps the prettiest and most fun-loving of the social, vivacious sisters, provided welcome excitement and even frivolity at Montpelier just as she had in the White House.

John C. Payne, fourteen years younger than Dolley, after false starts at seafaring and military life and some bouts of alcoholism and mental illness, had married and tried to settle down on a small farm in Orange, secured with the Madisons' help. The father of six girls and two boys, he supplemented his income by acting as Madison's secretary and amanuensis. His fine, distinctive handwriting appears everywhere in Madison's papers, evidence of the hours he spent copying, arranging, and taking dictation. So close was his family to the Montpelier family that upon James's death, Dolley adopted John's daughter Annie, seventeen at the time, as her own, only formalizing what had already become a fond attachment. John Payne never fully overcame his alcoholism and near poverty. Dolley, nonetheless, had written in 1834 to a niece that "your Unkle Jno. Payne . . . is an honorable & industrious man, with Eight children: Dolley, Lucy, & Anna, the last, lives entirely with me & the others are much with me also. They are very amiable girls, rather pretty, & so far, have good plain educations. The names of the three younger, are Mary, Louisa, and Susa. The boys are William Temple and James Madison." John moved his family, minus Annie, first to Kentucky and then to Illinois, in 1837, where knowledge of them largely disappears. We know only that his son William Temple Payne, then age twenty-one, returned to Montpelier in 1841 as farm manager during Dolley's earnest but failing attempts to make it prosper. He died two years later.

Dolley's youngest sister, Mary (1781–1808), married in 1800 John G. Jackson (1777–1825), a congressman and fervently republican political colleague of James from northwestern Virginia. They had two children before Mary's early death in 1808, the younger of whom, Mary Jackson Allen (1805–1881), became, after her father's death in 1825, a virtual ward of her Aunt Dolley, often visiting her at Montpelier and then in Washington as long as Dolley lived.

Anna Payne (1779–1832) was fourteen when she became virtually Dolley's daughter after the 1793 yellow fever epidemic in Philadelphia. She lived with the Madisons in Philadelphia, at Montpelier, and in Washing-

Anna Payne Cutts, by Charles Bird King. (Virginia
Historical Society, Richmond)

ton, where, Aaron Burr reported to his daughter Theodosia in 1802 echoing the gay, party-filled days the girls had shared in Philadelphia, that
"Anna [Payne] is a great belle." In 1804 she married Richard Cutts of Maine
and began raising her own family, living partly in New England. After 1817
she and her six children lived in Washington, in a house partly owned by
the Madisons, while Richard Cutts was supported by his job as second
comptroller in the Treasury, to which his brother-in-law had appointed
him. His efforts to recoup his shipping fortune, lost during the War of
1812, failed, however, carrying away as well about $5,000 loaned by Madi-
son. He went through bankruptcy and even to debtor's prison for a time.
Only desperate maneuvers saved their house on Lafayette Square, which
ended up in Madison's hands and became Dolley's residence when she
returned to Washington after her husband's death. For weeks at a time
during the hot summers, Anna and the children came to Montpelier. The

older boys, James Madison and Thomas, reached maturity during the 1820s, while the two girls, Dolley and Mary, were busy children running about the house and grounds after their Aunt Dolley.

The most promising of the Cutts children, however, was the youngest, another Richard, born in 1817, who became the favorite of the playful old man he called "Uncle Madison." When Richard was about ten years old, James, whose fingers were "a little sore," dictated to Dolley a letter addressed to "Richard Cutts, Tobaco Planter, Washington." With mock seriousness Madison asked the "experienced" planter whether he wanted his "three-ounce [crop] . . . made into pigtail or twist for chewing—or if you think it best to make it into snuff," which his Aunt Dolley had used regularly. Madison urged the boy to bring "Miss Modesty, her sister taciturnity, and above all, their cousin good humour" on his next visit, but "you need not trouble to bring your appetite for bacon and chicken—nor for warffle butter, custard, nor honey—particularly you'd better leave behind your relish for grapes, figs, and water melons." More seriously, harking back to his own education nearly seventy years earlier, the former president advised young Richard to read the *Spectator* papers of Joseph Addison, "the first rank among the fine writers of the age." James instructed Richard to read Addison's papers twice, to form the most correct and natural style (Benjamin Franklin had advised young students similarly), and to follow Jonathan Swift's dictum that good sentences consisted of "proper words in their proper places." Madison hoped his nephew would someday employ his pen "for the benefit of others and for your own reputation." He sent a copy of the *Spectator* "as a token of all the good wishes of your affectionate uncle."

This young man became Dolley Madison's helpful neighbor and dependable adviser after she moved back to Washington in 1837. In 1845 he married Martha Jefferson Hackley (named for her aunt, Thomas Jefferson's daughter), and they produced a distinguished line of lawyers, engineers, and army officers. The oldest Cutts boy, James Madison, married Ellen O'Neale in 1834, and came on his wedding journey to Montpelier, where Dolley Madison arranged a huge lawn party for the newlyweds. Ill and barely able to appear on the portico, the eighty-three-year-old former president mustered strength to raise his wineglass in a toast to the bride but then, supported by a servant, returned to his couch and fireside. Mary Cutts, always fervently devoted to the Madisons and the author of the most authentic, intimate sketch known of their family life and of Montpelier, wrote that her "Uncle Madison" was "a dear lover of fun and children" who often told anecdotes of his nieces and nephews with a swift transition "from sternness to brilliant mirth" delightful to his listeners. Mary's sister, Dolley Madison Cutts, also unwed, shared Mary's constant attention to the elder Dolley and also the elder's constant attention to their affairs of all kinds. During the twenty years of retirement, Montpelier was a congenial place for reminiscing adults, but it was also alive with the joys and vicissitudes of growing children and maturing adolescents, who, as had been true throughout their lives, kept James and Dolley in touch with youth in a way remarkable for a couple themselves childless.

James K. Paulding's Impressions

As the Madisons settled into their retirement routine at Montpelier in the summer of 1818, James K. Paulding came to gather information for a biography of the retired president. Madison had appointed Paulding in 1815 to the newly created Board of Navy Commissioners, after which the two men enjoyed a warm friendship. Madison also appreciated his vigorous patriotism and satirical critiques of England during the War of 1812. In their easy companionship and conversations, Paulding said, "I have several times made the President laugh in a manner altogether unbecoming to a great man." "This same Chief Magistrate," Paulding continued in his reminiscences, "is a confounded sensible fellow, and talks about every thing like a professor. He is generally grave, but of an evening when the business of the day is done, he loves to talk about this that and the other thing, and enjoys a joke hugely. . . . The other day I dined [at the President's House]. The old squire was in a good humour, and gave us some famous Claret and Champagne; whereupon Speaker [Henry] Clay, the little plump Vice-President [John] Gaillard, and General [John] Mason, and I, did get as it were a little beyond the line of gravity becoming great statesmen."

In a reflective commentary on "Our Presidents" written after he had been secretary of the navy under Martin Van Buren and near the end of his own career as one of the New York "Literati" writers, Paulding described his July 1818 visit to Montpelier of "some weeks . . . during which few visitors made their appearance, and I had him all to myself":

The Mansion at Montpelier, is situated in Orange County Virginia, at the foot of The South Mountain, I think it is called. The ground rises some-what abruptly in the rear, and in front is a broad level field of nearly a mile, bounded by a Forest, beyond which at a distance of some fifteen or twenty miles, the view is closed by the Blue Ridge, which forms a beautiful termination to the wide plain. The Estate comprised about Five thousand Acres; the House was of Brick, consisting of a centre with a fine Doric Portico, and two wings, one of them appropriated to the mother of Mr. Madison then upwards of ninety Years of age. The old Lady seldom joined the family circle but took her meals by herself, and was visited every day by Mr. & Mrs. Madison whom I used often to accompany. She was quite cheerful, in full possession of her faculties, and lived some Years after my visit.

Our daily routine, with little variation, except Sundays was as follows. After breakfast, between seven & eight, I took my Segar and Seated myself on the western Portico, looking towards the Blue Ridge, while Mr. Madison would commence a conversation, sometimes on Public Affairs, in connexion with his previous Public Life, in which he spoke without reserve, & from which I gathered lessons of wise practical experience; sometimes on Literary and Philosophical subjects; and not infrequently—for he was a capital story teller—he would relate anecdotes highly amusing as well as interesting. He was a man of wit, relished wit in others, & his small bright blue eyes would twinkle most wickedly, when lighted up by some whimsical conception or exposition [?].

By and bye, the Horses were brought, and we set out on a tour to visit the different parts of the Estate where farming operations were going on. As he never encumbered himself with a servant on these occasions, it fell to his lot to open the Gates, which he did with a crooked stick, without dismounting, a feat which required no little skill. He undertook to teach me, and in time I acquired something of the art, but never could arrive at his matchless dexterity in the maneuvres of the crooked stick.

Mr. Madison had undertaken to substitute Beer in the room of whiskey, as a beverage for his slaves in Harvest time, and on one occasion, I remember, stopt on a wheat field where they were at work to enquire how they liked the new drink—"O! ver fine—vere fine masser" said an old grey head—"but I tink a glass of whiskey vere good to make it wholesome." He was excessively diverted at this supplement of the old fellow, and often made merry with it afterwards. On another occasion we rode to a distant

part of the Estate bordering on the Rapidan River—I think it is called—a
ferocious stream, and subject to occasional inundations. There had been a
very heavy shower the day before; the river had overflowed its banks, and
covered two or three acres of fine meadow with gravel some inches deep,
so that it was completely spoiled. "Why this is a bad business Tony [possibly
the Anthony for whom Madison had lanced a boil on the arm in 1777, reliev-
ing swelling and high fever, perhaps saving his life]," said Mr. Madison. "Yes
masser ver bad—ver bad indeed"—answered Tony—then scratching his
grey head, he added with perfect simplicity, "I tell You what Masser—I tink
The Lor amighty by and large, he do most as much harm as good."

In the course of these daily rides Mr. Madison's conversation was
various,—sometimes didactic, sometimes scientific, and at others diverging
to lighter Topics. He excelled in Anecdote, and his memory was stored with
good things of past times gathered in the course of long experience. He
gave me the private history of many important transactions, from which I
gathered that many great events arise from little causes, and that as relates
to the real motives, and moving causes of Public measures . . .

I have always considered Mr. Madison, as emphatically the *Sage* of his
time. He had not perhaps so much genius as Mr. Jefferson, but in my opinion his mind was more consummate and his faculties more nicely balanced
than those of his predecessor, who though justly called the Great Apostle of
Democracy, I think sometimes carried his doctrines to the verge of Political
Fanaticism. Mr. Madison had the power of condensing in his speeches &
writings in great perfection, though he did not always exercise it, for such is
the appetite of the People of this country, for long speeches, and discussions, that they don't like to swallow the truth in an incontrovertible axiom
but prefer it strongly diluted with verbiage. . . .

Mr. Madison died at a great age, and one of the last acts of his Life, was
to sit up in his Bed while Durant [Asher Brown Durand] drew the likeness
which is now in my possession. The likeness is admirable, and exhibits all
the characteristic indications of extreme old age, venerable though to the
eye, and pleasant in the contemplation. He died without pain and without
fear. His wife is still living while I write, a model of all that is kind hearted,
gentle, and blameless, in woman. I never heard her utter an unkind word,
or saw her do an unkind act to any human being. If she was ever out of
temper, it never appeared; and if she ever disliked any one, it only showed
itself in acts of Kindness.

Paulding's account of his visit to Montpelier, like many documents about the Madisons there, has a complicated and interesting history. The manuscript was sent by Paulding's literary executors in the 1850s to William Cabell Rives for use in his biography of Madison. By then Paulding's son, William Irving Paulding, had added, without acknowledgment and in a flowery style unlike his father's crisp expression, the last paragraph to his father's recollections, perhaps thinking that the sketch required some Victorian piety about Madison's death and about the sterling character of his widow. The sketch remained unknown in Rives's papers at the Library of Congress until its publication in 1959.

Daily Life at Montpelier

Dolley Madison, of course, was fully occupied both managing the plantation household and attending to the many overnight as well as daytime visitors. This required supervision and care of the perhaps two or three dozen slaves who worked in or near the mansion as personal servants, housekeepers, cooks, food servers, gardeners, and other skilled workers. One of the most trusted was James's valet, Paul Jennings. Another was Mother Madison's personal servant, Sawney, a sometimes overseer of other slaves who had been at Montpelier since the 1760s. Another intimate slave, Dolley's maid and household servant, Sukey, was both a blessing and a problem for her mistress. In Dolley's service at least since they had fled the burning White House together in 1814, she was Dolley's "most efficient House servant," as Dolley told Richard Cutts, but also was apparently inclined to carelessness and even theft. Dolley wrote Anna Cutts in 1818 that "Sucky has made so many depridations on everything in every part of the house, that I sent her to Black Meadow [one of the satellite farms and quarters at Montpelier] last week but find it terribly inconvenient to do without her, & suppose I shall take her in again, as I feel too old to bring up another—so I must even let her steal from me, to keep from labour myself." Sukey seems to have reformed, and Dolley became reconciled; Sukey remained in her service, apparently valued and loyal, for nearly thirty more years.

Dolley's kitchen under the "new" north wing and Nelly Madison's under the south wing were part of largely separate households maintained for the two women. Each had outside access where servants could come and go to the slave cabins, smokehouses, kitchen garden, outside kitchen, and workshops clustered just south of the mansion. A slave community of household servants of perhaps two dozen persons, including children and disabled or elderly, lived here both close-knit itself and intertwined with life in the mansion. Three or four other slave clusters existed around the plantation housing field hands and their families, less attached to life in the mansion than those housed close to it.

At two in the afternoon, James and Dolley often visited the rooms of Nelly Madison, who usually took her meals separately. The old woman, nearly one hundred when she died in 1829 but no more marked with age than her son, was seldom sick or in pain and, except for some deafness, retained full command of her senses. She passed her time knitting and reading, visiting with her many grandchildren and great-grandchildren (dozens would have been in the vicinity in the 1820s), and was always glad to talk for a while with her son's many guests. She was, Mary Cutts reported, "a lady of excellent education, strong mind and good judgment, action, and will, . . . [with] an interest in modern events." She adored and appreciated Dolley Madison, saying to her one time, "You are *my* Mother now, and take care of me in my old age."

She sat on a couch in the center of the large, west-facing room, opening off the art-covered south passage, that had probably been the main dining and living room of the mansion since it had been built ca. 1760 and was thus familiar to James Madison since his boyhood. Here the aged woman greeted her guests and talked with them, after her dinner but before theirs. A table in front of her held her Bible, prayer book, and knitting. Mary Cutts recorded as a childhood "earliest recollection" seeing "Madam de Neuville (wife of the French Minister) sitting near this old lady talking of the French Revolution and darning a camel's hair shawl." It was probably during this visit that Madame de Neuville made the drawing of Montpelier that best shows its appearance early in the retirement years.

After this filial call, the Madisons dined with their company at about four o'clock, in a meal that usually lasted two hours. Visitors to Montpelier in 1825 reported that at dinner food was "not only abundantly, but handsomely provided; good soups, flesh, fish and vegetables, well cooked—desert and excellent wines of various kinds. . . . The table is very ample and elegant, and somewhat luxurious, . . . it seems to be [Madison's] habit

Montpelier, 1818, watercolor by Baronne Anne Neuville de Hyde. (Musée national de la Coopération franco-américaine, Blérancourt, France; Réunion des musées nationaux/Art Resource, NY)

to pass about an hour, after the cloth is removed, with a variety of wines of no mean quality." At the table, Margaret Bayard Smith reported in 1828, "Mr. Madison was the chief speaker. . . . He spoke of scenes in which he himself had acted a conspicuous part and of great men, who had been actors in the same theatre. . . . Franklin, Washington, Hamilton, John Adams, Jefferson, Jay, Patrick Henry and a host of other great men were spoken of and characteristic anecdotes of all related. It was living History!" Only the presence of strangers, Mrs. Smith wrote, could make "this entertaining, interesting and communicative personage . . . mute, cold, and repulsive." "After dinner," she continued, "we all walked on the Portico . . . until twilight, then retreated to the drawing room, where we sat in a little group close together and took our coffee while we talked. Some of Mr. Madison's anecdotes were very droll, and we often laughed very heartily. . . . When I retired for the night [at ten o'clock], I felt as if my mind was full to overflowing, . . . as if I had feasted to satiety."

The fullest account of the congenial hospitality of the Madisons at Montpelier recorded an earlier visit of Mrs. Smith and her husband, Samuel H. Smith, a longtime Washington newspaper editor and colleague of Dolley's husband. They arrived on a hot August afternoon while Madison was president and shortly after the addition of "Dolley's wing" on the north end of the mansion. According to Mrs. Smith's diary,

It was near five o'clock when we arrived, we were met at the door by Mr. Madison who led us in to the dining room where some gentlemen were still smoking segars and drinking wine. Mrs. Madison enter'd the moment afterwards, and after embracing me, took my hand, saying with a smile, I will take you out of this smoke to a pleasanter room. She took me thro' the tea room to her chamber which opens from it. Everything bespoke comfort, I was going to take my seat on the sopha, but she said I must lay down by her on her bed, and rest myself, she loosened my riding habit, took off my bonnet, and we threw ourselves on her bed. Wine, ice, punch and delightful pineapples were immediately brought. No restraint, no ceremony. Hospitality is the presiding genius of this house, and Mrs. Madison is kindness personified. . . . The house seemed immense. It is a large two story house of 80 or 90 feet in length, and above 40 deep. Mrs. Cutts soon came in with her sweet children, and afterwards Mr. Madison, Cutts, and Mr. Smith. The door opening into the tea room being open, they without ceremony joined their wives. They only peeked in on us; we then shut the door and after adjusting our dress, went out on the Piazza—(it is 60 feet long). Here we walked and talked until called to tea, or rather supper, for tho' tea hour, it was supper fare. The long dining table was spread, and besides tea and coffee, we had a variety of warm cakes, bread, cold meats and pastry. At table I was introduced to Mr. William Madison, brother to the President, and his wife, and three or four other ladies and gentlemen all near relatives, all plain country people, but frank, kind, warm-hearted Virginians. At this house I realized being in Virginia, Mr. Madison, plain, friendly, communicative, and unceremonious as any Virginia Planter could be—Mrs. Madison, uniting to all the elegance and polish of fashion, the unadulterated simplicity, frankness, warmth, and friendliness of her native character and native state. Their mode of living, too, if it had more elegance than is found among the planters, was characterized by that abundance, that hospitality, and that freedom, we are taught to look for on a Virginian plantation. We did not sit long at this meal—the evening was warm and we were glad to leave the table. The gentlemen went to the piazza, the ladies, who all had children, to their chambers, and I sat with Mrs. Madison till bed time talking of Washington. When the servant appeared with candles to show me my room, she insisted on going up stairs with me, assisted me to undress and chatted till I got into bed. How unassuming, how kind is this woman. How can any human being be her enemy. Truly, in her there is to be found no gall, but the pure milk of human kindness. If I may say so, the maid was like the mistress; she was very attentive all the time I was there, seeming as if she could not do enough, and was very talkative. As her mistress left the room, "You have a good mistress Nany," said I. "Yes," answered the affectionate creature with warmth, "the best I believe in the world—I am sure I would not change her for any mistress in the whole country." The next morning Nany called me to a late breakfast, brought me ice and water (this is universal here, even in taverns), and assisted me to dress. We sat down between 15 and 20 persons to breakfast—and to a most excellent Virginian breakfast—tea, coffee, hot wheat bread, light cakes, a pone, or corn loaf—cold ham, nice hashes, chickens, etc.

Another visitor found when he arrived in 1827:

Mr. and Mrs. Madison were out having gone over to a relation's in the neighborhood [perhaps to sister Sarah Madison Macon's nearby Somerset or to niece Nelly Conway Willis's Woodley, over the Southwest Mountains]. . . . In a little while, a fine portly looking lady, with a straw bonnet, and shawl on came in, whom I at once took for her ladyship. . . . Soon after Mr. Madison came in. . . . [He] is quite a short thin man, with his head bald except on the back, where his hair hangs down to his collar and over his ears, nicely powdered—he has gray but bright eyes, and small features—he looks scarcely as old as he is, . . . and seems very hale and hearty—the expression of his face is full of good humour—he was dressed in black, with breeches and old fashioned top boots, which he afterwards took off and sat during the evening in his white stockings, but the next day he had black silk on and looked very nice. Mrs. Madison slipped off to change her walking

dress, and made herself quite stylish in a turban and fine gown—she has a
great deal of dignity blended with good humour and knowledge of the
world. A number of her relations were staying with them, a party I suppose
of a dozen, and two or three pretty girls among them. . . . I talked with or
rather listened to [Mr. Madison] almost exclusively while I remained. We sat
up pretty late; . . . his favourite topic appeared . . . to be the early constitutional history of this country, the state of the confederacy originally, the
points involved in the constitution, the errors relative to many facts which
he pointed out, etc. We discussed too ancient and modern literature—
Herodotus, Gibbon, Sir Walter Scott and the Reviews. . . . The next morning I was down sometime before the ladies but found him reading in the
parlour.

An Italian traveler, Count Carlo Vidua, had similarly favorable impressions of Madison during a visit to Montpelier in May 1825. He found Madison "a small, thin old man, but of a kindly and pleasant face; his bearing
is very aristocratic, and without assuming the air of importance and dignity befitting one of his station, he displays an indescribable gentleness
and charm, which I thought impossible to find in an American. I have
heard few people speak with such precision and, above all, with such fair-
ness." Upon visiting with the four living former presidents and with President John Quincy Adams, Vidua found aged John Adams precise and
vivacious in answering questions but too old to sustain a long conversation. "Jefferson's intellect seemed . . . the most brilliant, Madison's the
most profound, Monroe's the least keen, and [John Quincy] Adams' the
most cultivated." Altogether, Vidua preferred Madison because his "reflections seemed . . . the most weighty, denoting a great mind and a good
heart."

Some of the visitors to Montpelier were doubtless not as interesting
and searching as the Italian intellectual but nonetheless contributed to
making it a busy and sociable place for James and Dolley. In 1827, for
example, after spring began to make its appearance, a Mr. Clarke and
J. T. Shepherd, the husband of one of James's nieces, visited Montpelier. A
month later, in April, neighbors and close friends James Barbour and John
Taliaferro came for a couple of days. Historian Jared Sparks, preparing his
edition of General Washington's papers, also came in April, pushing Madison to rummage both his memory and his archives for evidence of his

close workings with the first president. Martha Jefferson Randolph and her family visited in May for a few days, continuing the annual exchange of visits between Monticello and Montpelier enjoyed twice a year during her father's lifetime. She and Dolley had been close friends for more than forty years. A Mr. Willard from Massachusetts and a Mr. and Mrs. C. Tait also came in May, along with Virginia historian Hugh Blair Grigsby seeking Madison's help for his edition of the debates of the Virginia ratifying convention of 1788. July, as usual, was the peak of the season: Barbara O'Sullivan Addicks, Chapman Coleman, David Hoffman, Joseph W. Farnum, and Jared Sparks again, all came, while Madison gave a toast to his Revolutionary colleagues at the Fourth of July celebration at Orange Court House. Still, the busyness of the season did not prevent "Mrs. M. and myself" from inviting James K. Paulding to visit for a few weeks during the summer "when our mountain ether will bear the most favorable comparison with the damp breezes from the ocean." The visit would be especially gratifying, the Madisons added, if by then "you had exchanged the galling burden of bachelorship for the easy yoke of matrimony."

Dolley's Preoccupations

For Dolley especially, though, there were down sides as she moved from the exciting and interesting life in Washington to the sometimes dull and burdensome rounds at Montpelier. In April 1818 she reported "the Old lady [Nelly Conway Madison] is quite well," but by July she wrote that "Mother M is very sick again & Fanny [her daughter] here nursing her." Fanny (about to move to Alabama with her large family) was at Montpelier with her daughter, along with the daughters of Dr. Taylor and Mrs. Jirdon, together with William Madison, with Mr. and Mrs. Dade expected the next day with a "large party" for dinner. Dolley wrote her sister she "must stir myself to fix for them." Edward Coles and Payne Todd had been at Montpelier for some days that spring and could not "fix on the day to leave us." Edward, soon to take his slaves "to the West" to give them their freedom, was "a great fidget and is hard to marry." "I'm thinking Payne will be the same way," she opined, but she thought them both right to be cautious to be sure to marry well. "Though I should like a fine daughter much," wrote Dolley, it never happened. Dolley also was worried that Anna had been to only one "Drawing Room at the White House" that season, a remark that revealed the continuing social coldness between President Monroe's family and the Montpelier family. They did not like Monroe's wife and elder daughter, who had largely shut down the Washington social life Dolley had so cultivated and enlivened. James sent word to his wife from Monticello that summer that "President Monroe, *with his family,*" might be stopping at Montpelier on their way to Washington—obviously warning of an unwelcome visit.

At the University of Virginia examinations and board of visitors meetings in Charlottesville for ten days in July 1827, James was bedridden with cholera during some of the sessions. When Dolley heard of his illness, she feared a "relapse," but better news, she wrote, "revives my heart" and led her to hope he might be "safe at home on Wednesday night, with your own affectionate nurse." Anna Cutts and her three youngest children, ages ten, thirteen, and sixteen, doubtless came in August and September, as did again widowed sister Lucy Todd, with one of her sons and his wife. University of Virginia mathematics and science professor Charles Bonnycastle and historian Henry Gilpin (who eventually edited the posthumous publication of Madison's much-anticipated Notes of the Federal Convention) also came during those months, as did an R. Bayly. For four days in November antislavery and pro-manufacturing economist and prospective University of Virginia professor Jesse Burton Harrison came and recorded long conversations with Madison about everything from the life habits of Eskimos to the future of international law. Madison's protégé Nicholas Trist and his wife Virginia, one of Jefferson's granddaughters, came for a pre-Christmas visit. By mid-December, Madison was in bed with influenza. James wrote a young and sometimes demanding correspondent that

> it is an error very naturally prevailing, that the retirement from public service, of which my case is an example, is a leisure for whatever pursuit might be most inviting. The truth, however, is that I have rarely, during the period of my public life, found my time less at my disposal than since I took my leave of it; nor have I the consolation of finding, that as my powers of application necessarily decline, the demands on them proportionately decrease.
>
> Were it necessary to prove what is here observed, I might appeal to what continually passes to and from me through the mail [would Madison have enjoyed the age of e-mail?]; to the modes of neighbourly intercourse

unavoidable in rural situations, especially in this quarter of the Union [good hotels are still scarce near Montpelier]; and to the cares incident to the perplexing species of labour and of husbandry from which alone is derived the support of a complicated establishment; to all of which may now be added, the duties devolved on me since the decease of the late Rector of the University [Jefferson had died the year before, and Madison succeeded him as rector], as one of the standing Executive Committee and an organ of intercommunications among the Visitors when not in session. Nor must I omit, as a further addition, the effect of the age at which I am arriving in stiffening the fingers which use the pen, to say nothing of a concurrent effect, of which I may be less sensible, on the source which supplies the matter [that is, mental acuity] for it.

In December 1827 Madison had completed more than forty years in public office, had been ten years retired from the presidency, and was seventy-six years old. He would live another nine years with scarcely diminished demands on his time—and on Dolley's duties as hostess and as caregiver for an aging husband.

Yet, so contented were the Madisons at Montpelier with their daily round of life that the letters and diaries of those who visited them generally reflect euphoria. One lady found Dolley "a great soul—and her body not decreased." The old couple "looked like Adam and Eve in their Bower," she added. Another glimpsed an unpretentious former president, "quite the Farmer, enthusiastically fond of all its employments, and wearing Pantaloons patched at the knees." On rainy days, according to one report, James walked back and forth on the portico for his exercise, sometimes racing with Dolley, who could move very well for a woman of her age. In no other country, the visitor said, could one find an ex-ruler living so quietly and so simply. Surrounded by an affectionate family, visited by streams of (mostly) agreeable guests, serenely comfortable at last on his own farm, and able to bask in the adulation of his countrymen, Madison enjoyed a retirement often idyllic beyond what he had dared hope. Some commentators contrasted this with the poisoning or violent deaths of so many other rulers, or the sad fate of Madison's famous contemporary, Napoleon, sick and scorned, who died a lonely exile on the remote island of St. Helena in 1821.

Virginia Agriculture in Decline

The need to make a living, as well as Madison's agrarian convictions about the good life, though, did require him to remain an active farmer. Jefferson himself had declared, John Quincy Adams wrote in 1807, that "the person who united with other science the greatest agricultural knowledge of any man he knew was Mr. Madison. He was the best farmer in the world." The Montpelier plantation had prospered during the Napoleonic Wars, despite the inattentions of Madison's overseers during his long absences in Washington. He had shifted his production as much as possible to wheat and other grains, but the decline of European demand after the wars caused Madison to depend again on tobacco for a cash crop. His earliest letters from Orange after his retirement are filled with talk of fields, crops, market prospects, and the weather, marking his absorption in a farmer's concerns. Visitors commented on the sophistication of his farming methods, especially his interest in equipment and machinery. Like Jefferson, he experimented with plows that might "better stand the shocks of our rough and rooty land." He showed a European visitor, the baron de Montlezun, not generally impressed with American farms or farmers (he thought the latter had "badly formed manners, crude usages, religious fanaticism"), a wheat-threshing machine with "large cog-wheels" that, when attended by slaves and driven by four horses, could turn out two hundred bushels of wheat a day.

Madison also tried to improve livestock by adding imported merino sheep to his flock. He had sought to promote the idea by wearing a suit of merino wool at his inauguration ceremony in 1809—recalling for him, no doubt, his pride in a class at Princeton in 1770, protesting British trade restrictions on the colonies, that had, he wrote his father, graduated "all of them in American cloth." Madison agreed with his old Philadelphia friend from his service in the Continental Congress, Richard Peters, who wrote that "being a good Republican, I have a coat made for my own wearing" from the crossbred sheep he, like Madison, raised to diversify the market for farm products. Another longtime colleague, Tench Coxe, wrote that raising merinos and encouraging making homespun garments from them was patriotic because if war "shall be taken toward us, manufactures must support our Agriculture, and the woolen manufacture, with some aid from the cotton, must become necessary to effective war."

Altogether Madison sought earnestly to make the working and produce of his Virginia farm suit his republican ideology of the moral and civic benefits of an agricultural economy, but it was thwarted by what one of Jefferson's granddaughters termed "the canker of slavery" that for Virginians and other Southerners "eats into their hearts, and diseases the whole body by this ulcer at the core."

In recognition of his zeal for both the economic and political benefits of good farming, Madison's neighbors elected him president of the Agricultural Society of Albemarle. Madison saw it as a model of the scientific, practical self-help organization he and Jefferson thought could be the salvation of American agriculture. Their goal was to sustain in the country the life of rural virtue and prosperity vital to its republican character. Madison delivered a long address to the society in May 1818. Speaking before Jefferson, members of the board of visitors of the soon-to-be University of Virginia, and piedmont farmers anxious to apply the lessons of science to fields threatened with impoverishment, Madison first considered some questions of agrarian philosophy: What caused men to change from hunters to farmers? What instincts, if any, inclined men to become civilized? What ratio of plants to animals best suited human progress? And finally, What balances of nature must man be careful not to upset, lest he make the world unfit for human habitation? Especially important was plenty of pure air. "In all confined situations, from the dungeon to the crowded work-house, and from these to the compact population of overgrown cities," Madison declared, "the atmosphere becomes, in corresponding degrees, unfitted by reiterated use, for sustaining human life and health." Despite the dangers of upsetting natural harmonies, though, Madison insisted that man's reason and will, "by which he can act on matter organized and unorganized," enabled him to improve species of plants and animals, restore exhausted soil, and increase the proportion of living things useful to him. He insisted, too, that "the enviable condition of the people of the United States is often too much ascribed to the physical advantages of their soil and climate, and to their uncrowded situation." Much is certainly due to these causes, he said, but "a just estimate of the happiness of our country will never overlook what belongs to the fertile activity of a free people, and the benign influence of a responsible Government." Madison always believed that human effort, right principles, and proper institutions were vital adjuncts to the bounties of nature, separating the free, prospering portion of mankind from the degraded part. This remained throughout his life the center of his political and social philosophy, and it furnished the essential point of his lifelong agreement with Jefferson.

Applying his insights to Virginia agriculture, Madison recommended specific changes and improvements. First, he pointed out the futility of continued working of exhausted fields, which put both land and laborer in a downward spiral of diminishing returns. He then commended Thomas Mann Randolph's (Jefferson's son-in-law) system of contour plowing as of "inestimable advantage," particularly in "our red hills" and in the cultivation of Indian corn. Madison also spoke learnedly, and in great detail, of the benefits of various kinds of animal manure and of the relative merits of grain chaff and cornstalks as soil rejuvenators. He anticipated both the source and doctrine of Edmund Ruffin's landmark *An Essay on Calcareous Manures* in commending Sir Humphrey Davy's demonstration that chemical fertilizers, if properly applied, could be the salvation of Southern agriculture. Madison next noted the advantages of irrigation, the superiority of the ox to the horse for most farm purposes, and the need to rid the countryside of scraggly animals, especially dairy cows. The milk, manure, and hides of these cattle, Madison observed, seldom paid for the cost of feeding them, while the same feed given to a few fat cows would provide rich returns in the milk pail and elsewhere. Madison concluded with a plea for conserving and restoring the woodlots, toward which "the great effort . . . to destroy trees" in pioneer days seemed to have created an "antipathy." Estimating, for Virginia, that each fireplace required an average of ten cords of wood annually, that an acre of woods yielded twenty cords, and that it took twenty years for a woodlot to restore itself, Madison urged that every farm maintain ten acres of trees for every fireplace it wished to fuel. Madison's recommendations for scientific agriculture in Virginia embodied the reasoned, practical approach his disciplined mind over and over again applied to human problems. His listeners voted him their thanks for his "enlightened and important address" and ordered it printed and distributed for the edification of farmers everywhere.

Further Challenges to the Virginia Economy

Despite the confident tone of his address, Madison in fact faced, along with his neighbors, the calamitous consequences of agricultural depression. With the end of war-heightened demand for wheat in Europe, the bottom fell out of the grain market, and the revival in the tobacco trade immediately after the war proved short-lived. The former secretary of state wrote paragraphs of sophisticated discourse about Russian and Spanish efforts to extend their sway in the Western Hemisphere that would interrupt republican agricultural development. He even observed that Czar Alexander "mingles with ambition a spice of [religious and dynastic] fanaticism," which, Madison feared, "if it grows into stronger delusions of supernatural guidance, may transform the Saint into a Despot." He also wrote President Monroe in 1818 as one farmer to another complaining about the disastrous effects of bad weather: a "remarkable spring," with frosts in May, had "destroyed the peaches and cherries" and "deprived me of the . . . best of my wheat." Furthermore, his cornfields, put in the ground a month ago, had "but a small portion . . . getting above it." Though the "ravages" of the Hessian flies were perhaps less than usual, Jefferson's "best farmer in the world" concluded, the diminished crops, including even some new strands of "Lawler wheat," all suffered "from the peculiar unfavorableness of the [extended] winter." An unusual number of poor harvests during the 1820s, the steady exhaustion of the soil, and competition from rapidly opening rich farmlands in the West all intensified the distress.

Always short of cash, Virginia planters found it increasingly difficult to derive anything like the needed income from their crops. Farmers, large and small, faced grim alternatives: sell their land, sell their slaves, emigrate, or fall into impoverishment. Madison saw the results all around him: his sister Frances and her husband moved to Alabama; his nephew Robert Madison sought to go to New Orleans for his law career; his nieces increasingly married merchants and professional men living in cities; many of his Taylor cousins, following the family of future president Zachary Taylor, Madison's second cousin, moved to Kentucky. Dolley's brother John, unable to make a living first on a farm in Louisa County and then on one near Montpelier that James had helped him acquire, moved to Kentucky and then Illinois. Edward Coles left first for Illinois and then

Philadelphia. Many of Madison's neighbors were reduced to breeding slaves for sale "down the river." Both Jefferson and Monroe went broke. The prosperous way of life Virginia had known for nearly two centuries seemed in the 1820s to be near its end.

For ten or fifteen years Madison avoided the worst effects of the depression. His salary as president, $25,000 annually, was for that time a handsome one and permitted him not only to make improvements at Montpelier but also perhaps build up some reserve to carry him over hard times. His lack of expensive and dissipating habits meant he was without a burden many Virginia planters imposed on themselves, and he was also free of the steady drain of raising many children. Furthermore, the use at Montpelier of the best farm techniques, evident in Madison's letters from the 1780s on, made its fields unusually productive. Finally, Madison possessed in 1817 not only clear title to five thousand fertile acres in Orange County but also over a thousand acres of Kentucky lands, some stock in a turnpike company, a house in Washington, and other assets able to cushion him from the shock of crop failures. On the other hand, a gracious way of life filled with company and entertainment, a refusal to traffic routinely in slaves, and the vast expenditures needed to keep Payne Todd out of debtor's prison depleted Madison's cash reserves.

Through his retirement he gradually sold his Kentucky lands, disposed of his stock and other convertible assets, and even mortgaged, with little hope of regaining clear title, perhaps half of his Montpelier lands. Madison's credit and the prospects of Virginia agriculture were so poor by 1825 that even his personal appeal to Nicholas Biddle, president of the Bank of the United States, failed to procure a $6,000 loan. Nothing could have been more disappointing for Madison than the inescapable fact that by the time of his death, he had failed in his lifelong efforts to make Montpelier in particular, and Virginia generally, with or without slavery, a prosperous farmer's paradise. Though he was spared the pain and humiliation of bankruptcy, the threat of economic ruin grew stronger during his years of retirement. The enslaved population on his farm, of course, shared his distress and impoverishment. "Since my return to private life," Madison wrote Jefferson in 1826, "such have been the unkind seasons, and the ravages of insects, that I have made but one tolerable crop of Tobacco, and but one of Wheat; the proceeds of both of which were greatly curtailed by mishaps in the sale of them. And having no resources but in the earth I cultivate, I have been living very much throughout on borrowed means."

Struck by these grim realities, Madison admitted increasingly that social problems were unlikely to yield to panaceas. Echoing opinions expressed forty years earlier to Jefferson—"A certain degree of misery seems inseparable from a high degree of populousness," Madison had written then—he reasserted his Malthusian insights against the extravagant hopes of the English theorist William Goodwin. Though Madison admitted, as always, that enterprise and good government could vastly improve human life, he insisted generally that "all the . . . beings on the Globe, . . . animal and vegetable, . . . when left to themselves multiply until checked by the limited funds of their pabulum, or by the mortality generated by the excess of their numbers." In 1827, reflecting on Robert Owen's hope that socialist communities would eliminate want and evil, Madison wrote more bluntly. "Custom," he averred, "is properly called a second nature; Mr. Owen makes it nature itself." Though Madison hoped Owen's "enterprise" would "throw light on the maximum to which the force of education and habit can be carried," he had grave doubts that any social reorganization could wholly overcome the "desire for distinction," the harmful effects of fashion, and the tendency of leisure to produce ennui or "vicious resorts." And after all, Madison noted, "there is one indelible cause remaining of pressure on the condition of the labouring part of mankind; and that is, the constant tendency of an increase of their number, after the increase of food has reached its term. The competition for employment then reduces wages to their minimum and privation to its maximum." Thinking of war, famine, and pestilence, Madison said that "any checks on this iron law" (had he been reading David Ricardo, the leading English economist of the time?) were themselves only further and worse evils. He concluded that because it was impossible to banish evil from the world, "We must console ourselves with the belief that it is overbalanced by the good mixed with it, and direct our efforts to an increase of the good portion of the mixture."

Slavery, That "Dreadful Calamity"

Of all evils, however, none was for Madison more dangerous, more intractable, than slavery. His conviction of its immorality and its incongruity in a nation resting on the Declaration of Independence had been formed early and never slackened. His failure in the 1780s to free himself from dependence on slave labor and to secure a law for gradual abolition in Virginia doomed him, it seemed, to live within a system he abhorred. During the years of his public life, the revived economic utility of slavery in the fast-growing cotton fields of the lower South made its elimination, contrary to what Madison, Jefferson, Washington, and other eighteenth-century Virginians had supposed, more difficult as time passed.

In retirement Madison turned again to antislavery intentions. Though he insisted in 1819 that liberal principles and improved conditions made slaves much better off than they were before the Revolution, their degraded status was nevertheless intolerable under a supposedly free government. Any plan for emancipation, Madison declared, would have to be gradual, for only by gradual measures could any "deep-rooted and widespread evil" be corrected. Furthermore, because slaves were recognized as property under American laws, any emancipation plan would have to pay a fair compensation to the masters. This would also reconcile the masters and help prevent violence and bloodshed. It was further necessary, Madison reasoned, that the plan provide for the free blacks, so that a slave would consider "a state of freedom [to] be preferable, in his own estimation, to his actual one in a state of bondage." Madison felt using money earned by the sale of western lands to purchase slaves from willing masters, under supervision of the national government, would be a sufficient, fair, and efficacious means of gradual abolition.

The most serious problem in Madison's view, arose from "existing and probably unalterable prejudices in the United States [requiring that] freed blacks . . . be permanently removed beyond the region occupied by, or allotted to, a white population." "Physical and lasting peculiarities" among the blacks would mean, if they were "thoroughly incorporated" into white society, "a change only from one to another species of oppression." "Reciprocal antipathies," moreover, would leave a constant "danger of collisions" if the two races, each free, dwelled together. Madison thought that blacks, either innately or from long bondage in Africa and America, were so different from and possibly inferior to the white population generally, and that white prejudices against them were so indelible, that meaningful freedom and equality for blacks in an integrated society could not be achieved. He hoped, therefore, to find a refuge somewhere

in the world where freed slaves could develop their full human potenti-
alities entirely removed from the scene of their former degradation. For
a time both Madison and Jefferson thought the American West might
provide such a refuge, but by 1819 Madison looked upon thinly settled
parts of West Africa as the best place for a colony of freed slaves. To this
end, he joined with Henry Clay, Bushrod Washington, John Marshall, and
many other eminent men, mostly from the upper South, to support the
American Colonization Society, dedicated both to the freeing of slaves
and to their transportation to the west coast of Africa.

The idea of transport to Africa, discussed by Jefferson and others ever
since the 1780s, had been urged systematically in 1804 by Dr. William
Thornton, a frequent visitor at Montpelier, in a pamphlet dedicated to
Madison. Madison thought the plan practical if the national government,
over the course of a generation or so, would appropriate perhaps $600
million, the sum to be expected from a sale at $2 an acre of about one-
third of the western lands available after the Louisiana Purchase. Such a
fund would yield $400 to free each of the 1.5 million slaves in the country
and, omitting slaves unwilling or too old and frail to go to Africa, would
furnish a surplus to pay for transportation and for capital to develop Liberia, the nation founded in 1822 for the freed slaves. Madison challenged
those who raised objections to come forth with a better plan and to
remember the transcendent need to do something about the looming evil
that mocked the moral integrity of the nation and even threatened the
Union itself.

Shortly after thus expressing himself, Madison heard from his ex-sec-
retary and Dolley's cousin, Edward Coles, whose own antislavery feelings
had intensified. On an official mission to Russia, he had observed that
serfdom was "a form of servitude . . . infinitely of a milder and less oppressive character" than black slavery in America. Coles then took his
slaves to Illinois, announcing their freedom to them as they floated down
the Ohio River, gave each some land, and helped them become good
farmers. Madison was pleased Coles pursued "the true course" of providing for his slaves' happiness as well as their freedom because "with the
habits of the slave, and without the instruction, the property, or the
employments of a freeman, the manumitted blacks, instead of deriving
advantage from the partial benevolence of their Masters, furnish arguments against the general efforts in their behalf." Madison wished also

Edward Coles, lithograph by Albert Newsam, 1831.
(The Historical Society of Pennsylvania)

that Coles could change the color as well as the legal condition of his slaves, because without this "they seem destined to a privation of that moral rank and those social participations which give to freedom more than half its value." The two Virginians thus displayed again the vital difference that separated them: Coles felt so strongly the moral evil of slavery that he went ahead, with great personal sacrifice, to free his slaves. With such help as he could give them, he had faith in the ability of his freed blacks to thrive. Madison, on the other hand, "lulled," as Coles put it, by a lifetime of existence with slavery, and without Cole's zealous faith in the ultimate equality of the races, was unwilling to undertake the suffering and disruption, for him and for his slaves, of individual manumission. Furthermore, he placed his faith in a colonization plan that had serious practical difficulties and had as well supporters who saw it as a way to preserve slavery by getting rid of free blacks. That a man of Madison's realism and integrity should adhere in this instance to such an impractical and compromised program is painful evidence of the dilemma the existence of slavery posed for him.

In the agitation preceding the Missouri Compromise of 1820, Madison opposed the restriction on slavery in Missouri, both because it denied Missouri the right to determine the question of slavery for itself, as the other states had done, and because he thought the "diffusion" of slaves, once nonimportation was firmly enforced, was the best way to secure slavery's eventual abolition. Its abolition, he observed, thinking of the gradual end of slavery in the North, had proved attainable in proportion to the relative scarcity of blacks in the population of a state. He recalled, too, that the clauses in the Constitution protecting slavery had been put there in 1787 at the determined insistence of only two states, Georgia and South Carolina, where the concentration of slaves was greatest and where their "diffusion" was least contemplated. Madison phrased a number of questions about removing the restriction on slavery. Would not the "diffusion" of slaves, by "lessening the number belonging to individual masters," improve their condition? Large numbers of slaves held en masse by one owner were generally less well treated and less likely to be manumitted, Madison observed. Would not, he also asked, the diffusion of blacks amid a large white population lead to more benign attitudes toward them, promote their manumission, and lessen the violent controls and rebellions incident to the heavy preponderance of black slaves on large plantations, as were found in the West Indian islands? Madison also wondered whether imposing restrictions on the diffusion of blacks would extend "disqualifications . . . which degrade them from the rank and rights of white persons." The key question, always for Madison, was, "Will the aggregate strength, security, tranquility, and harmony of the whole nation, be advanced or impaired" by the proposed public measure? These questions, of course, rested on Madison's assumption that a total, immediate emancipation, however morally correct, was not presently possible in the United States. As always, Madison remained a gradualist, a nourisher of the overall republican character of the nation, rather than a tackler head-on of what he always acknowledged was the dreadful wrong and inconsistency of slavery in such a nation. But how, in Jefferson's metaphor, could a wolf held by the ears be safely let go?

Madison feared as well "a new state of the parties, founded on local instead of political distinctions, thereby dividing the Republicans of the North from those of the South." This tendency, so clearly encouraged in the inflammatory and widely publicized speeches of Senator Rufus King of New York and others (as well as those on the other side heightening Southern sectionalism) was to Madison, as to Jefferson, "a fireball in the night," gravely threatening the survival of the Union. In fact, as the Missouri Compromise controversy made painfully clear, the era of sectionalism with all the contentions, party politics, and division along North-South lines that Madison had long feared was underway fifteen years before his death. Though both James and Dolley Madison during their retirement had upbeat hopes for the future of the nation, they were discouraged by the growth of a divisive partisanship in its public life.

Madison wrote grimly to Lafayette in 1820 of "the dreadful fruitfulness of the original sin of the African trade." When the liberal Frenchman made his triumphal tour of the United States in 1824, he stopped for four days at Montpelier and never missed, according to his secretary, "an opportunity to defend the rights *that all men without exception have to liberty.*" Lafayette spent hours visiting with slaves at Montpelier, and though full of praise for Madison's humanity toward them, he made clear to his old friend that their joint efforts over a course of fifty years simply could not be reconciled with the existence of human slaves on the very plantations of those who talked so fervently of human freedom.

A few months later Fanny Wright, who had traveled in Lafayette's entourage, wrote Madison of her plan to gather slaves destined for freedom on large, collectivized plantations, where they could be educated while working to earn their independence. Madison replied that he doubted whether, under such an arrangement, "a competent discipline" could be maintained and whether "the prospect of emancipation at a future day will sufficiently overcome the natural and habitual repugnance to labor" on the part of blacks as well as whites. He doubted, too, whether "there is such an advantage of united over individual labor" as Wright took for granted. Malice and indolence, in Madison's judgment, tempered plans to abolish slavery, just as they have all aspirations for human reform. Commenting to Lafayette on the Wright plan and one he regarded as better—government purchase and manumission of all enslaved "female infants at their birth"—Madison insisted again that "no such effort would be listened to whilst the impression remains and it seems to be indelible, that the two races cannot co-exist, both being free and equal. The great *sine qua non,* therefore, is some external asylum for the coloured race."

In the 1830s, as hope dimmed for state action for abolition and as arguments upholding the virtues of slavery spread, the American Colonization Society seemed to Madison more and more to have the best plan. He accepted the presidency of the society and, in a letter written four months after the Nat Turner rebellion of 1831, thought colonization prospects "brightening." He hoped the "increasing . . . spirit of private manumission" would gradually end "the dreadful calamity" of slavery. A little over a year later, reading Thomas R. Dew's defense of slavery and effort to blame the ills of the South on the tariff, Madison turned again to the colonization society's plans as the best answer. The expense of wholesale manumission and transportation he thought within the resources of the Union, and he insisted that thinly settled portions of Africa, plus lands in the far West or asylums in the West Indies, would provide ample space for freed slaves to develop their own society and culture. Madison admitted that "I may indulge too much my wishes and hopes, to be safe from error," but he thought partial success in colonization preferable to giving up in despair or to turning instead, as Dew did, to embrace slavery. The aged former president, eighty years resident on a Virginia farm, concluded by demolishing Dew's argument that the tariff had caused agricultural depression. Slavery itself was to blame, Madison asserted, insofar as it resulted in poor farming practices and led to the exploitative development of lands in Alabama and Mississippi. Even a slow and uncertain progress toward abolition was preferable, Madison asserted, "to a torpid acquiescence in a perpetuation of slavery, or an extinguishment of it by convulsions more disastrous in their character and consequences than slavery itself."

In February 1835 Harriet Martineau, deeply concerned about slavery in America, visited Montpelier. She found Madison had "an inexhaustible faith that a well-founded commonwealth may . . . be immortal," a faith that "shone brightly" on every subject but slavery, where he was in despair. So great was his concern that Madison "talked more on the subject of slavery than on any other, acknowledging, without limitation or hesitation, all the evils with which it had ever been charged." It debauched young slave girls, who were expected to be mothers by the time they were fifteen. The Northern states, as well as foreign nations, treated freed blacks abominably. Though Madison thought treatment of slaves in Virginia had improved, in the new lands they were handled like beasts. He pitied as well the "slavery" of conscientious Southern women who could not trust their servants and had to superintend them in every detail. Masters lived "in a state of perpetual suspicion, fear and anger." Thus Madison extolled again the plans of the American Colonization Society, something Martineau could ascribe only to his "overflowing faith; for the facts were before him that in eighteen years the Colonization Society had removed only between two and three thousand persons, while the annual increase of the slave population in the United States was upward of sixty thousand."

As Madison's financial plight worsened, Virginia laws against manumission tightened. When prospects for freed blacks deteriorated, he withdrew from the promise Edward Coles asserted he had made to free his slaves in his will, as Washington had done, and Jefferson had done for a few of his slaves. Learning of Madison's hesitation, Coles wrote urging him not to let the practical difficulties of manumission deter him from an act of freedom that would be "the consummation of your glory." Madison agreed again to seek a plan to free his slaves, but difficulties accumulated. His slaves were terrified of Liberia, and of those remaining on the reduced Montpelier estate, two-thirds were too young, too infirm, or too old to make the uncertainties of freedom seem a blessing to them. From a peak Montpelier taxable slave population of 108 in 1801, there were 63 in 1828, 61 in 1832, 40 in 1834, and 38 when he died in 1836. In October 1834 he wrote Coles of his difficulties: "Finding that I have, in order to avoid the sale of Negroes sold land until the residue will not support them, concentered and increasing as they are, I have yielded to the necessity of parting with some of them [16] to a friend and kinsman [W. Taylor], who I am persuaded will do better by them than I can, and to whom they gladly consent to be transferred. By this transaction I am enabled to replace the sum you kindly loaned me." By thus disposing of surplus hands, for whom there was no longer work on his shrinking lands, Madison hoped to make Montpelier profitable enough to sustain plans to free the remaining slaves. Even this hope, however, was doomed. In his will Madison said of his slaves merely that none of them should be sold without each slave's consent as well as Dolley Madison's.

Dolley Madison herself, after her marriage to James in 1794, seems to have readopted the benevolent yet accepting attitude toward slavery common among the Virginia families to whom she was related and among whom she had grown up. In the eleven years she lived in Philadelphia, where her Quaker antislavery father had moved the family after freeing his few slaves for sake of conscience, she lived in an antislavery culture, married into it, and presumably shared its convictions. Her second marriage, into an established, slaveholding Virginia family, and her residence at Montpelier after 1794, however, left her in the rather conventional role of good plantation mistress. She was generally attentive and kind to the numerous household slaves and in a long-range, humane way looking forward to the eventual demise of the institution, but nonetheless dependent on and unable to imagine or manage existence without them. Her attitudes about and behavior toward the enslaved persons at Montpelier, though sometimes seeming more strict than her husband's, were much the same as his.

A lifetime of opposition to slavery (more in word than deed) had thus been reduced in Madison's will to a gesture, likely to be ineffectual, not of freedom, but only of decent treatment. As happened again and again in slave states, the demands of creditors and estate legatees subverted Madison's intentions. In the twenty years after James Madison's death, in litigation following the sale of Montpelier in 1844 and the deaths of Dolley Madison in 1849 and her children in 1852, many of the Madison slaves were subjected to the miseries and uncertainties of their bondage.

Beyond his invariably humane treatment, which made a slave's life at Montpelier as tolerable as possible, Madison failed utterly to do anything about what he always regarded as a moral evil and an economic catastrophe. He depended all his life on the labor of slaves; he did nothing effective to diminish the baneful place of the despised institution in the social fabric of Virginia. At his death, slavery in the United States was far more an anomaly, a curse to the nation, and an affront to the conscience of humankind than it had been in his youth. Furthermore, his sense of the immense gulf between the ways of life of blacks and whites, whether inherent or resulting from centuries of cultural difference, was impressed on him during a lifetime of contact with blacks always in a degraded condition. The situation prevented him from envisioning humans of different color living equally, freely, and congenially together. To him the only moral solution, fair to each race alike, especially in order to lift from blacks the "indelible prejudices" of whites confident of their own superiority, was division into separate societies. Only this, he thought, could complete the republican character of the United States, which could not happen as long as some people were slaves and others masters.

Continuing Public Involvement

I N JUNE 1824 AN ITINERANT BOOKSELLER, SAMUEL WHITCOMB, COM-
mented on two Virginia customers he had recently visited:

> Mr. Madison is not so large or so tall as myself and instead of being a cool
> reserved austere man, is very sociable, rather jocose, quite sprightly, and
> active.
>   . . . [He] appears less studied, brilliant and frank but more natural, can-
> did and profound than Mr. Jefferson. Mr. Jefferson has more imagination
> and passion, quicker and richer conceptions. Mr. Madison has a sound judg-
> ment, tranquil temper and logical mind. . . . Mr. Madison has nothing in his
> looks, gestures, expression or manners to indicate anything extraordinary in
> his intellect or character, but the more one converses with him, the more
> his excellences are developed and the better he is liked. And yet he has a
> quizzical, careless, almost waggish bluntness of looks and expression which
> is not at all prepossessing.

Whitcomb further observed that Madison took many newspapers and,
much more than Jefferson, remained well informed on current issues. In
fact, from the moment he left Washington, James Madison remained an
active elder statesman, fully abreast of public affairs and in close touch
with the nation's political leaders. Dolley maintained the same interest.

In the first years of Madison's "retirement," President Monroe and
Richard Rush, who had been in Madison's cabinet and was American minister in London, both forwarded diplomatic dispatches to Montpelier,
almost as if from force of habit, and consulted Madison on Latin America,

Florida border disputes, the increasingly harmonious relations with Great Britain, the tariff, internal improvements, and other matters. A stream of letters answered from Orange. Madison took special interest in the convulsions racking South America as the Spanish colonies sought independence, consciously and at almost every step seeking to emulate their revolution-founded northern neighbor. The former president urged his successor to give "every lawful manifestation" of United States approval of the revolutionaries, "whatever may be the consequences." He saw with pleasure Britain's inclination to prevent other European powers from helping Spain retain control.

In 1823, as the repressive intentions of the Holy Alliance became clear, French armies invaded Spain, and Russia declared its right to expand down the Pacific coast, Monroe sought his predecessor's advice on a crossroads confronting American foreign policy. Britain had proposed cooperation with the United States to prevent the Holy Allies from "reducing the Revolutionized Colonies . . . to their former dependence." Madison replied to Monroe's queries that United States sympathy with the "liberties and independence [of] . . . these neighbors . . . and the consequences threatened by a command of their resources by the Great Powers confederated against their rights and reforms" made it imperative "to defeat the meditated crusade." It was fortunate, too, he observed, that Britain, whatever its motives, sought the same object. "With that cooperation we have nothing to fear from the rest of Europe, and with it the best assurance of success to our laudable views." "In the great struggle of the Epoch between liberty and despotism," Madison observed to Jefferson, "we owe it to ourselves to sustain the former in this hemisphere at least." Madison suggested a joint proclamation with Great Britain on behalf of Latin American independence. "With the British fleets and fiscal resources associated with our own," he noted to Rush several days later, "we should be safe against the rest of the World, and at liberty to pursue whatever course might be prescribed by a just estimate of our moral and political obligations."

Later dispatches from London, John Quincy Adams's distaste at the United States being "a cock-boat in the wake of the British man-of-war," and Monroe's own inclination toward a unilateral American proclamation resulted in the famous Monroe Doctrine. Though Madison's proposed joint statement fell through, the effect was much the same. The

United States, with implicit British support and approval, had declared against colonialism in the Americas. Madison congratulated Monroe a few months later that despite the enmity of the Holy Alliance toward "free Government everywhere," the British-American stand had had "a benumbing influence on all their wicked enterprises." Madison's support of Latin American independence and of United States action with whatever friendly powers might help resist the spread of despotism were, of course, consistent with his lifelong views on foreign affairs. He had shown himself, as well, fully able to forget a half century of anti-British hostility should Britain prove by its conduct once again to be a friend of freedom. Madison expressed his basic faith to Lafayette: "Despotism can only exist in darkness, and there are too many lights now in the political firmament, to permit it to remain anywhere, as it has heretofore done, almost everywhere." Dolley Madison's letters to the wives of American and international statesmen and her cordial hospitality on their visits to Montpelier aided and reflected her husband's aspiration for a secure and freedom-friendly nation.

James Madison even speculated that "were it possible by human contrivance so to accelerate the intercourse between every part of the globe that all its inhabitants could be united under the superintending authority of an ecumenical Council, how great a portion of human evils would be avoided. Wars, famines, with pestilence as far as the fruit of either, could not exist; taxes to pay for wars, or to provide against them would be needless, and the expense and perplexities of local fetters on interchange beneficial to all would no longer oppress the social state." He nonetheless retained a realism about quick and easy solutions, as is evidenced in a remark to John Quincy Adams, who had delivered to Jeremy Bentham Madison's polite deflation of the English philosopher's scheme to rationalize and codify American law: "[Either] I greatly overrate or [Bentham] greatly underrates the task . . . not only [of digesting] our Statutes into a concise and clear system, but [of reducing] our unwritten to a text law." Blending high hopes, always important to Madison, with the limitations impressed on him by his experience in public life and his sense of human frailty was the supreme political task.

Chief Justice John Marshall's opinion in the *McCulloch v. Maryland* case (1819) also commanded Madison's attention as he dealt with the mass of papers and correspondence coming daily to Montpelier. Spencer Roane of the Virginia Court of Appeals and other jurists, incensed at Marshall's nationalist doctrines, sought Madison's support. Madison saw in Marshall's decisions, almost verbatim, Hamilton's arguments for the "latitudinary mode of expounding the Constitution," which Madison had denounced in Congress in 1791. He thus objected thirty years later to Marshall's obiter dicta again indiscriminately extending the power of the national government. Madison insisted that to place no restriction on the means Congress might choose to achieve its constitutional ends destroyed the whole notion of limited government. "To give an extent to the . . . means [of government] superseding the limits of [its objects] is in effect to convert a limited into an unlimited Government," Madison held. He agreed with Marshall, though, that the state of Maryland had no power to tax the Bank of the United States.

Two years later, following the *Cohens v. Virginia* decision, Madison again sympathized with Roane's disgust at Marshall's "practice of mingling with his judgments pronounced, comments and reasonings of a scope beyond them; . . . and an apparent disposition to amplify the authorities of the Union at the expense of those of the States." The great need, the former president declared, was to maintain impartially the constitutional boundary between the state and federal governments. Sometimes this required restraint on state encroachments and sometimes on federal invasions. Madison belittled Roane's wild fears of Marshall's "ingenious and fatal sophistries" and the Supreme Court's "usurpations," however, by observing that other agencies of government, when backed by the sense of the people, would be fully able to restrain the court. One such "usurping experiment," the Alien and Sedition Acts, had thus been "crushed at once." Then, aiming directly at Roane's argument that the federal courts had no power to set aside decisions of the highest state tribunals, Madison upheld the final jurisdiction of the federal Supreme Court: "Were this trust to be vested in the States in their individual characters, the Constitution of the U.S. might become different in every State, and would be pretty sure to do so in some; the State Governments would not stand all in the same relation to the General Government, some retaining more, others less of sovereignty, and the vital principle of equality, which cements their Union [would] thus gradually be deprived of its virtue."

Jefferson was seventy-three years old and had been retired at Monticello for eight years when the Madisons arrived back at Montpelier. The old friends were now a few hours' carriage or horseback ride from each other and often visited and conferred. In the *Cohens* case, however, Jefferson had agreed with Roane, placing him on the side of the burgeoning states' rights ideology in Virginia politics. Madison waited two years to politely but firmly set Jefferson straight. His plan to call conventions to settle disputes over state and federal jurisdictions Madison called "too tardy, too troublesome, and too expensive, besides its tendency to lessen a salutary veneration" for the Supreme Court. To suppose in such questions equal authority in state and federal courts would end, after consultations had left some matters still in dispute, in "a trial of strength between the Posse headed by the Marshal and the Posse headed by the Sheriff." Madison then reaffirmed his opinion (stated in *Federalist* No. 39 thirty-five years earlier, he reminded Jefferson) that to prevent inequalities and appeals to the sword, a federal tribunal must "ultimately" draw the line between state and national power. Madison also insisted, ten years later, on the primacy of the judiciary over the legislature and the executive in interpreting laws: "Notwithstanding [the] abstract view of the coordinate and independent right of the three departments to expound the Constitution, the Judicial department most familiarizes itself to the public attention as the expositor, by the *order* of its functions in relation to the other departments. . . . It may always be expected that the judicial bench, when happily filled, will most engage the respect and reliance of the public as the surest expositor of the Constitution." Madison clearly positioned himself as a foe of the nullification and secession arguments soon to come, while Jefferson left himself open to accusations that he was their originator.

While the split over interpreting the Constitution lingered in the background, letters from an old Federalist antagonist, Jedidiah Morse, revealed another difference between Jefferson and Madison during their retirement years. To lead the Indians into the ways of white civilization, Morse proposed a national society composed of former presidents, virtually all officers of the federal government, an array of state officials, Indian agents, and military officers, as well as all the college professors and clergymen in the nation. Jefferson estimated that of the total of perhaps 8,500 people, more than 90 percent would be clergymen. He wrote at once to Morse, refusing cooperation because the "gigantic" organization, however laudable its intention, would "rivalize and jeopardize the govern-ment." Writing to Madison, hoping he too would spurn Morse, Jefferson explained further that though voluntary organizations of "moderate" size were useful and "general associations coextensive with the nation" might be necessary in revolutionary times, in the United States, where no abuses called for revolution, "voluntary associations so extensive as to grapple with and controul the government . . . are dangerous machines, and should be frowned upon in every regulated government." The goal of Morse's society, Jefferson observed, was being pursued by the govern-ment "with superior means, superior wisdom, and under limits of legal prescription." He foresaw further that a few persons "clubbed together" in Washington under Morse's direction would use the society for their own, perhaps nefarious, and at any rate unrestrained, purposes.

Unknown to Jefferson, Madison had already accepted membership in Morse's society, esteeming its benevolent goal of rescuing the Indians from their own "vices" as well as from those "doubled from our inter-course with them." The Indians could not really be helped, Madison ob-served, "without substituting for the torpid indolence of wigwams and the precarious supplies of the chase the comforts and habits of civilized life." Madison also thought the intention to gather information about "the opinions, the government, the social conditions, etc. of this untu-tored race [might reveal] . . . a just picture of the human character" in its natural state. As to Jefferson's fears, Madison thought Morse's plan "rather ostentatious than dangerous." The proposed membership, wrote Madi-son, recurring to a favorite theme, was "too numerous, too heteroge-neous, and too much dispersed, to concentrate their views in any covert or illicit object." Furthermore, even the clergy, so apparently dominant, were "themselves made up of such repulsive sects that they are not likely to form a noxious confederacy, especially with ecclesiastical views." Mad-ison did concede that Jefferson had spotted an excessive concentration of power in the small board of directors, but even that, Madison thought, would be rendered harmless by the watchful eyes "of so many of every description of observers" in Washington. Madison here reflected the same sense of the self-regulating quality of a free society that again and again made him support or at least view with equanimity plans or asso-ciations to do things, wherein the less subtle Jefferson could see only the threat of bad men combining for evil purposes. Though Jefferson spoke, in dead earnest, on behalf of the people and their government, Madison in a crucial way displayed more faith in the beneficent effects of "the extensive republic."

Madison revealed further his unquestioned conviction that the civilized ways of agriculture, trade, and republican government were best for everyone when he wrote approvingly of another plan to improve the lot of the Indians. Though Madison acknowledged he was "less sanguine" of the result than its promoter, the student and advocate of Indian rights Thomas McKenney, he said, "I do not despair, and join in applauding the philanthropy and zeal that labour and hope for it." He advised, in estimating Indian character, further study of the advanced Aztec and Inca civilizations and the ability of Indians descended from them to live successfully and equitably in stable, Europeanized societies. Madison sent along to McKenney a copy of a "Talk to the Indians" he had given to a delegation of Sac, Fox, Osage, and Sioux chiefs brought to Washington for a treaty at the beginning of the War of 1812. The treaty was "one proof," the former president said, "of the spirit and policy of the Administration in relation to the Indians." Dolley Madison wrote that after the treaty, "We had 29 Indians to dinner with us, attended by 5 Interpretors & Heads of Depts. Making 40 persons." "Another set of the terrifick Kings & Princes," she said, would arrive the next day for more negotiations. In the "Talk" Madison (or perhaps some secretary or official helping him prepare for the treaty) had used the conventional language of Indian negotiation in speaking to "my red children" as "your father of the 18 fires" ("Chief" of the eighteen states then in the Union). He did reveal, however, his lifelong understanding of the culture and capacities of Native Americans:

> I have a further advice for my red children. You see how the country of the 18 fires is filled with people. They increase like the corn they put into the ground. They all have good houses to shelter them from all weathers; good clothes suitable to all seasons; and as for food of all sorts, you see they have enough & to spare. No man woman or child of the 18 fires ever perished of hunger. Compare all this with the condition of the red people. They are scattered here & there in handfuls. Their lodges are cold, leaky, and smokey. They have hard fare, and often not eno' of it. Why this mighty difference? The reason, my red children, is plain. The white people breed cattle and sheep. They plow the earth and make it give them every thing

they want. They spin and weave. Their heads, and their hands make all the elements & productions of nature useful to them. Above all; the people of the 18 fires live in constant peace & friendship. No Tomahawk has ever been raised by one agst. another. Not a drop of blood has ever touched the Chain that holds them together as one family. All their belts are white belts. It is in your power to be like them. The ground that feeds one Lodge, by hunting, would feed a great band, by the plow & the hoe. The great spirit has given you, like your white brethren, good heads to contrive; strong arms, and active bodies. Use them like your white brethren; not all at once, which is difficult but by little & little, which is easy. Especially live in peace with one another, like your white brethren of the 18 fires: and like them, your little sparks will grow into great fires. You will be well fed; well cloathed; dwell in good houses, and enjoy the happiness, for which you like them, were created. The great spirit is the friend of men of all colours. He made them to be friends of one another. The more they are so the more he will be their friend. These are the words of your father, to his red children. The great spirit, who is the father of us all, approves them. Let them pass through the ear, into the heart. Carry them home to your people. And as long as you remember this visit to your father of the 18 fires; remember these as his last & best words to you.

Native Americans, or Indians as they were called at the time, were to Madison fully equal to white Europeans in physical and mental capacities, had the same human rights, and should have the same opportunities to lead safe, happy, and prosperous lives. To do this, though, Madison thought they needed to abandon their dangerous, unhealthy, inefficient, and morally enervating lifestyle of hunting, hardship, and warfare and instead become skilled, settled farmers. Then, like new residents of the American republic, they would absorb and learn the ways and attitudes of "the people of the 18 fires." This knowledge would enable them to be free, responsible, and prosperous citizens who could "live in constant peace & friendship" with their neighbors.

James and Dolley were thus, like many Europeans on both sides of the Atlantic, utterly convinced of the superiority of the Enlightenment ideals of a moral, economic, and political culture based on yeoman farming and responsible citizenship. Those not sharing or possessing this culture, whether Native Americans or Europeans who had lived as oppressed peasants or as "mobs in great cities," as Jefferson had put it, "added just so much to the support of pure government, as sores do to the strength of the human body." Only with an equitable, agrarian, republican way of life under good government, Madison believed, could the problem of the "red race on our borders, . . . next to the . . . black race within our bosom . . . the most baffling to the policy of our country," be handled with humanity and any hope of success. Yet the aggressive and violent lifestyle of the frontier, always pressing against Native Americans, in fact largely overwhelmed and made a mockery of Madison's aspirations and policy.

In the extended controversy over the tariff, Madison stuck to his support of the mildly protective duties he had proposed as president. When the tariff of 1824 was before Congress, Madison wrote Thomas Cooper that he considered the general principle of free industry and free trade "unanswerably established," and furthermore a policy "certainly most congenial with the spirit of a free people, and particularly due to the intelligent and enterprising citizens of the United States." He therefore told Henry Clay that he could not concur entirely in the extent of the proposed tariff or "in some of the reasonings by which it is advocated." The only industries that might be protected indefinitely, Madison wrote Clay, were those producing military supplies, other "indispensable" strategic materials, and goods calculated to be so expensive in wartime as to justify the higher cost of tariff-protected domestic manufacture in peacetime. Furthermore, there might be a "*temporary* [protection to] introduce a particular manufacture, which once introduced will flourish without that encouragement." "In every doubtful case," Madison wrote, "the government should forbear to intermeddle." Foreseeing the heated sectional dispute of a few years later, he added that "particular caution should be observed, where one part of the community would be favored at the expense of another." A "moderate tariff," Madison asserted, would "answer the purpose of revenue and foster domestic manufactures" without an undue interference with the economically and politically beneficent principle of free trade. Remembering Hamilton's national economic planning schemes, which he had fought in Congress in the 1790s, Madison urged caution, though, about more grandiose aspects of Clay's "American System."

In 1828 Southern hostility to the so-called Tariff of Abominations engendered arguments denying the constitutionality of any protective

duties and even asserting the right of states to nullify tariffs deemed injurious to themselves. From Montpelier, Madison wrote long public letters
addressed to House of Delegates member Joseph C. Cabell of Nelson
County reaffirming his arguments to Clay on the advisability of a tariff in
some instances and upholding the constitutionality of a protective tariff.
With his usual thoroughness and unique authority, Madison pointed out
that regulation of commerce in the national interest had been a prime
reason for adopting the Constitution in 1787, that this power had not been
questioned in the ratifying conventions, and that in the tariff debates during the First Congress, Southern states no less than Northern ones had
sought protective tariffs useful to themselves. Forty years of "uniform
and universal" acceptance by every state in the Union of national regulation of commerce, Madison insisted, settled that question. Finally, he
noted that if one accepted the extreme states' rights doctrines, "there
would be an end to that stability in Government and in Laws which is
essential to good Government and good Laws; a stability, the want of
which is the imputation which has at all times been leveled against Republicanism with most effect by its most dexterous adversaries." Though
Madison's requirement that tariffs be brought "to the test of justice and
the general good" implied objection to the inequitable burden the 1828
tariff imposed on the South, he was perfectly clear that the line of resistance taken by South Carolina and the "Richmond Junto" (a group of
Virginia Republicans long opposed to Madison) countenanced far graver
dangers.

Publication of Madison's views had great influence in Richmond and
in Washington, Attorney General William Wirt and others reported.
Niles' Weekly Register remarked that throughout the country Madison had
"silenced the *constitutional* croakers [like] . . . frogs frozen up in a pond."
Nevertheless, Madison wrote Clay in 1832 that he hoped the "deep and
extensive discontent" caused by the tariff might be relieved by compromise. It was "impossible to do perfect justice in the distribution of burdens and benefits," Madison admitted, but "equitable estimates and mutual concessions are necessary to approach it."

Virginia Convention of 1829–30

Madison's only formal resumption of public life during his retirement came in 1829, when he accepted election as a delegate from Orange County to a Virginia convention to draft a new state constitution. Then, as he had done in 1776 and in 1788, he journeyed to the state capital to consider the fundamental law under which free people would choose to live. He was now seventy-eight years old and recovering from flu. But with the draft of another constitution at stake, how could he not go? Leaving the Orange-Charlottesville region for the first time in twelve years, in October 1829 James and Dolley rode the ninety miles to Richmond. For three months James attended the convention, and Dolley enjoyed Richmond society.

The trip to Richmond came after a year of stress and grief at Montpelier. Mother Madison had died at age ninety-seven on February 11, 1829. Her death and funeral, Dolley wrote her sister, *"was near, causing another;"* her son came down with a serious influenza that he took months to shake off. Dolley's letters to Anna Cutts were filled with the "Petticoat Affair" in Washington over the refusal of many cabinet wives to visit, despite President Jackson's insistence, Peggy Eaton, the wife of Secretary of War John Eaton, whom Washington society ladies regarded as a tavern keeper's daughter and woman of ill repute. Dolley was astonished at the controversy's "melancholy perspective, as well as retrospect to our country," destroying the amicable, polite republican lifestyle she had established twenty years earlier. She was glad Anna had not visited Peggy "as you had nothing to lose by her." Dolley seemed pleased to hear, in the politics associated with the imbroglio, that "Mr. Kalhoon is a little on the wane" and that "Mr. V. B. [Van Buren] is the favorite with you all for the next President."

National politics crowded on the visit to Richmond when the Madisons were able to politely refuse the official invitation of Governor William B. Giles, long a thorn in Madison's side, to stay with him. Instead they stayed congenially with a favorite cousin of Dolley's, Sally Coles Stevenson, wife of Speaker of the United States House of Representatives Andrew Stevenson. Anna's husband, Richard Cutts, had been fired under the Jacksonian spoils system, and their son James Madison Cutts, along with many old friends and colleagues, seemed likely to lose federal jobs, too. Dolley wrote she "would *myself* rather be my own cook and keep a respectable boarding house than have the Dept. of State under Genl. J——n [Jackson] because I think there w'd. be more honor and independence in it." Dolley also sought to channel some desperately needed funds from her cash-strapped husband to the Cutts in Washington, to failing farmer brother John C. Payne in Orange County, to a niece in western Virginia, and to son Payne Todd "boarding within Prison bounds for a debt of 2— or 300$." The "Jacksonian Revolution" of 1829 was generally a social and political horror to the Madisons as the harmonious, elite, republican culture they had worked for a generation to nourish seemed to be displaced by the hordes of new politicians and office seekers who trampled the carpets and tore down Dolley's rich red damask drapes at the White House during Jackson's inaugural ball. Departing president John Quincy Adams believed that the Age of the Argonauts was over; what Theodore Roosevelt, when he studied Jacksonian public life, would call "the millennium of the minnows" had begun. Altogether, Dolley wrote Anna in June 1829 as James struggled to throw off the effects of influenza, "I loath the idea of going to Richmond, but if M. goes, so I must."

In Richmond, even though Dolley worried that "Mr. M. is not yet well of his influenza, . . . [he] goes every day to convention, just a little walk" from the Stevensons' comfortable home. George Tucker found Madison "rejuvenated; . . . his cheerfulness and amenity and abundant stock of racy anecdotes were the delight of every social board." Dolley, of course, was in her glory. Anne Royall, who came to interview the famous sixty-year-old hostess, was astonished to find, instead of "a little old dried-up woman," one "tall, young, active and elegant." With a full, oval face and large, expressive dark eyes set off by a silk checked turban and black glossy curls, Dolley Madison "captivated by her artless though warm affability." She was "as active on her feet as a girl" and seemed to be "young enough for Mr. Madison's daughter." "Her power to please, the irresistible grace of her every movement shed such a charm over all she says and does," Mrs. Royall exclaimed, "that it is impossible not to admire her." A young man who came to visit Madison found him "in tolerably good health, thin of flesh, rather under the common size, and dressed in his customary black, old-fashioned clothes. His form [was] erect, his step firm but somewhat slow, walks without a staff, his visage pale, and abounding in small wrinkles, his features well-proportioned but not striking, his head bald on top but excessively powdered showing a point in front. . . . His forehead of common size, his brow grey, heavy, and projecting, his eyes small and faded, his nose of ordinary size and straight, his mouth rather small, . . . his ears obscured by whiskers and hair, his sight and hearing both somewhat impaired."

The convention gathered the surviving leaders of Virginia public life in the past half century. At the opening session Madison nominated former president and former governor James Monroe as presiding officer and then with Chief Justice John Marshall escorted him to the chair. Madison was the sole surviving member of the 1776 convention, while Monroe and Marshall, Washington's comrades in arms, had each served the state and nation for more than fifty years. Among those whose careers dated from the 1790s were three longtime antagonists of Madison's, Littleton W. Tazewell, John Randolph of Roanoke, and William B. Giles. Of the younger members, many of whom would remain active in public life through the Civil War, dozens saw the seventy-eight-year-old Madison as a demigod whose thought and career had been guides for them for as long as they could remember. Thus preeminent among the distinguished company crowded into the old House of Delegates chamber in the state capitol (now a restored museum room long dominated by a statue of Robert E. Lee), Madison appeared daily for the convention sessions, taking his seat, as he had done so often before in deliberative bodies, near the front in order to pay close attention to the proceedings.

Two great issues faced the convention. On the first, whether to extend the suffrage to those who did not own land, Madison stopped short of advocating universal suffrage, but he did succeed in pushing through the committee on legislation he headed an extension of the vote to all householders and heads of families who paid taxes. He noted that the rapidly increasing population of the United States, despite the vast expanses of unsettled land, would force large numbers, possibly even a majority, and perhaps within a century, to live in cities. Madison declared that republican government could not, in justice or in safety, be rested on a minority. Therefore citizens who had "a sufficient stake in the public order and the stable administration of the laws," even though they did not have freeholds, should be allowed to vote.

Insisting as he and Jefferson always had that in good government a

Madison speaking at the Virginia constitutional convention on December 2, 1829, by George Catlin. (Virginia Historical Society, Richmond)

sense of responsibility and attention to the public good had to accompany the right to participate, Madison could not accept the simple solution of universal suffrage. In urging the extension he did, however, he satisfied the demands of most of those who sought the vote. He stood on the liberalizing side in the convention and broadened his own understanding of the needs of majority government. To the safety gained by eliminating a large portion of the disenfranchised, and therefore potentially rebellious, citizens, Madison sought by extending "the partnership of power" to add the constructive "political and moral influence emanating from the actual possession of authority and a just and beneficial exercise of it." This position, accepting the beneficent effects of political participation, put Madison clearly on the road to advocating universal suffrage, once it became clear that possessors of property were not always responsive to the public welfare, any more than those without it always acted irresponsibly. His theory of suffrage, far from seeking to protect vested interests by exclusions, in fact required a steady expansion (eventually to include blacks, women, and eighteen-year-olds). Madison sought a citizenry responsible not only to the rights of property but even more, in a priority he always insisted on, to the natural and political rights that were part of republican government.

The even more divisive issue of whether to count slaves in apportioning the state legislature caused Madison to consider again the deep contradiction between the existence of slavery and the principles of republican government. In notes taken in the early 1790s when contemplating a political essay on the "Influence of domestic slavery on Government," Madison had noted that "the southern States of America" were in fact "aristocracies." Because blacks as slaves were of course excluded from power and because nonslaveholding whites without sufficient land ownership were also denied the franchise, power was exercised "for the most part by the rich and easy." Thus "power lies in a part instead of the whole; in the hands of property, not of numbers." The situation of slaves in Virginia, Madison thought, illustrated perfectly "the danger of oppression to the minority of unjust combinations of the majority." This injustice, he felt, was all the more pernicious when implanted in the provisions and structure of a constitution. "Were the slaves freed and the right of suffrage extended to all," he wrote, looking far into the American future, "the operation of the government," truly resting on majority rule, "might be very different."

In 1829 as in 1792, though, Madison still felt it politically counterproductive to raise directly the question of abolishing or even restricting slavery. To do so as the convention opened, he wrote Lafayette, "would have been a spark to a mass of gunpowder." Madison had not changed his basic position on the incongruity of slavery in a republican government, but he also as much as ever felt forced to compromise with the slave power in order to avoid a breakdown in the more than half-century-long effort to sustain constitutional self-government. Madison thus again advocated, not abrupt change, but a liberalizing course. The portions of the state east of the mountains wanted their numerous slaves counted in legislative apportionment to retain their heavy preponderance, while the western counties insisted on a "white basis" that would give them, with proportionally far fewer slaves, a much stronger voice in the legislature. Under the old constitution, counting slaves, white votes in the east had at least twice as much weight as white votes in the west (but slaves, of course, had no voice; their masters, in effect, voted for them). Madison managed, narrowly, to move through his committee on legislation a "white basis" for the lower house, while retaining the old provision in the less powerful Senate. Having expected Madison to stand with them, eastern delegates fumed about his "fatuity" and "treason." Madison's compromise caused hotheads on both sides to bemoan "the effect of putting old men in active life." Shaken by the violence of eastern denunciation, and sensing defeat, Madison shifted to advocate the use of the federal three-fifths ratio in apportioning the lower house. Monroe stood with him, while Marshall voted against any movement toward a "white basis." Petitions poured in on the convention from eastern constituencies, threatening disunion and violence unless their position was protected. Madison later explained his compromise as due to "the necessity of securing an effective and tranquil result by indulging the party, whose defeat would have been pregnant with danger." His critics thought this cowardly; his supporters, a wise act of prudence.

In this tense atmosphere Madison, in old-fashioned powdered hair, black clothes, and shoe buckles, rose on December 2 to deliver his only speech before the convention. "*Members from all parts of the Hall* (with the exception of not more than ten) gathered round him to catch the lowest accents from his tongue," a Richmond *Enquirer* reporter wrote. "His voice was low and weak, but his sentences were rounding and complete; and his enunciation, though tremulous and full of feeling, was distinct to those who heard him." Madison began by noting that he was deeply sensible of the disqualifications imposed by his extreme age and long retirement. He asked time to make only "a few observations." He affirmed his lifelong insistence that "in republics, the great danger is, that the majority may not sufficiently respect the rights of the minority." Generosity, social feelings, and even conscience were insufficient guards against selfish drives, whether in minorities or majorities. Though the "favorable attributes of the human character are all valuable, as auxiliaries," Madison observed, repeating language he had used before in the 1788 Virginia convention, "they will not serve as a substitute for the coercive provision belonging to the Government and Law. . . . The only effectual safeguard to the rights of the minority, must be laid in such a basis and structure of the Government itself, as may afford, in a certain degree, directly or indirectly, a defensive authority in behalf of a minority having right on its side." Therefore Madison urged the convention to accept the three-fifths basis for the lower house, both to give a security to the "peculiar" property of the easterners and to give some recognition, even though a degraded one, to the humanity of the slaves.

Madison hoped further that the interests of the slaves might receive a little protection, sometimes by eastern members anxious to protect them as property and sometimes by western members sympathizing with them against the oppressive designs of their masters. To abolitionists, of course, beginning to loom larger and larger on the national scene, Madison's course seemed unjust and evasive in the extreme, but as usual he preferred a perhaps achievable lesser of evils to unattainable perfection. He concluded with a plea for "the spirit of compromise" that found him, consciously and almost word for word, reenacting the role played by the aged Franklin at the close of the 1787 Federal Convention. He asked his fellow delegates not to despair, "notwithstanding all the threatening appearances we have passed through," but instead to "agree on some common ground, all sides relaxing in their opinions, not changing, but mutually surrendering a part of them."

Madison's efforts at compromise failed, however, in the face of unyielding pressure from eastern delegates determined to retain their favored position as slave owners. With the help of westerners, now seeking to disrupt the convention rather than accept less than a full "white basis," eastern delegates defeated Madison's three-fifths compromise and then pushed through provisions maintaining eastern control of both houses of the legislature. Partly through his own shifting tactics and failure to stand resolutely for majority rule and against slavery, Madison had vitiated his own influence and helped put the convention under the control of men with less subtle, less ambiguous intentions. Though, at adjournment, universal respect for "the venerable Mr. Madison" led to an affecting scene where all members, some with tear-filled eyes, shook his hand, he admitted after he got home that the convention, "by indulging the party whose defeat would have been most pregnant with danger to it," had surrendered to those "fixed in their hot opinion."

Madison's report to Lafayette nonetheless tried to put the best construction possible on the convention. It had been, he said, "pregnant with difficulties of various sorts, and, at times, of ominous aspects": conflicts concerning the structure of government, peculiar local interests, severe sectional differences, taxation, and "above all the case of our coloured population" and slavery. "Every concession of private opinion not morally inadmissible," he said, had been necessary to prevent a dissolution of the convention that would have "inflict[ed] a stain on the great cause of self-government." Madison thus hoped the framing of a new constitution and its adoption by the people, flawed as it was but still some improvement, would make it "new evidence of the capacity of men for self-government, instead of an argument in the hands of those who deny and calumniate it." Madison was proud, too, that he, Monroe, and Marshall, though "mindful of the years over our heads," had nonetheless taken part in the "great talents in the discussions" exhibited at the convention. Though he thus sought to put as good a light as possible on the presence and practice of good republican government, Madison was also deeply troubled by the power of the slave-owning minority. "A government resting on a minority is an aristocracy, not a Republic," he noted severely, "and could not be safe with a numerical and physical force against it, without a standing army, an enslaved press, and a disarmed populace."

The 1829–30 Virginia constitution was not a document of which Madison was proud, nor did he entirely admire the tenor of the convention debates. Though he maintained an outward equanimity, he must have sensed that in Virginia, and the rest of the South, slavery and its defenders had become, as he had always feared they would, a grave threat to the survival of republican government. Madison's unwillingness, though, to confront the slave power directly and his faith that self-government had again "triumphed" in the compromise were further evidence of his own deepening self-delusion about the eventual demise of slavery.

As the convention had moved toward its rather rancorous adjournment, Dolley Madison wrote that though "all Richd. allmost, had been afflicted with Influenza," the city had been filled with gaiety and "quiet but thorough hospitality" during their three-month visit. On Christmas Eve, Dolley went to a party where a dozen people appeared in masks, dancing and "causing a deal of amusemt." (Dolley "staid only til 10 oclock," she said.) One dancer impersonated Rob Roy, part of the rage for Sir Walter Scott novels that so excited Dolley and her literary friends. The ladies also quoted Shakespeare (the first lines of "Macbeth"), read James Fenimore Cooper's *The Wept of Wish-Ton-Wish* ("too full of horrors" Dolley told her niece), deplored the dissipated low life described in *The Oxonians* (too close for Dolley's comfort to her son Payne's real life), and hoped to see Thomas Moore's exciting and romantic *Letters and Journals of Lord Byron*. As for the Christmas Eve party, Dolley reported that "Mr. M. did not want to go though he has generally gone to parties with me." On Christmas

Day the Madisons "dined at Major Gibbon's," and cousin Betsy Coles "had a large party in the Evg." When Dolley got back to Montpelier in January 1830, she wrote Anna Cutts that "we had a very pleasant visit of 3 months and more," and, given the Peggy Eaton embroilment in Washington, she "wd. Prefer Richd. for a residence," for she had been "surrounded . . . by the kindest, & most agreable people" there. James simply reported wearily that in Richmond "every moment of my time was, in some way or other, exacted by my public situation, and of the accumulating arrears of a private nature requiring my attention."

Nullification, "a Deadly Poison"

Madison's most important and fateful confrontation with forces defending the South and its "peculiar institution," however, came during the South Carolina nullification crisis, 1828–33. He saw at once that the doctrines of nullification and secession posed a fundamental threat to the Union, and he took an active part in the war of words waged against them. His public defense of the constitutionality of the tariff had aroused the ire of states' righters, but that was only a mild foretaste of the storm that broke over him when Governor Giles, Vice President John C. Calhoun, and others insisted that the doctrine of nullification rested on the Kentucky and Virginia Resolutions drafted by Jefferson and Madison in 1798. In holding that the Constitution countenanced state nullification of federal laws deemed in violation of the Constitution, states' rights theorists asserted they did no more than the two earlier leaders had done in resisting the Alien and Sedition Acts in 1798–1800. Calhoun's South Carolina "Exposition" of December 1828 declared that Madison's 1800 "Report on the [Virginia] Resolutions" so ably upheld the doctrine of state sovereignty that no further argument was needed. Giles, in anonymous newspaper articles defending nullification, quoted at length from Madison's "Report" and from Jefferson's letters declaiming against expansion of federal authority that had appeared in a recently published edition. As if expecting Madison to rebut him, Giles asked his readers to "rely on [Madison's] opinions of fifty," rather than on any senile effusions he might make at age seventy-nine.

To state senator Joseph C. Cabell, who led the antinullificationists in Richmond, Madison outlined arguments against the doctrine. The people composing the states, not the state governments, were the parties to the constitutional compact, delegating certain powers to the general government and reserving others to the states. The Constitution further provided that the Supreme Court of the United States should decide disputes over the boundary between state and federal powers. Admissible remedies for "usurpations" accepted by the court, Madison said, included remonstrances and instructions such as those used by Virginia in 1798, "recurring elections and impeachments," and amendments to the Constitution. Declaring federal laws invalid, "nullified," and thus unenforceable within a state, by executive or legislative action, or even by state conventions, was illegal and unconstitutional, not admissible. Finally, the ultimate resort, the natural right of resistance and revolution, was available to states or to individual citizens, but this exercise dissolved government and could not be claimed under the Constitution. Short of such extremities, Madison insisted nullification made a farce of national law and supposed the Constitution established a mere league rather than a government. "The awful consequences of a final rupture and dissolution of the Union," which nullification certainly foreshadowed, Madison declared, "must be shuddered at by every friend to his country, to liberty, to the happiness of man."

Early in 1830 the Webster-Hayne debate in the United States Senate heated up the controversy and drew Madison further into its center. Each orator claimed Madison's support. Daniel Webster of Massachusetts noted Madison's "impregnable" defense of the constitutionality of the tariff in his published letters to Cabell. Surely the Father of the Constitution could not approve a nullification doctrine almost certainly fatal to the Union. Robert Y. Hayne of South Carolina cited the "Report" of 1800 at length, quoting (out of context) phrases such as Madison's reference to the federal Constitution" as "a compact to which the States are parties." Though Madison did not wholly approve of Webster's sweeping insistence that "the people of the United States in the aggregate" had established the Constitution, he unequivocally took Webster's side in the argument. Madison was delighted to hear from his young friend Nicholas P. Trist, who had sat enthralled in the Senate galleries during the debate. He reported that Webster had been "the mammouth deliberately treading the canebreak," so devastating was his reply to Hayne. To Senator Hayne, who immediately sent copies of his speeches to Montpelier, Madison acknowledged their "ability and eloquence," but he then explained in detail why he was "constrained to dissent . . . from the doctrines espoused in them."

Madison gradually gave in to the mounting pressure to speak out and thus arrest, as the Richmond *Whig* put it, "the deadly poison circulating under the authority of his name." In June 1830 South Carolina and Virginia newspapers printed a letter from Madison to a South Carolina Unionist warning against interpretations of the Constitution that gave the federal government virtually unlimited powers but nonetheless denying that state sovereignty was supreme and indivisible or that states could revoke or alter federal laws or the federal Constitution on their own authority alone. Richmond politicians began to shift ground and declared that Virginia, despite its belief in states' rights, would not join South Carolina in nullification. As a Madison-suggested alliance of Unionists and moderate states' righters emerged in Richmond, Cabell pronounced that "nullification is dead in this state." Sensing the power of Madison's support, Congressman Edward Everett of Massachusetts, also editor of the influential *North American Review,* asked permission to print Madison's rebuke to Hayne, which had somehow come to his attention. Madison agreed but recast the letter into one to Everett. It was printed in October 1830, Madison's final, most carefully considered interpretation of the nature and powers of the federal Constitution.

The aged statesman, weak from an attack of bilious fever, began by pointing out again, as he had in *Federalist* No. 39, that the Constitution established neither a consolidated (national) government nor a confederated one, but rather a composite, or mixture of both. Because this was a unique form, it had to be interpreted in and of itself, and could not be expounded by "similitudes and analogies." Because the Constitution had been formed by the people of the states—the same authority that established the state constitutions, Madison noted—it shared sovereignty with the state governments. Furthermore, it could be altered or annulled only with the consent, according to the prescribed modes, of the other parties to it, all the states and the federal government itself. Turning to the division of powers between the federal and state governments, Madison pointed out that the general government was no less sovereign, supreme in its prescribed realm, than the states themselves. In the vital matter of "controversies . . . concerning the boundaries of jurisdiction," Madison

insisted that the clauses of the federal Constitution making federal statutes the supreme law of the land, binding state judges to the federal Constitution, and giving the federal judiciary jurisdiction in all cases arising
under federal law indicated clearly that the Supreme Court of the United
States was to be the final arbiter. To give this power to the states would
violate the "vital principle [of] . . . a uniform authority of the laws." To
make it a matter of "negotiation" among the parties overlooked the resort
to arms that was the only recourse among "independent and separate
sovereignties" when negotiations broke down, as invariably would happen on occasion. Many provisions within the Constitution guarded against
federal usurpations, such as state control of senators and frequent elections, which had proved effective against the Alien and Sedition Acts. On
the other hand, the doctrine of nullification allowed the general government no means to defend itself against state pretensions and hence would
lead certainly to its demise.

Turning to "the expedient lately advanced," Madison pointed out
that the proposal that state nullifications stand unless rejected by three-
fourths of the states was hopelessly cumbersome. He insisted instead that
changes, including nullifications, be made only with the approval of that
proportion of states, a provision already existing under the Constitution.
As to the claim that the Virginia Resolutions of 1798 and "Report on the
Resolutions" of 1800 sanctioned nullification, Madison apologized for language perhaps insufficiently guarded, but he went on to assert that not
the resolves, nor the "Report," nor the debates in the Virginia legislature
anywhere disclosed any "reference whatever to a constitutional right in
an individual state to arrest by force the operation of a law of the United
States." The intent was entirely to call for concurring statements from
other states and other modes of cooperation among them, as had soon
transpired in the political campaign that ousted the government responsible for the offending laws. Nothing was said in the Virginia proceedings,
Madison observed, "that can be understood to look to means of maintaining the rights of the states beyond the regular ones within the forms of
the Constitution." Further action could be justified only under the natural
right, "extra and ultra constitutional," of resistance and rebellion, which
of course would cancel the constitutional compact and return society to
a state of nature.

Antinullificationists thrilled at Madison's performance. Cabell called its effect "as great as ever was produced by any document in any age or country." Edward Coles thought it "the clearest exposition of the Constitution" he had ever read, and even Chief Justice Marshall wrote of his "peculiar pleasure . . . [that Mr. Madison] is himself again, [avowing] the opinions of his best days." Nullifiers, having depended so heavily on the "doctrines of '98," felt injured and betrayed. Some who had recently praised and revered Madison became "his most embittered revilers and denouncers," while others argued at length that the resolves of 1798 and "Report" of 1800 had declared the states the final arbiters of the meaning of the Constitution. Madison's recent letter was a tissue of sophistries, demonstrating only his own inconsistency and senility.

Meanwhile, events conspired to place Madison's friends, and hence his ideas, close to President Jackson's ear. Nicholas Trist, appointed a State Department clerk by Clay in 1827, became a White House aide and finally, in 1830, one of Jackson's private secretaries, through his close friendship with Jackson's nephew Andrew Jackson Donelson. From then through the early months of 1833, Trist wrote at length to Montpelier of the problems faced by the administration, while Madison supplied Trist, and hence the president, with arguments and information useful in resisting nullification. Trist filled Washington and Virginia newspapers with anonymous articles that were often little more than paraphrases of Madison's notes and letters to him. Madison also advised the increasingly influential Martin Van Buren on interpreting the Constitution. Perhaps most strategic of all, after Jackson's expulsion of the Calhounite, anti–Peggy Eaton members of his cabinet in April 1831, Edward Livingston became his secretary of state and draftsman for documents on nullification.

Livingston had been Madison's supporter in 1798, resisting the Alien and Sedition Acts. Though not always political allies, by 1831 they were again on friendly terms, and Madison responded to Livingston's inquiries with helpful advice on the best formulations to use against the nullifiers. Finally, the hero-president himself, informed by Trist of Madison's personal responsibility for his appointment as major general in 1814 and grateful for Madison's refusal to speak out against him in the 1828 election, maintained an affectionate respect for his former commander in chief. Jackson's visit to Montpelier in the summer of 1832 strengthened the personal bond between the two old patriots and afforded them a congenial opportunity to attune their defenses of the Union. Madison was careful to assure that the president's visit did not overlap with that of Senator Clay, his rival in the 1832 presidential election. At the same time, by retaining his ties to the leading anti-Jackson foes of nullification, Clay, Webster, and John Quincy Adams, Madison was the nonpartisan elder statesman, the "honorary chairman" of an informal national committee to preserve the Union. Madison's still-powerful mind and unique prestige permitted him, though past eighty and long retired, to perform a final, vital service to his country.

Through 1831 and 1832 Madison wrote long letters, not published over his name but obviously intended for public use, upholding the constitutionality of the tariff but at the same time both resisting nullification and denying that the "general welfare" or "necessary and proper" clauses of the Constitution gave Congress virtually unlimited authority, as Clay, Webster, and others at times seemed to assert. Madison, the living sage of Montpelier, also wrote at length to repudiate efforts by nullificationists to claim for their side the by now dead sage of Monticello. Finding unguarded expressions of states' rights in the recently published edition of Jefferson's letters and pointing out that the word *nullify* had been used in the Kentucky Resolutions drafted by Jefferson, the nullifiers argued that Jefferson was their source. Insofar as Madison claimed otherwise, nullificationists argued that he simply betrayed or misinterpreted his departed friend. Though letters in Madison's possession confirmed more certainly than he liked Jefferson's authorship of the incriminating Kentucky Resolutions and his unequivocal appeal at times to state sovereignty, Madison insisted that a fair overall view of Jefferson's public and private writings afforded little comfort to the nullifiers, who "make the name of Mr. Jefferson the pedestal for their colossal heresy . . . [and] shut their eyes and lips, whenever his authority is ever so clearly and emphatically against them." Further, Madison observed, "allowances . . . ought to be made for a habit in Mr. Jefferson, as in others of great genius, of expressing in strong and round terms, impressions of the moment." To Madison, the South Carolina doctrines of 1830 and 1833 echoed the peripheral and occasional and distraught rather than the essential, enduring Jefferson, who in fact had worked for half a century, along with Madison, to establish a viable Union.

As the crisis deepened, Madison's concern for the Union and disgust at its foes grew. "The idea," he wrote to Trist in May 1832, "that a Constitution which has been so fruitful of blessings, and a Union admitted to be the only guardian of the peace, liberty and happiness of the people of the States comprizing it should be broken up and scattered to the winds without greater than the existing causes is more painful than words can express. It is impossible that this can ever be the deliberate act of the people, if the value of the Union be calculated by the consequences of disunion." The "preposterous and anarchic" proposals of the nullifiers for state conventions to approve acts of the Union had "no shadow of countenance in the Constitution," Madison asserted, and contained "such a deadly poison" that the Union would not last a year under them. He begged for equitable distribution of burdens among the states and urged "mutual concessions," but all within prescribed constitutional modes.

In December 1832 Madison read the recently passed South Carolina nullification ordinance. In effect it denied the authority of the federal government to enforce the tariff within that state's boundaries and embraced, theoretically, the even more dangerous heresy of secession. He sent long treatises to Trist, used in newspaper campaigns against nullification, and approved the conclusion, if not all the arguments, of Jackson's antinullification proclamation of December 10, written by Livingston. Pleas from Richmond for help against states' righters seeking to place Virginia at South Carolina's side prompted letters from Montpelier denying that the proceedings of 1798 in any way furnished a precedent for South Carolina's recent action. Virginia withheld its vital support. In Washington, Senator William Cabell Rives of Virginia, recently returned from France, spoke brilliantly for the Union, using materials furnished by Madison. "Mr. Rives . . . has met Mr. Calhoun on his own ground," wrote one correspondent sitting in the galleries, "and by one of the ablest speeches delivered this session, has demolished the doctrine of nullification, root and branch. . . . You have no idea how Mr. Rives's facts and arguments made Mr. Calhoun wince in his seat." Madison declared Rives's speech "very able and enlightening" and hoped it would confound those who sought to label defenders of the Union "as Innovators, heretics and Apostates." It made perfectly clear that "whilst a State remains within the Union it cannot withdraw its citizens from the operation of the Constitution and laws of the Union," nor was "the more formidable" doctrine of secession any more within the meaning of the Constitution. Madison also praised a speech by Webster that "crushes 'nullification,' and must hasten the abandonment of 'secession.'"

Early in 1833 Henry Clay, claiming he "adhered to the doctrines of that ablest, wisest and purest of American statesmen, James Madison," arranged the compromise tariff that led to South Carolina's repeal of its nullification ordinance. Madison hoped this would be "an anodyne on the feverish excitement under which the public mind was laboring." He nonetheless was alarmed by "the torch of discord" lighted by the South Carolinians and kept burning by Northern hotheads who proclaimed "unconstitutional designs on the subject of . . . slaves." With a deep emotional breach opening between the sections, Madison hoped that "as the gulf is approached the deluded will recoil from its horrors, and that the deluders, if not themselves sufficiently startled, will be abandoned and overwhelmed by their followers." "What *madness* in the South," Madison lamented, "to look for greater safety in disunion. It would be worse than jumping out of the Frying-pan into the fire: it would be jumping into the fire for fear of the Frying-pan." Calhoun's defensive "Exposition" of 1828 was as much anathema to the architect of the "extended republic" as was fearful Antifederalism in 1788 or timorous New England Federalism from 1808 to 1814. It was fitting that virtually the last remnant of Madison's strength should be expended against an effort to deny to the nation the benefits of mutual accord that could only come in union.

Fears and Sorrows at Montpelier

James Madison's intense and effective defense of the Constitution against nullifiers, secessionists, and sectionalists occurred, though, during months and years of ill health for both James and Dolley, financial disarray, illness and death of cherished relatives and friends, and multitudes of sometimes troublesome guests. James had influenza in April 1830, a "billious attack" while attending a Board of Visitors meeting at the university in Charlottesville that lasted all summer, and the onset of severe rheumatism just before Christmas. Dolley found herself "over head in business" after returning from Richmond, down with a bout of cholera morbus in September, and busy, perhaps oppressed, with visits from relatives, friends, and strangers. All were eager to meet and talk with the famous couple who

had, in now legendary fashion, presided over the birth and then the building of the national republic already a model for the world.

Alexis de Tocqueville's tour of the United States about this time, for
example, was planned to include Montpelier, but that visit was omitted
because of severe weather and fear of the cholera pandemic that in 1831
ravaged Europe and in 1832 crossed the Atlantic, killing thousands in Philadelphia, Washington, Richmond, and other American cities in August and
September 1832. All at Montpelier watched with apprehension and dread.
Chief Justice Marshall wrote of the Richmond epidemic, called "Asiatic
cholera," that he was "not sure that a single person actually seized with it
has survived." The feared disease, he thought, was "sporatic," jumping
from place to place, and "confined chiefly to people of colour." He took
"measures of precaution"; the Montpelier "family" did likewise. Nonetheless, James had had influenza again during the "severe cold and snow"
of winter 1831, and his rheumatism was worse again that summer. More
rheumatism in January 1832 and a long bout of "bilious fever" from March
to May that year kept him in bed most of the time. Dolley reported that
the "Norwegian Winter [of 1830–31] . . . proved too cold for me," drag-
ging her, too, down with an influenza that lasted even longer than her
husband's. "So you see," she wrote hyperbolically to "dear cousin" Elizabeth Coles, "how much younger & stronger he is, than I am."

Often it seemed that only bad news came to Montpelier. Dolley's letters sometimes express pleasure at events but often are full of apprehension, worry, and even disdain and anger over what has been reported to
her. She sought to know of all the "manoeuverings" of the ladies in Washington over the Peggy Eaton affair and herself tried to be neutral in "the
contention of parties," but she was pleased her sister Anna did not visit
Peggy or the ladies who supported her and President Jackson. Former
president Monroe, dispirited and mortally ill, was in Washington with his
daughter Mrs. Hay, whom Dolley supposed was as cold-tempered and
unpleasant as ever. Dolley was pleased to see the husband of her niece
Mary Jackson Allen but was sorry that some of Mary's recently deceased
father's relatives were bringing suit against and spoke "harshly" of Richard Cutts, who seems to have owed money to Mary's father (husband of
Dolley's long deceased sister Mary). Cutts could not repay it because,
under President Jackson's spoils system, he had been fired from the gov-

ernment job James Madison had procured for him more than a decade earlier.

The problems of the Cuttses, raising their family in Washington and visiting Montpelier for months each summer, were always of concern to Dolley. She worried even more as Anna's health deteriorated. In January 1831, as her sister passed through an "extreme illness," Dolley begged her seventeen-year-old niece Mary to write "by every post" of her mother's improvement to "relieve my oppressed heart." In the meantime, Dolley, always Anna's mother as well as sister, instructed her nieces that "you must keep [Anna's] room quiet and herself from the slightest agitation or uneasiness, [and] . . . let no one approach her, who is not sensible of the importance of smiles and comfort to one who has been so near the grave!" Anna, with her children, was able to make what turned out to be her last visit to Montpelier that summer. She was sick again in September as Dolley worried as well about the "alarm of Insurrections"—the Nat Turner rebellion of August 1831—that she hoped "all will be on guard" against in the future.

Another hard winter in 1831–32 left Dolley worried about her husband's health; "he could not travel unless conveyed on his bed" and was "too feeble to sit up but to have it made." If that was not enough, she was fearing the approach of "the Alarming Cholera" when Anna's health again failed. Anna's last letter arrived at Montpelier on August 4, 1832, telling, in Dolley's words, of "great and many sufferings [that] . . . fall heavily on my heart," but Dolley hoped, as always, that the crisis would pass. But as Dolley was replying, Anna, age fifty-three, had already died in Washington that very day. Upon receiving the news from Richard Cutts two days later, Dolley wrote him, "The heart of your miserable sister mourns with you, with your precious daughters, with your sons!" She asked Richard to give her "gratitude and love to" all who "to the end, extended their kindness & consolations to my lamented sister." This circle of friends, who had been Dolley's social colleagues during her sixteen years as First Lady in Washington, included some whose husbands, like Richard Cutts, had recently lost their jobs to Jackson's spoils system. "Mr. Madison," she added, "partakes in our sorrows, & in my wish to see you all here. . . . Come as soon as you can, & bring [the children] with you." The Cutts children, especially Richard, fifteen when his mother died, and

Mary, eighteen then, continued to come to Montpelier as long as Dolley kept the plantation. She looked after them as their grandmother as well as aunt as long as she lived. James, of course, was always the attentive, pleasing grandfather. Yet Anna, the person probably closest to both the Madisons, who had come to them as a fifteen-year-old "daughter" at their marriage in 1794, was gone.

James Madison supported as best he could some of his numerous nieces and nephews, especially William Madison's son Robert, whose promising career in Virginia politics was cut short by his early death in 1828. Both Madisons continued to worry about Dolley's younger brother John's struggle to raise his family on a farm in Orange County. Low prices for crops (also a problem at Montpelier), the steady enlargement of his family, and his continuing bouts of alcoholism meant, however, that he barely held on and was a constant worry at Montpelier. The progeny and in-laws of Dolley's other vivacious and beloved sisters, Mary and Lucy, also continued to be a care, but the hardest burden to bear was the profligate and wayward life of Dolley's son, John Payne Todd. He wandered about the East from Boston to Richmond, coming occasionally for a month or two to Montpelier at his mother's urgent, desperate pleas. He was in debtor's prison in Philadelphia in June 1829, in Washington again a year later, back at Montpelier in February 1832, and then back in Washington in July. He was never other than a source of worry, embarrassment, and financial hemorrhage to his mother and stepfather, and he supplied the constant refrain in his mother's letters of anxiety and anguish over him.

Furthermore, Mother Madison's death on February 11, 1829, at age ninety-seven brought anguish and family adjustments. She was buried in the family graveyard next to her husband, who had died twenty-eight years earlier. Her funeral was in Orange Court House on May 7. On June 30 her estate, including her slaves, her farm animals, and the furnishings of her part of the Montpelier mansion were evaluated by her grandson-in-law Orange County clerk Reynolds Chapman. Sons James and William Madison, granddaughter Nelly Conway Willis, and grandson Dr. Erasmus T. Rose signed papers to clear up old and perhaps contentious debts in the family. Probably to provide an equitable way, monetarily, to divide up her estate for settlement on dozens of heirs, a friendly sale of its assets was held on July 30. Prominent among the buyers was Sarah Madison

Nelly Conway Madison. (Belle Grove Plantation)

Macon, the major purchaser, who bought two bedsteads, three dozen chairs, a walnut table and a pine table, "8 knives & 10 forks & knife box," four wineglasses and an "old" tumbler, a "ball metal" skillet, two teakettles and other kitchenware, a large trunk, blankets, counterpanes, sheets, and towels, and two large looking glasses. John C. Payne acquired some less expensive items including a "pine table painted," five plates, an old trunk, and three iron pots, and Reuben Conway got a walnut table, "2 Dutch ovens," and a black heifer and a red one. Even the slave Sawney bought "7 bottles, Coffee Pot & Turene Top" for $12. Michael Hasey got two red cows and one old one, plus two calves, for $31.75. Thos. Brown bought a mousetrap.

In a final settlement, Chapman brought Mother Madison's eighteen evaluated slaves before him to complete the instruction in her will that the slaves go to masters or mistresses of their choosing. They registered their choices and presumably were distributed accordingly: Joshua (evaluated at $375), Edmund ($380), Frank ($350), Reuben ($300), Simon ($50), Betty ($275), Milly and child under fourteen ($350), and Daniel ($340) went to "Genl William Madison"; Moses ($375) went to Ambrose Madison; Sam ($50), Pamela and her son Solomon ($275) and daughter Judy, eight years ($200), Peter ("nothing"), and James ($300) went to Sarah Macon. In a different arrangement, Sawney, Violet, and Lucy, "old negroes" (Sawney was seventy-eight) not evaluated, were allotted to James Madison who was to provide "necessary support including clothing for the remainder of their lives," estimated to cost $60 each.

Altogether the years from Mother Madison's passing through Anna Cutts's early death in August 1832 were replete with bouts of illness, fears of cholera and slave insurrection, and family worries. Montpelier housed as much, perhaps more, sorrow than joy.

Establishing the University of Virginia

James Madison nonetheless sustained both his deep interest in national affairs during the nullification controversy and his work to help establish and guide the University of Virginia. In 1816 he had been appointed, with Jefferson and Monroe, one of the trustees, or visitors, of the university, at first called Central College, to be established, Jefferson hoped, in Charlottesville, with the support of the state of Virginia. Though Madison did not leave Washington in time to attend a meeting of the board called for April 8, 1817, he did go to Charlottesville on May 5. He met there with Jefferson, Monroe, and John Hartwell Cocke of Fluvanna County to launch Central College, which, according to Jefferson's strategy, would soon become the University of Virginia, standing at the apex of the state's educational system. At the next board meeting, held at Montpelier in July, the visitors went ahead with building plans and agreed to ask Dr. Samuel Knox of Baltimore to "accept the Professorship of Languages, Belles Lettres, Rhetoric, History, and Geography." In October the visitors gathered again in Charlottesville to lay the cornerstone, "with all the ceremony and solemnity due to such an occasion," and because Dr. Knox had refused an appointment, to increase professorial pay and privileges. Madison was present when the board agreed to invite his longtime friend Thomas Cooper to be professor of chemistry, zoology, botany, and anatomy, but he had to go home the next day, before the minutes could be copied, so Jefferson signed the secretary's book for him.

During the following winter Madison watched anxiously as a fund drive progressed and the legislature in Richmond struggled with a general education bill providing for primary education throughout the state, colleges or academies in each of nine districts, and a university to cap the system. The fund drive soon had subscriptions of nearly $50,000, including a $1,000 pledge from Madison. It was enough to begin building in Charlottesville, even though sectarians hostile to "godless" higher education, sectional jealousies over location of the university, and provincial, economy-minded opposition to elegant plans for education in general, and to Jeffersonian speculations in particular, combined in the legislature to threaten the whole scheme. Joseph C. Cabell, sponsor of the bill in the legislature, found every effort to garner votes met "the imputation of management and intrigue" and despaired at one point that only the election of Madison and other "enlightened" men to the House of Delegates could ever secure passage of the bill. A letter supporting the plan, signed by Jefferson, Madison, and the other visitors, did help, however. In late February 1818 the legislature authorized a general system of education, including a university, but referred the vital question of location to twenty-four "discreet and intelligent" commissioners to be appointed by the governor and to meet in August at Rockfish Gap in the Blue Ridge between Charlottesville and Staunton. Jefferson wrote Cabell that Madison would serve as a commissioner, of course, but because "fanatics both in religion and politics . . . consider me as a raw head and bloody bones, . . . I believe the institution would be more popular without me than with me." It was not "mock-modesty," therefore, Jefferson said, that caused him to urge his own omission from the list of commissioners. He and Madison were both appointed, however.

In Charlottesville in May 1818 the board hastened the building of Central College, pushed the fund drive, and otherwise sought to strengthen the claims of Charlottesville at the upcoming Rockfish Gap meeting. It was during this visit that Madison found time to address the Agricultural Society of Albemarle, extolling, in the physiocratic tradition he shared with Jefferson, the republican benefits of yeoman farming and the application of science to the tillage of the soil, along with the parallel moral and social improvements possible through education. Three months later he returned to Charlottesville, arriving at Monticello only a half hour before sunset after a hot ride from Montpelier. "The ladies" there, James wrote his wife, "enquired affectionately after you," disappointed that she had not accompanied her husband for the visit. The next day he and Jefferson went west to visit "Mr. Divers, with whom we shall dine and pass the night," at his home with a wing designed by Jefferson. The next morning they went on to Rockfish Gap in the Blue Ridge where the commissioners were to have the historic meeting that in effect designed and founded the University of Virginia according to Jefferson's plan.

In May and June wagonloads of beds had passed through Charlottesville on their way to Rockfish Gap, where, Jefferson heard, the commissioners would be "tolerably" accommodated in forty lodging rooms. At the comfortable but unpretentious inn near a falls on a branch of the James River and commanding broad vistas in all directions, they gathered for four days on homemade split-bottom chairs around a large dining room table in a low-ceilinged whitewashed room. Present were twenty-one eminent Virginians, many of them long known to Madison, including his brother-in-law John G. Jackson, Senator Armistead T. Mason, Archibald Stuart of Staunton, and Judge Spencer Roane. Jefferson, of course, was the center of attention, "the soul that animated the meeting," one of his admirers reported. He was chosen both president of the commissioners and chairman of a committee to deal with all matters except that of location. The committee accepted, probably with little amendment, a carefully drawn philosophical plan Jefferson had brought with him, both for education in Virginia generally and for organizing the university.

Jefferson proposed that the primary schools, established with public support throughout the state, teach the rudiments of learning, so that all citizens would be able to transact their own affairs, understand the elements of morality, and be trained in the responsibilities of community life and citizenship. He further envisioned preparatory academies scattered about the state in places other than Charlottesville, to teach "the easier authors" in Latin and Greek and the intermediate stages of mathematics and natural science. Such a plan, the commissioners noted, would enable the university to be truly an institution of higher learning, unbothered by "the noisy turbulence of a multitude of small boys" characteristic of pre-paratory schools. Then the commissioners reaffirmed their faith in education generally, against the opinion of "some good men, and even of respectable information, [who] consider the learned sciences as useless acquirements." Scorning "the discouraging persuasion that a man is fixed, by the law of his nature, at a given point; that his improvement is a chimera, and the hope delusive of rendering ourselves wiser, happier, or better than our forefathers were," the commissioners declared that "each generation succeeding to the knowledge acquired by all those that preceded it, adding to it their own acquisitions and constant accumulation, must advance the knowledge and well-being of mankind . . . indefinitely to a term which none can fix or foresee." In this, as in Jefferson's other views on the vital place of education of all citizens as well as of leaders in a self-governing society, Madison fully and profoundly agreed.

The commissioners approved Jefferson's plan for ten divisions in the university, each to be taught by a distinguished professor: ancient languages, modern languages, pure mathematics, physics (including geography), chemistry (including geology), biology, anatomy and medicine, government (including history and economics), law, and a humanities division to teach philosophy, ethics, rhetoric, literature, and fine arts. In a startling departure from the usual prescribed curriculum, Jefferson proposed that students be allowed to choose freely which of these divisions they would emphasize. In explaining his plan, Jefferson endorsed the ancient languages as "the foundation common to all the sciences" but insisted that French, Spanish, Italian, and German, and also Anglo-Saxon, "the earliest form [of the language] . . . which we speak," be taught with equal earnestness. He emphasized the practicality of his curriculum by pointing out that mathematics would include military architecture; chemistry, "the theory of agriculture"; and medicine, all studies necessary to that art except, temporarily, "practice at the bedsides of the sick." Finally, Jefferson observed that though Virginia laws on freedom of religion precluded a professor of divinity, the professor of ethics would teach those proofs of God and moral obligations "in which all sects agree," while otherwise leaving "the different sects . . . to provide, as they think fittest, the means of further instruction in their own peculiar tenets." In fact, far from seeking to distance the university from moral training and character development, Jefferson set forth as its goals "to develop the reasoning faculties of our youth, enlarge their minds, cultivate their morals, and instill into them the precepts of virtue and order," and "to form them to habits of reflection and correct action, rendering them examples of virtue to others, and happiness within themselves." Though this plan and the arguments supporting it were Jefferson's, Madison again agreed entirely with the philosophy behind the University of Virginia, providing for modern, nonsectarian, but morally grounded higher learning.

In regulating the university Jefferson left broad discretion in the hands of the visitors, but he did seek to establish a creative, mature atmosphere in which learning would go on easily and enjoyably, rather than under the customary stern discipline. He designed the buildings to provide tranquility and comfort for professors and students, with congenial access to each other. Gymnastic exercise, "the use of tools in the manual arts," militia drill, and "the arts which embellish life, dancing, music, and drawing," would be encouraged to broaden the experience of all students. To govern the whole system, Jefferson hoped that "pride of character, laudable ambition, and moral dispositions" could replace "the degrading motive of fear." "Hardening [students] to disgrace, to corporal punishments, and servile humiliations cannot be the best process for producing erect character," he admonished with pointed understatement. "A police exercised by the students themselves," Jefferson thought, would also be useful to initiate the students "into the duties and practices of civil life." Following Jefferson's lead, the commissioners accepted a transforming vision of educational needs and practices in a self-governing republic. To realize it, Madison did all he could to assist while Jefferson lived. Then for eight more years, when more than seventy-five years old himself, Madison took the lead.

Before and after philosophizing about education, however, the commissioners wrestled with the vexing question of site. They found all three proposed places, Lexington, Staunton, and Charlottesville, "unexceptionable as to the healthiness and fertility." Lexington offered the advantages of an existing institution, Washington College, willing to transform itself into the state university. It promised a subscription of nearly $18,000 and the will of John Robinson conveying property worth perhaps $100,000 to the university if it located in Lexington. Jefferson noted shrewdly that debts of unspecified amount against Robinson's estate and other uncertainties compromised the value of the bequest and that "questions may arise as to the power of the [Washington College] trustees to make the [pledged] transfers." Furthermore, Washington College stipulated that its present faculty be used by the state university, a provision fatal to Jefferson's hope to acquire really distinguished professors and an indication to skeptics that self-interest motivated the Washington College offer. Against this Jefferson set the larger subscription in favor of Charlottesville, the buildings already under way there, and the fully certified transfer of Central College properties to the state university. Finally, in debate before the full Board of Commissioners, Jefferson demonstrated Charlottesville's more central location with demographic calculations and underscored the healthy climate of its vicinity by offering a long list of the octogenarians, soon to include himself, who lived there. The commissioners concluded, "after full inquiry, and impartial and mature consideration," and by a 16-to-5 vote, that Charlottesville was the "convenient and proper" place for the university.

As the meeting adjourned, Jefferson declared he had "never seen business done with so much order, and harmony, nor in abler nor pleasanter society." He went on to the Warm Springs seventy-five miles to the west, but Madison rode back through Charlottesville, confident at last that the ground was now firm beneath the truly republican institution of higher learning rising in the "academical village" he passed on the way. He hoped, he wrote Dolley, "not [to] lose a moment in getting home," both to help his sister Fanny Rose look after their ill mother and to relieve "my anxiety [to] be again with you." He hurried back to Montpelier, making the long trip in one day.

Early the following winter the Virginia legislature approved the proceedings of the commissioners. The university thus came into being much as Jefferson and Madison had hoped, though as Cabell pointed out, "the very same interests and prejudices which arrayed themselves against the location at Charlottesville, will continue to assail that establishment, [and] seize upon every occasion, and avail themselves of every pretext, to keep it down." Jefferson hastily called the Central College visitors to a nearly snowbound midwinter meeting at Montpelier, where he, Madison, and Cocke authorized additional buildings at the new university and passed their assets into its hands. Then, on March 29, 1819, Madison went to Charlottesville for the first of many meetings of the Board of Visitors of the University of Virginia. With the two former presidents on the board were Joseph C. Cabell and John Hartwell Cocke, who from the first had been Jefferson's able and diligent allies in planning the university and who would remain on its board into the 1850s. They were preeminent among the younger generation of Virginians who retained Enlightenment liberality and enthusiasm for reform, and they always revered Jefferson and Madison as paragons of virtue and statesmanship. Also on the board were Chapman Johnson, representative of Valley interests but nonetheless a warm friend of the university; General Robert B. Taylor, a Norfolk Federalist; and James Breckinridge of Botetourt County, another Federalist but long respected by his Republican colleagues.

The visitors immediately elected Jefferson the chairman, or rector, thus placing on him, as everyone had always assumed, the executive guidance of the university. The board quickly approved filling the offices of bursar, secretary, and proctor and provided for Jefferson and Cocke to oversee the construction of buildings, which, it was agreed, should take precedence at first over hiring professors. The board nonetheless affirmed the Central College commitment to Thomas Cooper as professor of chemistry, despite Cabell's warning that Cooper's unorthodox theology would greatly abet political opposition to the university. The board followed its rector on this point, partly out of "unaffected deference . . . for his judgment and experience," an early observer reported, "and partly for the reason often urged by Mr. Madison, that as the scheme was originally Mr. Jefferson's, and the chief responsibility for its success or failure would fall on him, it was but fair to let him execute it in his own way." Thus were fixed the informal relationships animating the board during its early years: Jefferson, as Madison put it, "the great projector and mainspring," Madison his trusted associate in everything, Cocke the executive assistant on buildings, Cabell the legislative liaison, and the other members friendly aides as well as watchdogs on the board for various sectional and political interests.

Even before this meeting, Madison had pronounced himself "uneasy on the subject of Cooper." Though he agreed entirely with Jefferson that Cooper was "the greatest man in America, in the powers of mind, and in acquired information," his touchiness, his reputation (undeserved, Jefferson insisted) for heavy drinking, and his unitarianism if not atheism seemed likely to arouse exactly the controversy and emotionalism so dangerous in launching a university under public sponsorship. The board stuck with Cooper for a time, but by the spring of 1820, "the hue and cry raised from the different pulpits on our appointment of Dr. Cooper, whom they charge with Unitarianism . . . as presumptuously as if it were a crime, and one for which, like Servetus, he should be burned," caused the visitors to accept Cooper's resignation. "For myself," Jefferson observed, "I was not disposed to regard the denunciations of these satellites of religious inquisition; but our colleagues, better judges of popular feeling, thought that they were not to be altogether neglected. . . . I do sincerely lament that untoward circumstances have brought on us the irreparable loss of this professor, whom I have looked to as the corner-stone of our edifice."

When the board convened again in October 1819, Dolley Madison went with her husband to stay at Monticello, but the Monticello family was unable to make the usual return visit to Montpelier "before the roads become impracticable." Jefferson's granddaughter Ellen Randolph wrote Dolley that "My dear Grandfather" had suffered a "sudden . . . violent and obstinate colic lasting about thirty hours." With advice James might have done well to follow himself, Jefferson's doctor told him to *take care of himself,* during this winter." But, Ellen wrote, "he does not know how, to *take care of himself,* to be very attentive to his diet, to use less exercise, and to avoid all fatigue of body or mind, and especially give up letter-writing." Despite such advice, each man continued university-related travel, farm management, social visits, and much letter writing. Madison made semiannual visits to Monticello and Charlottesville in 1820 and 1821, occasionally accompanied by Dolley.

The charges of irreligion at Charlottesville continued strong enough to endanger legislative support. The board, in October 1822, approved Jefferson's recommendation "to give every encouragement" to religious instruction by permitting the various denominations to establish seminaries adjacent to the university and to use its library and other buildings. Jefferson hoped that "by bringing the sects together and mixing them with the mass of other students, we shall soften their asperities, liberalize and neutralize their prejudices, and make the general religion a religion of peace, reason, and morality." Justifying this policy, Madison observed that "a university with sectarian professorships becomes, of course, a Sectarian Monopoly; with professorships of rival sects, it would be an Arena of theological Gladiators. Without any such professorships, it may incur for a time at least, the imputation of irreligious tendencies, if not designs. The last difficulty was thought more manageable than either of the others." "On this view of the subject," Madison concluded, "there seems to be no alternative but between a public University without a theological professorship, and sectarian Seminaries without a University." Jefferson and Madison intended no hostility to religion and hoped vital religious institutions near the university would help sustain among the students such values as "peace, reason, and morality." They were determined, though, both to keep inviolate the separation of church and state in Virginia and to nourish at the university an atmosphere of impartial, undogmatic inquiry rather than the shrill defense of sectarianism that engulfed so many of the religiously founded colleges of their day.

Madison clarified his attitude toward theological learning when Jefferson asked him to prepare a catalog of books on religion for the university library. Madison declared that "although Theology was not to be taught at the University, its Library ought to contain pretty full information for such as might voluntarily seek it in that branch of learning." He therefore undertook the "extremely tedious" task, considering "the immense extent" of theological books, of separating the "moral and metaphysical part" suitable for a university library from the unfruitful "doctrinal and controversial part." He had prepared a detailed list of authors, covering the first five centuries of the Christian era, before Jefferson's request for speed caused him merely to sketch lists for later periods. For the early centuries he included the works of the Alexandrian fathers including Clement; Athenagoras, Tertullian, and Irenaeus; and Latin authors including Augustine, as well as Flavius Josephus and other corroborative accounts. Among the books noted hastily, only Thomas Aquinas, Duns Scotus, the Koran, and some critical books on the popes and saints represented the Middle Ages, while Erasmus, Luther, Calvin, Socinus, Bellarmine, and William Chillingworth were listed for the modern era. The major speculative works of the seventeenth and eighteenth centuries concluded the list, with emphasis, of course, on the rationalists: "Grotius on the truth of Christian Religion," John Tillotson, Hooker, Pascal, Locke, and Newton (his "works on religious subjects"), Bishop Butler, Samuel Clarke, Wollaston's *Religion of Nature Delineated,* Jonathan Edwards on *The Will and Nature of True Virtue,* Cotton Mather's *Essays to Do Good,* William Penn, John Wesley, Joseph Priestley, Richard Price, Leibniz, William

Paley, and even the Boston Unitarian Joseph Buckminster. Madison intended students to have all the source materials they needed to investigate religious doctrine and history, but he meant as well to emphasize the critical approach so influential in rational and deistical writings. Students should form their own religious convictions; at least so thought the now-aged legislator who nearly forty years earlier had secured passage of Jefferson's bill for religious freedom in Virginia. However much a Roman Catholic or a "Baptist enthusiast" might have felt slighted, Madison thought his list included all the books necessary for earnest youths seeking, rationally, to understand divinity and theology.

To ensure both freedom from narrow sectarianism and a genuinely learned faculty, Jefferson and Madison soon saw they would have to recruit European professors. Two brilliant New Englanders, George Ticknor and Nathaniel Bowditch, had refused good offers from the University of Virginia. The Board of Visitors concluded that "it was neither probable that [first-rate American professors] would leave the situations in which they were, nor honorable or moral to endeavor to seduce them from their stations; and to have filled the professorial chairs with unemployed and secondary characters" would not fulfill the needs and expectations of the university. To progress, the board was convinced, "we must avail ourselves of the lights of countries already advanced before us." Jefferson's young friend Francis W. Gilmer was dispatched to Great Britain, "the land of our own language, habits and manners," to find and entice to Virginia young men "treading on the heels" of the unobtainable "men of the first eminence" at Oxford, Cambridge, and Edinburgh. With the help of Richard Rush and others, Gilmer signed up five brilliant scholars: George Long in ancient languages, Thomas H. Key in mathematics, Charles Bonnycastle in physics, Robley Dunglison in medicine, and George Blaettermann, a German previously recommended to Jefferson, in modern languages. Appointment of the young Irish-American John Patton Emmet as professor of natural history completed the scientific faculty. Though the enormous problems of settling these learned foreigners happily and fruitfully in the isolation of Charlottesville plagued Madison for years, he enjoyed their cultivated company and approved their youth. "They will be less inflexible in their habits, the more improvable in their qualifications, and will last the longer," he wrote Jefferson. Cabell too, exulted at "our corps of Professors . . . full of youth, and talent, and energy," while Jefferson declared "the five professors procured from England" so morally upright, congenial, zealous for the university, and learned in their fields that "as high a degree of education can now be obtained here, as in the country they left."

To complete the faculty, Jefferson and Madison insisted on finding Americans for the chairs in ethics and in law, fields especially subject to legislative oversight and thought to embrace peculiarly American understandings best taught by natives. Congressman George Tucker of Virginia seemed an admirable choice for the chair in ethics and literature because, as Madison wrote, to a style of "acuteness and elegance" he added a wide understanding of philosophy, literature, and American history. Tucker responded favorably and in his twenty years at the university became a fervent admirer of both the former presidents, writing, with Madison's help, a biography of Jefferson and a two-hundred-page unpublished memoir of Madison. Six eminent Virginia lawyers and judges could not be persuaded to trade their public posts for academic ones, but the seventh, a Fredericksburg attorney, John Tayloe Lomax, finally accepted and served for four years as an able, fair-minded professor of law.

Establishing the school of law, or government, confronted Jefferson with a delicate problem. He opposed the usual pattern of textbooks prescribed by the trustees, he wrote Cabell and Madison, "because I believe none of us are so much at the heights of science in the several branches as to undertake this [selection] and therefore that it will be better left to the professors, until occasion of interference shall be given. But, there is one branch in which we are the best judges, in which heresies may be taught, of so interesting a character to our own State, and to the United States, as to make it a duty in us to lay down the principles which shall be taught. It is that of government." Jefferson would not allow "a Richmond lawyer [states' rights extremist], or one of that school of quondam [former] federalism, now consolidation [like John Marshall or any number of New Englanders]" to be the professor of government in an institution designed to produce the "aristocracy of talent and virtue" he hoped would provide leaders in a republican government. "It is our duty to guard against the dissemination of such principles among our youth, and the diffusion of that poison, by a previous prescription of the texts to be followed in their discourses." He therefore proposed to require that the Declaration of Independence, *The Federalist,* and the 1798 Virginia Resolutions and 1800 "Report," together with works of John Locke and Algernon Sidney, be the basic texts for the study of public law.

Madison saw at once that this was another notion formed in Jefferson's passion for republicanism rather than upon careful reflection. "It is certainly very material," Madison noted tactfully, "that the true doctrines of liberty as exemplified in our Political System, should be inculcated on those who are to sustain and may administer it." He was as convinced as Jefferson of the universal truth of their republican doctrines and of the need to ensure that later generations of leaders remained steadfast in them. But it was difficult, Madison cautioned, "to find standard books that will be both guides and guards for the purpose." Though Madison thus appeared to propose only practical objections, he in fact proceeded to demolish Jefferson's whole notion of prescribed texts for the school of law. The Declaration of Independence, like the works of Sidney and Locke, "though rich in fundamental principles," did little to combat "constructive violations" of existing constitutions. *The Federalist,* "an authentic exposition" of the federal Constitution, nonetheless failed to anticipate many "misconstructions" and moreover was not accepted as authoritative by everyone in either of the political parties. Its use at Harvard and Brown, Madison observed, furnished merely the precedent of selection by the faculty, not "injunction from the superior authority." The Virginia Resolutions and "Report" were even more partisan, probably being objectionable even to some of the visitors, and so obnoxious to "the more bigoted" as to cause them to "withhold their sons" from the university. Madison finished his critique with a pointed comparison he knew would strike powerfully with Jefferson: "In framing a political creed, a like difficulty occurs as in the case of religion, though the public right be very different in the two cases. If the Articles [framework, basic principles] be in very general terms, they do not answer the purpose; if in very particular terms, they divide and exclude where meant to unite and fortify."

Madison suggested instead a listing of "the best guides" to the distinctive principles of American government, hoping that this would set useful standards for both students and professors while relaxing Jefferson's impractical, absolute prescription. Furthermore, to balance the list, Madison proposed adding Washington's Farewell Address to the three documents chosen by Jefferson. Madison concluded, however, with a remark of his own, as unwelcome to later defenders of academic freedom as Jefferson's impulse to shelter youth from "poisonous" ideas: "The most effectual safeguard against heretical intrusions into the School of Politics, will be an Able and Orthodox Professor, whose course of instruction will be an example to his successors, and may carry with it a sanction from the Visitors." Madison's point, however, was not as restrictive as it might seem. Because in its early stages the university would have but one professor of government, it seemed necessary that he be disposed to present republicanism sympathetically. The diverse library, as well as teachers in other fields and an abundance of current magazines and newspapers, offered an easy hearing to critics, even those referred to by Madison and Jefferson as "heretical."

Both revolutionists, moreover, retained a sense that the nation was still so new as to require special nourishment of its peculiar and still vulnerable principles and institutions. Madison's letter persuaded Jefferson that prescribing textbooks to guard against "poisonous opinions" was inadmissible in a university dedicated to free inquiry. Later libertarian concepts of "a marketplace of ideas," where no idea is regarded as heretical, were to Madison and Jefferson both impractical at their new, small institution and unacceptable in theory within a worldview not yet relativistic but still assuming that free, republican government was best for all humankind. They intended, as Madison explained four months after Jefferson's death, to make their university "a nursery of Republican patriots, as well as genuine scholars." They meant to nourish republicanism and in fact did so at the University of Virginia, in ways deeply and practically useful to the state and to the nation. In no way relevant at the time did they give aid or comfort to enemies of academic freedom. Instead, they stood firmly for an innovating, elective curriculum and insisted that scholarship, rather than national or religious standing, be the vital qualification for professors. Liberalizing reforms such as theirs were not accomplished in most American colleges and universities until a half century or more later.

In November 1824 Lafayette made a celebratory visit to the largely constructed but unopened university, with Madison proudly joining in showing him the buildings and plans. After Lafayette's return to Monticello in August 1825, Madison explained his idea of the university to a New York clergyman, Frederick Beasley, who had inquired about it. It was a "peculiarity," Madison admitted, that the university did not have a theological professor, as did virtually all other colleges and universities in the world. That omission was necessary, Madison explained, because of "its incompatibility with a *State* Institution, which necessarily excludes sectarian preferences," but this did not indicate any hostility to religious faith or practice at the university. The visitors had authorized that "the public rooms [be] open for Religious uses, under *impartial* regulations," and allowed "the establishment of Theological Seminaries by the respective sects contiguous to the . . . University" but separate from "the obligatory pursuits of the students." Furthermore, there were already "congregations and clergymen of the sects" in the nearby village of Charlottesville, less than a mile away, "to which the students will mostly belong." Religious practice, instruction, and even encouragement, voluntary and conveniently available, would, in Madison's lifelong conviction and support, better nourish the important moral and spiritual lives of the students than would official or obligatory measures in support of churches or religious instruction.

Madison also explained his support for Jefferson's plans for a faculty and student-based "system of polity for the University." Instead of a powerful "President or Provost as Chief Magistrate, . . . superintending and executive duties" would be exercised by the faculty, with "the professors presiding in rotation." All regulation, though, "will be at all times alterable by the Board of Visitors." The code of discipline would thus be developed from the experience of "the most distinguished seminaries" and from the needs and experience of the faculty and students. Madison hoped, though, acknowledging the often disorderly and immature behavior of college students, that University of Virginia students not under sixteen years of age, and thus "approaching to manhood," would have a "better chance for self-government, . . . [and hence] give efficacy to a liberal and limited administration." He hoped to confirm, that is, his long-held conviction that human beings are capable, given the proper circumstances and education, of governing themselves equitably and effectively. He and Jefferson were really proposing an experiment in a theory of democratic citizenship in the "regulation" of an institution of higher learning. Madison concluded his letter by pointing out that Beasley had "allotted to me a greater share in this undertaking than belongs to me. . . . Mr. Jefferson has been the great projector and the mainspring of it." Also, though he thanked Beasley for a book he had sent, which seemed worthy and interesting, to read it carefully would "be difficult to reconcile . . . with demands on my time, the decrease of which does not keep pace with the contraction of its remaining span."

In March 1825 the pavilions were ready, the European professors arrived, forty students were present, and the university began instruction. In the fall the number of students had increased to more than one hundred and seemed likely soon to exceed the 218 for whom accommodations were available in the rows of student rooms between the pavilions and in the ranges on the east and west. Cabell declared ecstatically that "the University will advance with rapid strides, and throw into the rear all the other seminaries of this vast continent." Before long, though, "incipient irregularities" under the loose code of discipline threatened to destroy the infant university. Disorder had erupted fitfully during the summer. Then, in late September, while Madison, Monroe, and other visitors were at Monticello for the semiannual meeting, full-scale riots broke out. Undisciplined students, some of them wealthy and dissipated, left classes, attacked professors, caroused in Charlottesville taverns, and made gambling dens of their rooms. One night they threw a stink bomb into Professor Long's room, and the next, surged about the grounds shouting, "Down with the European professors!" When Emmet and Tucker challenged the masked leaders, drunken cohorts set upon the courageous professors with canes and bricks. Sixty-five of the rioters had the effrontery to sign a petition condemning Tucker and Emmet for ganging up on a lone student. Disgusted, and perhaps frightened, Long and Key threatened to resign unless the visitors reestablished order.

The visitors then confronted the unruly students across a large table in the Rotunda. Seeing before him three former presidents and other men already legendary in Virginia, one of the students thought the visitors "the most august body of men I have ever seen." Jefferson rose to speak, Margaret Smith recounted, "with the tenderness of a father and it required an evident struggle to repress his emotions. . . . His lips moved, he essayed to speak—burst into tears and sank back into his seat. The shock was electric." Chapman Johnson, eloquent and austere, rose and delivered the admonition, but one of the students reported, "it was not his words, but Mr. Jefferson's tears that melted the stubborn purpose" of the rioters. Jefferson subsequently asked the board to adopt a stricter code of discipline. In his annual report he noted merely that because the original regulations had proved incapable of preserving order, "coercion must be resorted to where confidence has been disappointed." He explained to his grand-daughter that "four of the most guilty [students have been] expelled, the rest reprimanded, severer laws enacted, and a rigorous execution of them declared in the future."

This action gave the students "a shock and struck a terror," Jefferson concluded, "the more severe, as it was less expected." The new rules pro-vided that henceforth "minor . . . irregularities alone" would be handled by student courts, while unlawful riots would be quelled "on the spot by imprisonment and the same legal coercions, provided against disorder generally, committed by other citizens, from whom, at their age, [stu-dents] have no right to distinction." Thus, though Jefferson's principle "of not multiplying occasions of coercion" had proved too visionary to han-dle the fifteen or twenty students "disposed to try whether our indulgence was without limit," the new regulations remained, for their day, relatively permissive while at the same time allowing the proctor and faculty to deal rigorously with inveterate troublemakers. Madison voted for the new code, and his reputation while rector, as "no visionary or enthusiast," leaves no doubt of his support of the firmer regulations.

The careful balancing of freedom and discipline must have worked because a few months later "perfect subordination" had been restored and "industry, order, and quiet the most exemplary" again prevailed. Then came, however, one of the frequent refusals of the Virginia legislature to grant funds Jefferson considered essential to the university. The timing could not have been worse, coinciding as it did with Jefferson's ill health, near bankruptcy, and family crises. "Overwhelmed with every form of misfortune," Jefferson wrote of his "comfort" at being able to leave the university under Madison's care. Madison replied protesting that however deep his interest in the university—"the Temple through which alone lies the road to that of Liberty"—to suppose he could be Jefferson's successor in guiding it "would be the pretension of a mere worshipper [replacing] the Tutelary Genius of the Sanctuary." Madison hoped Jefferson could live until "stability and self-growth" could replace the unique care lav-ished on the university by its founder.

Jefferson's premonitions proved sound, however. He died on July 4, 1826, beginning for Madison eight years as rector of the university. Unless Madison was sick, he never missed meetings of the Board of Visitors or

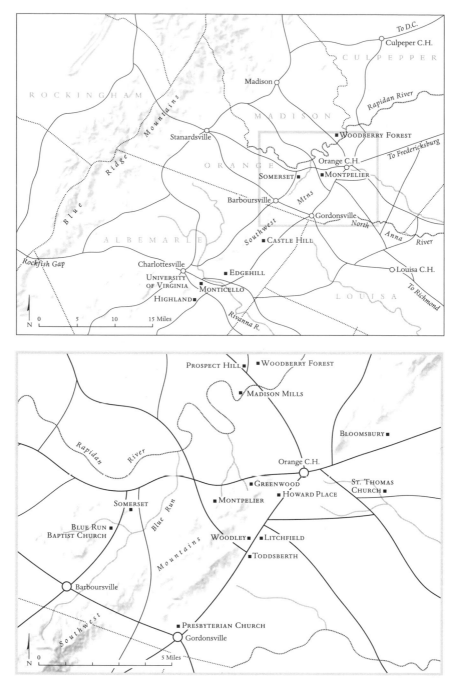

Orange County, Virginia, and vicinity

public examination periods, for which he traveled to Charlottesville, often with Dolley. One student remembered the old couple walking arm in arm about the university lawn, with the taller, more vigorous Dolley sometimes helping the frail, crippled man, seeming somehow, in their old-fashioned dress, to be representatives of a bygone era. A new pattern was set, though. Replacing the friendly, family semiannual visits to Monticello were less congenial and more frequent visits to Charlottesville for examinations and for Board of Visitors business.

At a university meeting six months after Jefferson's death, James had to go to Charlottesville without Dolley but accompanied by his manservant, Paul Jennings. They stayed in a "snug . . . warm room" at "Mr. Conway's University" hotel, where the students took their meals, but it must have been hard not to be able to be at Monticello. Jefferson's daughter and most of her family had gone to Boston "to pass the winter with Mrs. [Ellen Randolph] Coolidge." This "change of season had become essential to her health, as well as to her feelings," Madison had written earlier to Lafayette, especially with the impending forced sale of Monticello to satisfy Jefferson's creditors. Nicholas Trist, left at Monticello "in . . . new quarters," had, Madison reported, "got down thro' the snow" from the mountain and could help return the books Dolley had loaned to the young women at Monticello. Otherwise there was little personal news to report to Dolley from the ladies he did meet. "The first question from them," he wrote, "was whether you were with me, followed by regret at my answer."

Getting down to business, James reported on Monday, December 4, that though he had managed to "escape from the storm" that had hindered his trip from Montpelier, other members had had trouble. Joseph Cabell had finally made it up from Nelson County "travelling the whole way with this snow and hail in his face. . . . General Cocke is detained by a sick son," while James Monroe had detoured on his way to visit his brother, only to learn that he "had died the day before." Cocke arrived by Tuesday afternoon to "make up a board" that then was "chiefly engaged with the Examinations, which go on very well," as the students appeared for their exams individually before the august board. James hoped a week later that he might leave by Tuesday, but was still at work on Thursday, and was not even certain he would get away by Friday. The examinations had lasted into the night, the other business of the board had thus been left "undone," and it had proved to be more important and voluminous "than was first apparent." Exhausted by the labors of his first meeting of the board for examinations since he had succeeded Jefferson as rector, tired from the travel in the severe winter storms, and deprived of the usual comfortable stay at Monticello, James was desperate to get home. "I can not express my anxiety to be with you," he wrote Dolley. "I hope never again to be so long from you, being with devoted affection ever yours."

The long absence was hard on Dolley, too. An early letter to James reported that "the four days passed without you my beloved, seem so many weeks." Despite "the snow storm [that] had put an end to my hopes of rideing," "Sister Macon" and her son had come for dinner one day, and brother John Payne and his wife Clary had come for Sunday, bringing their daughter, another Dolley Payne, whom her aunt would, she said, "keep to sleep in your place" while her husband was away. "Mama [Mother Madison] is quite well," Dolley said, but otherwise she was stressed with chores. She was busy "attending to the blankets" and preparing "for Pork which will come in from Black Meadow and Eddens." "In truth," she complained, "I am too busy a House keeper to become a poetess in my solitude." On Wednesday at "2 oclock" she reported receipt of James's first letter of Monday night from Charlottesville. She rejoiced in his safety despite "exposure to the weather" and hoped he would get through his work soon. He did not; exams lasted a week longer. "Inform me," she said, "what figure the youths make, in their exhibition." She asked, "Please to present me to the ladies around you" (mostly the wives of the professors), and she was "sorry for Mr. Monroe's troubles, of any sort," but mostly she thought of her husband: "I must bid you adieu—or become troublesome, as some of your other long winded correspondents, who love to write you, because it pleases themselves. Forever your own DPM."

Though Rector Madison kept well informed of university affairs and took responsibility for major decisions, neither physically nor psychically could he replace Jefferson in the university's guidance. Increasingly he depended on much younger colleagues, especially Nicholas Trist, Jefferson's grandson-in-law, who even prepared the annual report for Madison for a time. Madison continued to search in the United States or abroad for professors of distinguished, enlightened scholarship, to repel sectarian efforts to dominate the board, the faculty, or the grounds, and otherwise to maintain the university in the character given to it by Jefferson. Under Madison's leadership the university maintained its enrollment, reaching 208 in 1834, the year Madison retired as rector. Its library acquired over ten thousand volumes; the number of graduates each year rose toward fifty, and the first master of arts degree was conferred in 1832. Though Madison's role in founding and sustaining the University of Virginia was in no sense comparable to Jefferson's, he provided constant support during Jefferson's lifetime, and he served much longer as rector of the university with students in attendance than did Jefferson.

While reserving his primary attention and support for the University of Virginia, Madison also befriended other Virginia colleges; supported his alma mater, Princeton; sent money to infant Allegheny College, struggling to bring learning to western Pennsylvania frontiersmen; and in his will left $1,000 to a college in Uniontown, Pennsylvania, named in his honor. He left the bulk of his huge library to the University of Virginia (though this bequest was not fulfilled) and provided particularly for the education of three of his nephews. He summarized the grounds for his devotion to education in a letter advising an old friend in Kentucky on its school system:

Learned institutions ought to be favorite objects with every free people. They throw that light over the public mind which is the best security against crafty and dangerous encroachments on the public liberty. They are the nurseries of skilful Teachers for the schools distributed throughout the Community. They are themselves schools for the particular talents required for use of the Public Trusts, on the able execution of which the welfare of the people depends. They multiply the educated individuals from among whom the people may elect a due portion of their public Agents of every description; more especially of those who are to frame the laws; by the perspicuity, the consistency, and the stability, as well as by the just and equal spirit of which the great social purposes are to be answered. . . . Throughout the Civilized World, nations are courting the praise of fostering Science and the useful Arts, and are opening their eyes to the principles and the blessings of Representative Government. The American people owe it to themselves, and to the cause of Free Government, to prove by their establishments for the advancement and diffusion of Knowledge, that their political Institutions, which are attracting observation from every quarter, and are respected as Models, by the new-born States in our own Hemisphere, are as favorable to the intellectual and moral improvement of Man as they are conformable to his individual and social Rights. What spectacle can be more edifying or more seasonable than that of Liberty and Learning, each leaning on the other for their mutual and surest support?

Nothing is more central to Madison's career and thought than this linking of learning and good republican government.

3

"I May Be Thought to Have Outlived Myself"

INCREASINGLY AS THE TWENTY YEARS IN RETIREMENT STRETCHED OUT, however, attention to public affairs and even to cherished educational projects gave way to the perennial concerns of old age: health, reminiscence, and reflection at the loss of lifelong associates. To an earnest plea in 1834 that he speak out against Jackson's war on the Bank of the United States, against nullification, and against the spoils system, Madison replied that those evils seemed to thrive despite his known opposition to them and that, in any case, the public had "the habit now of invalidating opinions emanating from me by a reference to my age and infirmities." He insisted more and more that whatever the issues of the third and fourth decades of the nineteenth century, younger men, not one who had begun his public life as a subject of George III, would have to deal with them.

Madison left the presidency at age sixty-six in excellent health, his system largely immune, it seemed, to tuberculosis, cholera, typhus, and other periodic scourges of the countryside. For ten years after 1817, visitors found him spry and active, he took daily rides to manage his farm, and he looked forward to short trips in the piedmont countryside. Through 1826 and 1827, however, he had premonitions that the debilities of old age would soon be upon him. A severe attack of influenza before Christmas 1827 weakened him, and late the following summer his old complaint, "bilious indisposition," so prostrated him that he missed, for the first time, the fall meeting of the Board of Visitors. Recovery from a long and severe round of influenza allowed him an exceptional period of good health for three months in Richmond while attending the Virginia Convention of 1829–30, but generally he felt less and less felt able to leave Montpelier. A year later a painful rheumatism (or was it what is now known as arthritis, or rheumatoid arthritis?), especially bad in his hands, became a serious, if intermittent, disability. He tried a medication supplied by Dr. Carr of the University of Virginia, but with little success. By midsummer of 1831 the stiffness had become so general he had again to miss the meeting of the Board of Visitors.

In the fall and winter of 1831–32, as Dolley Madison wrote fearfully of Nat Turner's insurrection, her husband was so weak from rheumatism and fever that she scarcely left his side for months at a time. His hands were so sore and swollen "as to be almost useless, and so I lend him mine," she wrote. She played a music box as they sat together before the fire, looking out at the snow on the mountains while the winter wind whistled "loud and cold." Wrapping his legs in oiled silk and taking tepid salt baths failed to give much relief. Though the coming of spring helped some, and Dolley even hoped her husband might be able to take the prescribed journey to the Warm Springs, this proved too optimistic. In late May, Madison wrote, "I am still confined to my bed with my malady, my debility, and my age, in triple alliance against me. Any convalescence therefore must be tedious, not to add imperfect." That summer he was well enough to greet President Jackson and Senator Clay, each campaigning for the presidency, from his sickbed. Clay found his old friend "feeble in health but his mind and memory . . . perfectly sound. He spoke with more freedom than is usual on public affairs, and appeared to take a lively interest in passing events." Then, as cold weather again stiffened Madison's joints, and after a year spent almost entirely in bed, he nevertheless wrote cheerfully to Andrew Stevenson (husband of Dolley Madison's cousin, Sally Coles), thanking him for a gift of a cap and gloves:

> It is as comfortable as it is fashionable, which is more than can be said of all fashions. . . . [The] excellent pair of gloves [made by] Mrs. Stevenson . . . being the work of her own hands . . . will impart the more warmth to mine. . . . Mrs. Madison has also provided well for my feet. I am thus equipt cap-a-pied, for the campaign against Boreas, and his allies the Frosts and the snows. But there is another article of covering, which I need most of all and which my best friends can not supply. My bones have lost a sad portion of the flesh which clothed and protected them, and the digestive

and nutritive organs which alone can replace it, are too slothful in their functions.

The next three years Madison was a semi-invalid, having periods, especially in the spring and summer, when the stiffness in his joints eased, the fevers subsided, and he resumed work at his writing desk. He complained to one correspondent, though, that his severe rheumatism "has so crippled my hands and fingers that I write my name with pain and difficulty, and am in a manner disqualified for researches that require the handling of papers." Dolley wrote her niece in August 1833 that "Uncle Madison mends his health, but often relapses." She reported having "more company this summer than I can describe—I could not go to breakfast with a party of eight, two ladies among them, on account of illness," she complained, but she added cheerfully that "I have taken a ride with my husband and shall join them for dinner." In September, James was well enough to "ride out every day, three or four miles," and the visits of the Riveses, the Stevensons, and others "on their way from the White Sulpher Springs" again became enjoyable. Dolley wished fondly she could get away to the springs herself, but even a journey five miles to Orange Court House was "quite an event." Madison often "walked only from the bed in which he breakfasts to another." Both the Madisons suffered eye inflammations that robbed them of their favorite pastimes, and in the summer of 1833 Dolley joined her husband on the sick list with "a violent though short illness brought on . . . by indulging a fancy for Raspberries and milk." Altogether, from his eightieth birthday on, James again and again failed to muster the strength to partake even vicariously in public affairs, and weeks and months passed with him able to do little more than nurse his aching limbs.

Living and Making History

Madison devoted much of his waning strength to arranging his papers and commenting on the past. A year after he retired, he gave to a Washington printer a list assigning authorship to *The Federalist Papers*. To validate his list Madison not only noted cogent internal evidence but remarked that Hamilton's conflicting lists had been jotted down hastily, and thus errors in them could be ascribed to oversight, while his own list, prepared upon full and careful consideration, had obviously superior claims, which he implied Hamilton himself would accept were he alive. Hamilton's misstatement, Madison declared, "was involuntary, and . . . he was incapable of any that was not so."

In 1818 and 1819 Madison supplied information to John Quincy Adams for his edition of the *Journal of the Federal Convention of 1787*. Controversy aroused by its publication and the appearance a year later of notes taken during the first five weeks of the convention by Robert Yates of New York caused renewed interest in the much fuller record of the debates known to be in Madison's possession. He continued to insist that this record be made public only after the death of all members of the convention, including himself. Rumors circulated that Madison guarded his notes for narrow political purposes or to write a history of the United States himself. He disclaimed such a project, assigning it instead "to those who have more time before them than the remnant to which mine is limited." Because "a personal knowledge and an impartial judgment of things rarely meet in the historian," Madison observed, "the best history of our Country therefore must be the fruit of contributions bequeathed by contemporary actors and witnesses, to successors who will make an unbiased use of them." Nonetheless, curiosity remained intense over Madison's archives because, as Edward Everett told him, "next to those of Washington, and in some respects not second even to his, your papers must possess a higher interest with your countrymen, than those of any of your contemporaries."

One publication project Madison heartily approved was Jonathan Elliot's to publish the debates of the state ratifying conventions of 1787–88. Madison had long believed that these debates, as an insight into the people's understanding of the Constitution upon its adoption, were the vital source for aid in interpreting the document, rather than the debates of the convention of 1787. He supplied Elliot with scarce printed copies of the debates in North Carolina and Pennsylvania. When Elliot asked Madison to "correct" his speeches in the Virginia convention, however, he declined because "it might not be safe, nor deemed fair, after a lapse of 40 years . . . to undertake to make [the speeches] what it might be believed they ought to be." "If I did not confound subsequent ideas, and varied expressions, with the real ones," Madison added, "I might be supposed to do so." Though Madison often approved excluding personal or prejudicial material from publication, he did not believe in altering records with the benefit of hindsight.

Another way Madison encouraged publication of source material was in responding to dozens of appeals from editors, historians, and archivists for information about or letters from famous people Madison had known. He pronounced George Mason "a powerful Reasoner, a profound Statesman and a devoted Republican," and he extolled the "brilliant careers" of Generals Nathanael Greene and Henry Lee during the Revolution. Requests for material about others not always favored by Madison, such as Gouverneur Morris, John Jay, and General William Winder, drew restrained but polite responses.

Madison's most sustained aid to a historian, however, was to Jared Sparks. The diligent young Bostonian impressed Madison during a brief visit to Montpelier in 1827 and thereafter received invaluable aid and support from the aged Virginian. Madison allowed him to use over twenty letters from George Washington, which inexplicably, or perhaps purposely, had not been copied into the general's letter books. They exchanged information about the origins of Washington's famous state papers and commiserated that the first president's archives had "been very extensively mutilated by rats" while on loan to Chief Justice Marshall. Then, in April 1830, when "the blossoms and verdure of the trees [were] springing into perfection," Sparks spent five delightful days at Montpelier. "The intellect and memory of Mr. Madison," Sparks noted, retained "all their pristine vigor," and in conversation he was "sprightly, varied, fertile in his topics and felicitous in his descriptions and illustrations." Sparks listened avidly to Madison "on general topics," copied frantically from the piles of unique and interesting papers Madison showed him, and recorded anecdotes of "revolutionary times." Some of the comments were candid remarks about famous people. John Jay's hostility to France, Madison observed, arose from "two strong traits of character, suspicion and religious bigotry." He thought Washington had never "attended to the arguments for Christianity" nor had any definite opinions on religion, but rather "took those things as he found them existing" and observed faithfully the Episcopal rituals "in which he was brought up." He also insisted that Washington had been most reluctant about both Hamilton's funding plans and the national bank, accepting them, not because he approved them as such, but because there seemed no practical alternatives. Hamilton, though personally incorruptible, Madison said, was so "hostile to France" that at times he made "perverted" and deceitful uses of public money. He thought "the talents of Richard Henry Lee were respectable, but not of the highest order"—dim, in fact, when compared to those of John Adams, who "was a bold and decided champion of independence from the beginning." Sparks also recorded Madison's observations on the usefulness of secret sessions during the Federal Convention and on Washington's disgust at the pompous ceremonies arranged for him by his aides in 1789. Sparks set down some of Madison's quips and puns, including a favorite story of a French officer during the American Revolution who fancied himself quite a lady's man. A friend, tired of his boasting, when asked by the vain fellow to divulge what others thought of him, replied, "The opinion of the world is divided; the men say you are an old woman, and the women say you are an old man." Altogether, Sparks was enthralled at the "social happiness" at Montpelier and, as a historian, was beside himself with excitement at the treasures residing in Madison's memory and archives.

Among the papers Sparks pored over were Madison's letters, copies of which he had not retained, written to his contemporaries forty or fifty years ago. Even before retirement Madison had begun to gather them as best he could from the recipients or their heirs. By 1830 he had retrieved many of his letters to Jefferson, Joseph Jones, Monroe, Edmund Pendleton, Edmund Randolph, and Washington. These letters, added to ones he received and notes he had made for his own speeches and state papers, were virtually a documentary history of the nation from 1780 until 1817, and even subsequently, because Madison preserved copies of the hundreds of letters he wrote on public affairs during his retirement (now readily available on the Library of Congress "American Memory" Web site). By the time of his death, Madison had arranged his papers through the convention of 1787. He used letters to supplement his notes on debates in the Continental Congress and, of course, his own full, uniquely valuable account of the Federal Convention. Madison wrote an introduction to this record, and with the help of Dolley and her brother John C. Payne, had selected and edited other papers to be published after his death. He was, therefore, virtually his own editor for the three volumes of *The Papers of James Madison* published in 1840 under the supervision of Congress, to which Dolley sold domestic publication rights for $30,000. It was much less than the $100,000 or more Madison had expected his widow would receive from the posthumous printing of the eagerly awaited 1787 debates.

He had also arranged a fourth volume, on constitutional topics, largely from his post-1787 correspondence, which appeared in 1853. Beyond that, he organized his papers in large bound folios or bundles, intending the publication of three or four additional volumes under Dolley's supervision. Unable to make favorable contracts, though, she sold the papers remaining in her possession to the federal government for $25,000 in 1848. Hundreds of the most valuable letters had already been withdrawn by Payne Todd, to pay gambling debts, however, and through him reached a Washington, D.C., collector, James C. McGuire. These papers, following sale by his heirs, and further boxes of Madison's letters, found among the papers of his editor and biographer William Cabell Rives, were in the twentieth century, with some major exceptions, reunited with the collections sold earlier to the federal government. Thus Madison's intention that his papers furnish a readily available resource for scholars has at long last been largely realized—minus, of course, an indeterminable number of the letters taken by Payne Todd. The collection and publication of a modern edition of *The Papers of James Madison,* begun in 1956 and continuing with nearly thirty volumes now in print, represents a modern fulfillment of Madison's labors and wishes.

Lafayette Comes to Virginia

Reflections on the past and a sense of settling his accounts with it, incessantly before Madison as he labored over his papers at Montpelier, became immediate and poignant as he had last meetings with old friends or heard of their deaths. Lafayette's visit to Monticello and Montpelier in November 1824 and his return visit in August 1825 recalled vividly for the Frenchman and his two venerable hosts the lifetime each had devoted to human liberty. Madison wrote Jefferson that Lafayette's "visit to the United States will make an [epoch?] in the history of liberty"—as indeed it did. Lafayette and his party had arrived in Charlottesville about noontime and, after ceremonies there, had proceeded with a large throng to Monticello. At the top of the hill, Lafayette left his carriage and, through a crowd assembled on each side of the path to the house, walked toward Jefferson, who had come down the front steps to greet his visitor. "They embraced, again and again; tears were shed by both and the broken expressions of 'God bless you General,' 'Bless you my dear Jefferson' . . . interrupted the impressive silence of the scene." A few of the dignitaries and Jefferson's family accompanied Lafayette into the house.

Madison went to Monticello to greet Lafayette, whom he had not seen since their wilderness journey in 1784 to negotiate the Fort Stanwix Indian treaty. James arrived at Monticello "about sunset," he wrote Dolley. Jefferson's grandson Thomas Jefferson Randolph and Joseph Coolidge, who was seeking the hand of Jefferson's granddaughter Ellen, had "just arrived from Boston" and were, with the rest of Jefferson's company, "commencing their Desert" when Madison arrived. "My old friend embraced me with much warmth," Madison reported to Dolley. "He is in fine health and spirits but so much increased in bulk and changed in aspect that I should not have known him."

Dinner over, the usual conversation began among the men. Afterwards Madison retired to what is still known as "Mr. Madison's room" at Monticello. Writing to Dolley at "7 oc" the next morning, he warned his wife of the coming visitation to Montpelier: Lafayette had not said how long he would stay at Monticello, only that "he will divide the time [November 5–19] not required for the road and appointed festivities, between Mr. Jefferson and myself." It was probable, then, that Lafayette, "his son and Secretary, the two [University of Virginia] Councillors, and such of the company of Orange [County hosts] . . . as may chuse to stop at Montpellier" would be arriving "near or quite the middle of next week." Dolley thus thought she had four or five days to get ready, though in fact Lafayette's party did not leave Monticello and Charlottesville until more than a week later, on November 15. James added somewhat uneasily that Frances Wright and her sister, Camilla, probably would be coming to Montpelier, too. "The Miss Wrights," he said, seemed to travel with the Lafayette entourage, but had not yet arrived at Monticello; "the General [Lafayette] thinks they may make a call [at Monticello] as a morning visit only." James worried (and surely then, Dolley too) about "whether they will . . . precede or accompany or follow the General . . . in the visit to us."

He hoped to find out more later that day and would let Dolley know as soon as he was able. In any case, Lafayette had quickly offered to "take charge" of Madison's letter inviting the Wrights to Montpelier; "it was given to him of course." The problem was that the Wrights' presence with Lafayette was ambiguous. They had been guests for extended periods at his La Grange estate in France. Fanny was a tall, attractive, vivacious, intelligent, public-spirited, and, it seems, an effusively friendly young woman, about thirty when she came to Monticello. She and Lafayette had been together enough to excite scandalous rumors and a warning coolness from Lafayette's family. She and her sister had taken an apartment in Paris near his city residence while Fanny helped him with his papers and invitations and worked on a biography of him; she had followed him to England where she seems also to have charmed Jeremy Bentham, as she had the American ministers to France and Great Britain. The sisters, Lafayette wrote Jefferson, "have passed the last three years in the most intimate connection with my children and myself," and he wished "to present these two adopted daughters of mine to Mrs. Randolph and to you." Of Fanny the Frenchman wrote, "You and I are the two men in the world the esteem of whom she values the most."

Stories had circulated about the women in Lafayette's life—in 1824 he was nearly seventy and long a widower—and he had a reputation, in the idiom of the day, as a "prober of the placket" (the slit then fashionable in the back of women's dresses), less frowned upon in France no doubt than across the Atlantic. On the other hand, he also had told Jefferson that "my way of traveling does Not Admit female Companions." Jefferson replied that as there were as yet no quarters for ladies at the university, the Misses Wright "will nowhere find a welcome more hearty than with Mrs. Randolph." His daughter, that is, would take care of them at Monticello, apart from Lafayette's party. At both Monticello and Montpelier as well, apparently, as elsewhere on Lafayette's long tour, however, the question of their full common itinerary with Lafayette and presence at overnight stops remained in question. As it tuned out, the Wright sisters did stay at Monticello but did not go on to Montpelier with Lafayette because one of them was ill.

James prepared to join Jefferson and Lafayette for the triumphal procession in Jefferson's landau to Charlottesville, hoping, he wrote Dolley anxiously, that he might be able to return to Montpelier the day after the celebrations at the university. At 10:00 a.m. the three aged Revolutionary companions left Monticello accompanied by "the cavalry and a numerous body of citizens," for a reception at the Central Hotel in Charlottesville. At noon a huge procession, with "The General, Mr. Jefferson and Mr. Madison in a landau drawn by four grey horses," went to the university for a great banquet with four hundred male guests at three o'clock in the top floor of the Rotunda, newly finished but as yet not in use (ladies apparently ate outside on the lawn between the colonnades). Lafayette sat with Jefferson and Madison, and when his turn came, Madison offered the toast "To liberty, with virtue for her guest, and gratitude for the feast." Lafayette's secretary, Auguste Levasseur, recorded that "Transports of applause" greeted Madison's toast. Levasseur found Madison "especially remarkable for the originality of his expressions, and the delicacy of his allusions," among "the enlivened sallies of wit and humour" that characterized the event. At Jefferson's eloquent and nostalgic speech, read by a young friend, Lafayette "grasped the hand of the venerable friend who penned it, and sobbed aloud." James Dinsmore, the skilled builder of Monticello, the Rotunda holding the banquet, and fifteen years earlier, the enlarged Montpelier, toasted "Thomas Jefferson, founder of the University of Virginia." "James Madison, the ablest expositor of the Constitution—his commentaries of '98 will be forgotten only with the text" was the toast to the fourth president, perhaps enjoyed more by the states' rights Richmond Junto guests than by Madison himself. The next toast addressed the Constitution: "The Rubicon of Federal Power: may the Caesar who dares pass it meet the dagger of a Brutus." Perhaps Madison frowned again. At the close of the banquet, he accompanied Lafayette and other guests on a tour of the new university. James seems to have been able, as he had hoped to Dolley, to leave for Montpelier the next day, while Lafayette (and the Wright sisters) stayed on at Monticello for another week. Doubtless James and Dolley worked busily preparing for Lafayette's long expected and much delayed arrival.

"At an early hour of Monday morning last [November 15]," the Charlottesville *Central Gazette* reported, "The General and Suite" left Monticello for Montpelier. In Gordonsville they were met by dignitaries headed by Madison's lifelong friend Senator James Barbour and had "refreshments" at "Mr. Thornton's Tavern." At two o'clock, according to Levasseur, they resumed the journey to Montpelier, "the charming residence of ex-President Madison . . . , [where] he retired to cultivate his fields, and devote himself to letters, which he had never wholly relinquished, amid the multifarious occupations of his active political life." "Mr. Madison at the time of our visit," he continued, "was seventy-four years of age, but his well-preserved frame contained a youthful soul full of sensibility, which he did not hesitate to show, when he expressed to general Lafayette the pleasure he felt at having him in his house. Although the habit of reflection and application give to his countenance an aspect of severity, all the impressions of his heart are rapidly depicted in his features, and his conversation is usually animated with a gentle gaity." The Frenchman went on to note that "Mrs. Madison also contributes much by the graces of her mind, and the amenity of her character to exalt the excellence of that frank hospitality with which strangers are received at Montpelier."

For four days James and Dolley and their guests "were agreeably employed in promenades over his beautiful estate, and still more agreeably by our evening conversations, particularly concerning all the great American interests, which are so dear to general Lafayette." He and Madison reminisced about the campaigns of Washington, about the great events of the French Revolution that were so fateful to Madison's political career in the 1790s, and about the incomplete struggles for liberty and national independence in Europe (especially Greece), South America, and the United States, so long linked to the careers of both of the old revolutionaries. They also doubtless recalled the monthlong expedition Madison and Lafayette had taken together years earlier from Philadelphia up the Hudson River valley to Fort Stanwix, near what is now Rome, New York, and to the Indian village of Oneida Castle, to negotiate a treaty with the Iroquois. The two young men, one nearing thirty and the other just past it, had shared the rigors of wilderness travel on horseback and nighttime respites before campfires as temperatures dipped well below freezing. At the treaty, Madison reported to Jefferson after returning to New York City, Lafayette had been "the only conspicuous figure," eclipsing the official delegates representing the Continental Congress. Madison continued with a candid assessment of his friend and traveling companion: "With great natural frankness of temper he unites much address, with very considerable talents, a strong thirst of praise and popularity. In his politics he says his three hobby horses are the alliance between France and the United States, the Union of the latter, and the manumission of the slaves. The two former are the dearer to him as they are connected with his personal glory. The last does him real honor, as it is proof of his humanity." "In a word," Madison had concluded in 1784, Lafayette was "as amiable a man as his vanity will admit, and as sincere an American as any Frenchman can be, one whose past services gratitude obliges us to ac-knowledge and whose future friendship prudence requires us to culti-vate." When Madison arranged his papers for publication, including this letter to Jefferson, he softened the phrase "his vanity will admit" to "can be imagined," perhaps reflecting both his desire to be more gracious to his guest and his heightened view of Lafayette's character as shown in his career in the forty years between the journey to the New York frontier and Lafayette's much relished visit to Montpelier during his triumphal tour in 1824.

As the conversations around the plantation, in the drawing room, and on the portico looking out at the Blue Ridge continued, Levasseur ob-served that "the society of neighboring planters assembled at Montpelier were as well-versed in all the great political questions as in agriculture." Perhaps Levasseur was impressed, in Orange, to find the farmers there already in the mode of Jefferson's idealized husbandmen, moved by their daily rounds to think beyond their usual talk of the state of crops, prices, and the weather, to attend to the "great American interests" of public affairs and citizenship, which both Jefferson and Madison always saw as a crucial part of good republican government.

They discussed freely two topics always of special interest to Lafay-ette, which were also much on the minds of the Madisons: slavery and religious liberty. Lafayette "never missed an opportunity to defend the right *which all men without exception* have to liberty," Levasseur wrote. The Frenchmen were fascinated with the life of "Granny Milly" at the log cabin "in the Walnut Grove" where, as Mary Cutts remembered, the 104-year-old slave lived with her daughter and granddaughter. Lafayette was impressed that leftovers from the sumptuous breakfasts from the mansion were taken to the old woman, and in exchange she gave her visitors "the gift of a potato or fresh egg." But these kindnesses could not, for the French hero of revolutions for freedom, in any way condone the terrible injustice of slavery. They found the Virginians understood the "deplorable circumstance" of their slaves and had "noble sentiments" about its eventual demise. Nevertheless, they fell under the condemna-tion of the Frenchmen, who could not understand the contradiction of slavery existing in a nation Madison had recently toasted as committed "to liberty, with virtue for her guest."

Levasseur was pleased, though, that on "the equally important question of spiritual slavery" (as compared to chattel slavery), the Virginians were in the vanguard, compared to the existence of dominant or state religions still prevalent in Europe. One Virginian took pains to tell Levasseur of an interesting event in the "formation of our institutions" that had not been mentioned "for fear of offending the modesty of our host." He then recounted Madison's role in bringing religious liberty to Virginia. First had been his removal in 1776 of the idea of toleration from the Virginia constitution, an "insult," the Virginian explained, to the idea of freedom of conscience. Then had come his role in defeating a bill to support teachers of the Christian religion in Virginia, through the "Memorial and Remonstrance against Religious Assessments" (1785), and in winning passage of Jefferson's "Act for Establishing Religious Freedom." Having seen the country churches where Madison, as a fresh college graduate before the Revolution, had defended the right of Baptist ministers to preach and noting the flourishing state of those unestablished churches in 1824, the Europeans all the more appreciated the lessons of this epochal achievement.

On November 19 Madison (and apparently not Dolley) accompanied Lafayette to Orange Court House where he was "introduced to the ladies, who manifested their gratitude and joy, in their own bewitching way, so readily performed by them, but so impossible to be described." Did the ladies attempt a *tableau vivant*? Lafayette and Madison passed between "citizens formed in double lines in the street," shaking hands and paying special attention to "several revolutionary soldiers." The "cordial and affecting" event, a newspaper account pronounced, created "a scene whose pathos reached every heart." "At 3 o'clock" Lafayette, Madison, "the revolutionary soldiers, and about 200 guests . . . sat down to a dinner prepared with great taste and elegance by Messrs. Verdier and Shephard." Among the thirteen toasts came one to "Our countryman, James Madison—First in private, as illustrious in public life: we love the man and venerate the statesman."

In reply, Madison of course praised Lafayette for "his persevering devotion to the great principles of our Revolution, and by his zeal, truly American, in maintaining our rights, our honor, and our interests, as a free and independent people," but he had to omit, he said, "much, which I cannot trust my feelings to utter in his presence." Madison noted especially his pleasure that the toast to him came "from those, in the midst of whom I have lived, and for whom I have such sincere respect." "The worthy citizens of the county of Orange," he continued, through "their suffrages introduced me into the public career which occupied so great a portion of my life, and in every stage of which I experienced from them all the kindness and support I could hope for or desire." Other toasts were offered by relatives and lifelong friends: Philip P. Barbour, Reynolds Chapman, John Gibson, Robert L. Madison, Philip Slaughter, C. C. Macon, George Spotswood, and many others.

When the banquet broke up about five o'clock, Lafayette and his company went through yet another double line of cheering citizens and under a triumphal arch, at the entrance of Marquis Road, named for Lafayette, and on to a narrow path in a thick wood, which "young ladies were scattering with flowers." At that very place "Lafayette on the 15th of June 1781 . . . in a rapid march," had surprised and defeated Cornwallis, who was attempting to "gain possession of the magazines of the southern states at Albemarle." Recalling this important engagement in the Virginia campaign that would soon corner Cornwallis and the British army at Yorktown, Lafayette told the crowd "it was exactly here, . . . in a movement which might have proved very injurious to me," that the farmer militia of Orange County had responded to Lafayette's plea that they endure "the ruinous neglect of their crops, the difficulty of obtaining provisions, . . . the separation from their families, [and] fatigues of all sorts" to continue on the campaign to Yorktown. He thus cemented his bond with the people with whom he had struggled and fought half a century before at the very point of their battles, five miles from Montpelier.

Lafayette then went on through "The Wilderness" to Fredericksburg and another round of parades, banquets, and toasts. Madison had been invited to those festivities, but he had declined partly because he would "enjoy opportunities within my reach" for honoring Lafayette. Actually, fatigued by the strenuous all-day celebrations in Orange, Madison had "mounted his horse with activity" after the banquet there, "not withstanding his seventy-four years," Levasseur recorded, "and set out through the woods for his peaceful dwelling."

Madison and Jefferson likely thought Lafayette's busy, nationwide schedule would prevent his coming back to Virginia, but after traveling thousands of miles and attending hundreds of celebrations, he made a hurried return in August 1825, just before his departure for home. He saw this visit as a culmination of his reunions with the surviving heroes of the Revolution, both statesmen and soldiers, and of his respect for the flourishing condition and good government of the nation he had helped found. He had seen ninety-year-old John Adams, who had welcomed the then twenty-year-old marquis to the Revolutionary struggle nearly fifty years before, and then had been welcomed to Washington by his son, the newly inaugurated president, John Quincy Adams, who had been a teenager serving as his father's secretary during the Revolution when he met the young Frenchman. From there Lafayette had gone, accompanied by the new president, to the Virginia home, Oak Hill, of the recently retired president, James Monroe, who was himself also a Revolutionary War hero, comrade in arms of both Lafayette and Washington.

Lafayette was enormously impressed with the good government of what was in 1825 a free, strong, growing, and prosperous nation, that his Revolutionary friends, including every president from Washington to John Quincy Adams, had created. It seemed of great significance to Lafayette to continue on for one last visit to the civilian heroes of good government, the now failing Jefferson and his friend and colleague at Montpelier. Accompanied by Monroe, Lafayette and a reduced entourage rode toward Monticello and were met by Madison for the last part of the journey. After another nostalgic gathering there, Madison wrote Fanny Wright on September 1 that "General Lafayette took his final leave of us a few days ago. . . . He carries with him the unanimous blessings of the free nation which has adopted him." He wrote a year later to Lafayette, with effusive recollections of his visit, that "my mother, now touching her ninety-sixth year, received your kind remembrance with much sensibility. She forgets many things she says, but shall never forget General La Fayette, the great and good friend of her country." Altogether the sojourn of Lafayette, replete with large parties, the greetings and hospitality of James and Dolley, tours of the plantation, and long conversations about the great events through which they had passed, may have been the most memorable of all visits during the Madisons' retirement at Montpelier.

Farewell to Thomas Jefferson

When Jefferson prepared wearily but excitedly for Lafayette's return to Monticello in August 1825, his stamina and sense of well-being had diminished from the generally good health he had enjoyed during the first years of his retirement and the busy years of planning and building the University of Virginia. A visitor to Monticello in 1820 had described Jefferson as "straight as a young man; compared with him, Madison, although ten years younger, looks like a little, old man." Always, indeed, Jefferson was known for his tall, vigorous good looks, and Madison, his smaller, rather frail, and sallow appearance. In the last year of his life, though, Jefferson began to fail and become increasingly aware of his approaching death. In May 1825 his doctor had diagnosed increasingly troublesome lower abdominal pains as dysuria, a urinary tract inflammation, which today might have been diagnosed as prostate cancer or enlargement. Jefferson was turned over as a patient to the newly appointed medical professor at the university, Dr. Robley Dunglison. He prescribed doses of laudanum (opium extract in brandy), which Jefferson used for the rest of his life. Dr. Dunglison made regular visits to Monticello, coming several times a week during the summer of 1825 while Jefferson again received Lafayette and struggled through crises as instruction began at the university. Dr. Dunglison became at the same time Madison's physician, making occasional visits to Montpelier and seeing him at Board of Visitors meetings in Charlottesville.

In this declining, perhaps depressed and anxious state, Jefferson had yet another occasion to seek Madison's help and good judgment as he faced, for what he sensed was his last time, an unwelcome and dangerous course in the nation's public life. Controversy over high tariffs to protect American industry and the "internal improvements" that were part of Henry Clay's "American System" came to a head with President John Quincy Adams's first annual message of December 1825. Adams endorsed not only higher tariffs and internal improvements generally but also a broad array of positive actions by the federal government, including establishing a national university and naval academy; building roads, canals, and an astronomical observatory; and supporting scientific expeditions and explorations around the world—all under powers possessed, Adams assumed, by the national government within the Constitution. In a "dark" mood brought on by ill health, by his frightening experience with sculptor James Browere's hammering of the hardened pieces of the plaster mask from his face, and by his accumulating financial worries, Jefferson panicked when he read the president's message and bitter critiques of it in Richmond newspapers. He also received a letter from an Albemarle delegate to the Virginia legislature asking what could Virginia do to ward off Adams's abuse of the Constitution? And would Jefferson help?

In an astonishing burst of energy, Jefferson drafted what he entitled "The solemn Declaration and Protest of the commonwealth of Virginia on the principles of the constitution of the U.S. of America and of the violations of them," a three-page polemic explaining how the particular measures proposed by Adams exceeded any of the powers granted the federal government by the Constitution. More problematically, though, he restated the compact theory of that document, echoing and even going beyond the states' rights doctrines he had expressed in the 1798 Resolutions protesting the Alien and Sedition Acts. The states, preexisting the Declaration of Independence, had called the Articles of Confederation, and then the Constitution, into existence, authorizing only clearly specified powers, and retaining to themselves all others. The states, or the people constituting them, remained the ultimate judges of the terms of the compact and were obliged to resist violations of it. Though Jefferson explicitly asserted the obligations of citizens to obey even federal laws they regarded as unconstitutional, he also clearly sustained his arguments of 1798, which states' rights Virginians were already using to validate some form of nullification. Jefferson thought releasing his "Declaration and Protest" would bolster those who believed in limited government, "intimidate the wavering" of anyone who might thus be kept on the right track, and derail the Clay-Adams proposals.

With the document hastily and vehemently drafted and intended for delivery to Virginia politicians, but still lying on his table, Jefferson held back. He knew Madison now paid more careful attention to public affairs than he. He even wrote his friend confessing candidly that he had "long ceased to think of subjects of this kind" and paid little attention to public proceedings. Indeed, Jefferson had long since canceled all but one of his newspaper subscriptions, while many still came to Montpelier. He thus forwarded the unsent document to Madison, writing that he supposed "a bolt shot critically may decide the contest [over the unconstitutional

enlargement of federal powers] by its effect on the less bold." He hoped
Madison had already responded publicly; if so, he would "stop here
. . . [and] be satisfied to adopt implicitly anything which you may have
advised. . . . I would not hazard so important a measure against your
opinion, nor without its support." He wished Madison would look over
the "Declaration and Protest," he wrote, and "make whatever alterations
you please" before it was released to the public. Ill, worn-down, but still
intensely committed to the principles of self-government he and Madison
had nurtured for half a century, Jefferson turned as he had so often to his
younger friend, possessed of better judgment if less genius, as Henry Clay
would observe, and of the most profound understanding.

Jefferson's letter enclosing the document, written the day before
Christmas, reached Montpelier three days later. Madison responded at
once. Though he too, "in his retired position," felt out of touch with "the
precise tendency of [public] measures, and of the opinions and feelings"
of legislators and the people (both he and Jefferson were overmodest in
disclaiming their attention to public affairs), he nonetheless had already
perused Adams's message elaborating federal power. He was much more
sympathetic to it than Jefferson. Indeed, it was much in the mood of his
own message to Congress exactly ten years earlier proposing national
measures after the successful conclusion of the War of 1812. He did his
best, though, to comfort and calm his upset friend. He had, ten days
before, written a long letter to the Richmond editor and influential states'
rights advocate Thomas Ritchie answering his urgent queries about how
Virginians might respond to what Ritchie, like Jefferson, regarded as federal usurpations. This letter was already or soon to be public. Also, by the
time Madison got Jefferson's letter and "Declaration and Protest," he had
also heard of a proposal in Congress ("coming from the President himself," Jefferson supposed) for a constitutional amendment specifically
empowering Congress to build roads and canals. Virginia congressmen
were inclined to support this idea, perhaps to stall or compromise the
president's plans. Madison ten years earlier and Jefferson twenty years
earlier had urged the amendment route to avoid the stretching of the
existing Constitution until it was no longer a limited government at all.

So, again, Madison agreed with Jefferson's broad principle of protecting limited government. He warned, however, against measures that
"might lead to a stile and tone irritating rather than subduing prejudices"

and insufficiently "mingling gentleness of manner . . . [with] firmness in acting." He proposed, therefore, that his letter to Ritchie, explaining how the Constitution divided sovereignty between the state and federal governments in a way that required obedience of the people and of the states to federal law as arguments and protests went on, be accepted as the response to the crisis by the two elder statesmen. Discussion of Adams's proposals, especially in New England and New York, was likely to lead to temporizing changes and delays, Madison thought, and perhaps would result in the passage of an internal improvements amendment, some form of which he had long advocated. Madison urged, as Jefferson had offered, that the latter's "Declaration and Protest" be suppressed. Then Virginia authorities could look hopefully at the amendment proposals and further discussion as likely to result in modified action, if any at all. At least the sweeping proposals of Adams's message, so dangerous, Jefferson thought, to the idea of limited government, would fail—as they did.

Jefferson replied at once, after New Year's: "I have read . . . Ritchie's letter and your answer with entire approbation and adoption of its views. When my paper was written all was gloom, and the question of roads and canals was thought desperate at Washington after the President's message." He never released the "Declaration and Protest," but he was still upset by the doctrines of Adams and his supporters. Before receiving Madison's wise and patient response, he wrote, still agitated and filled with gloom, to former senator William Branch Giles. He had been a colleague of Madison's in Congress in the 1790s and occasionally in Virginia politics, but their relationship had turned bitter when Giles had first sought to prevent and then to hamstring Madison's presidency. Jefferson again upheld in unguarded language his compact-among-the-states view of the Constitution and, theoretically at least, seemed to justify nullification in words like those he had used in 1798.

When this letter became public after Jefferson's death, Madison did his best to defend and more accurately explain Jefferson's argument of 1798 and 1825, but his effort was only partially successful. Having carefully examined the Jefferson and Madison documents on interposition, nullification, and secession when he prepared his eulogy of Madison in 1836, John Quincy Adams concluded that "there was a wide difference of opinion between Jefferson and Madison. I believe them both to have been in error, but the error of Madison was comparatively harmless." Both state and federal governments were of limited and delegated powers, he agreed with the Virginians, but they were mistaken in supposing the states, or their people, had "the authority to declare acts of Congress unconstitutional." "The deadly venom of Jefferson's nullification," Adams intoned severely, "points directly to the dissolution of the Union." Madison was equally wrong in supporting state authority, Adams insisted, but by "reducing his right of interposition by the State legislatures to mere declarations, remonstrances, and arguments," he rendered his disagreement constitutional as well as "comparatively harmless." Madison correctly shrunk from Jefferson's baneful conclusions, but, scolded Adams, he "admitted rather too many of [Jefferson's] premises."

Adams's critique of the arguments of the two Virginians clarifies their position on the Constitution as a frame of limited but still empowered government. Adams, of course, was not entirely objective in his assessment of the two men. He later recorded that Madison, along with Washington and Monroe, were his "friends and benefactors," while Jefferson had been "a hollow and treacherous friend." He did, however, identify the key relationship between them. Jefferson was the bold and eloquent proposer of principles of liberty; Madison the wise and profound analyst of the government suited to them. Daniel Webster captured the combination in his famous peroration, "Liberty and Union, one and inseparable, now and forever." Sick, discouraged, stressed, and aware of impending death as the last new year of his life approached, Jefferson had once again needed his steady friend at Montpelier to protect him from his tendency, a curse as well as a blessing, for "bold" if ill-considered "shots" to move those of less clear principles.

Jefferson's decline also affected his supervision of the university and its Board of Visitors meetings, where he always met James and often Dolley Madison. He reported to Madison in October 1825 that "my rides to the University have brought me great sufferings, reducing my intervals of ease from 45 to 20 minutes [achieved with laudanum]. This is a good index of the changes occurring," he noted ominously. He told another friend on New Year's Day 1826 that he was reading "one newspaper only and forgetting immediately what I read in that."

The visit in October 1825 of J. H. I. Browere, who made a plaster life mask of Jefferson, was another trying experience, as he reported to Madison.

It was a bold experiment on his part on the health of an Octogenary, worn down by sickness as well as age. Successive coats of thin groat plaistered on the naked head, and kept there an hour, would have been a severe trial of a young and hale person. He suffered the plaister also to get so dry that separation became difficult and even dangerous. He was obliged to use freely the mallet and chisel to break into pieces and cut off a piece at a time. These thumps of the mallet would have been sensible almost to a loggerhead. The family became alarmed, and he confused, till I was quite exhausted, and there became a real danger that the ears would separate from the head sooner than from the plaister.

Granddaughter Virginia, who viewed the whole scene with horror, called Browere "the vile plaisterer." She thought the application of oil to her grandfather's face and then the successive coats of thin plaster "seems really like burying [him] alive." However, Browere had failed to put on enough oil "to prevent adherence to the skin," and removing the plaster became so "excessively painful . . . we expected Grand-papa to faint from exhaustion." Horrified, the family fled the room but could still hear the usually long-suffering and patient Jefferson sobbing from his ordeal. "I now bid adieu forever to busts and even to portraits," the sick and exhausted man exclaimed.

Madison doubtless was particularly chagrined at his friend's bad experience because he had himself introduced Browere to Jefferson as a talented artist who had just done face masks of James and Dolley. They were proof, James said, that Browere deserved his excellent reputation. The face mask could "be taken with but little fatigue to the patient," Madison had explained to his friend—or so apparently had been his and Dolley's experience. When Lafayette heard of Jefferson's contrary experience, though, he resonated more with Jefferson than with Madison: "I have seen in the papers the High price You Have paid on your person for Your Bust, and do the more sympathize with it as I had my Share of plaistering on one of the Hottest days in New York." Browere somehow managed to reconstruct the "chiseled" and shattered pieces of the mold for Jefferson's mask, and the life masks of the three Virginians made from the molds, plus that of Lafayette, repose today in a museum in Cooperstown, New York.

In February 1826, burdened more than ever it seemed with visitors,

Life masks of James Madison
(*above*) and Dolley Madison
(*right*), by John Henri Isaac
Browere, 1825. (Fenimore
Art Museum, Cooperstown,
New York)

Life masks of Thomas
Jefferson (*right*) and the
marquis de Lafayette (*below*),
by John Henri Isaac Browere,
1825. (Fenimore Art Museum,
Cooperstown, New York)

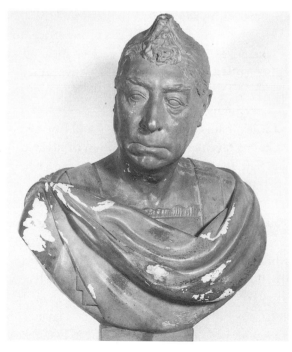

letter writing, impending financial disaster, family problems, and university affairs and sensing the end of his life more and more strongly, Jefferson wrote Madison in a somber yet nostalgic mood. First he worried about how the good Whig principles of Lord Coke on law, of Rapin on English history, and Locke and Sidney on political ideas could be sustained at the university against the increasing prevalence of the Tory doctrines of Mansfield and Blackstone in law and of David Hume in history and elsewhere. With "nearly all the young brood of lawyers" having mostly taken a "slide into toryism, . . . [they] no longer know what Whigism and republicanism means," Jefferson complained. He hoped, because his own influence would soon rapidly decline, that Madison "or some other will mark out the path to be pursued by us." Only then could the "vestal flame" of republican good government be kept alive and "spread anew over our own and sister states." Madison replied, hoping cautiously that the "truly distressing" condition of the law school might be improved in the long run by the choice of a proper law professor.

Second, Jefferson laid out the full and catastrophic state of his finances. Paying the interest on the defaulted loans of friends for whom he had generously but unwisely cosigned, plus the "maintenance of my family," had made "deep and rapid inroads on my capital," he reported. All this might have been managed had not a succession of years of low prices for crops and a depression of land prices by as much as 80 percent meant that his "property has lost its character of being a resource for debts." A legislative scheme in Richmond to float a public lottery to relieve him of his distress showed some signs of coming to fruition, he thought (in fact this one did not), but without it Jefferson foresaw that he would lose all his property in Albemarle, including Monticello, and even most of his land in Bedford County. He would have to "move thither with my family, where I have not even a log hut to put my head into."

Madison replied with his usual understatement that he "had not been without fears that the causes you enumerate were undermining your estate" but he had not realized how really bad things were. Jefferson's distresses were similar to his own. "Since my return to private life (and the case was worse during my absence in public)," Madison noted, "such have been the unkind seasons, and the ravages of insects, that I have made but one tolerable crop of tobacco, and but one of wheat. . . . Having no resources but in the earth I cultivate," he added, "I have been living very much throughout on borrowed means." If his debts were called for with any "rigid pressure" (happily not threatened at the present), his situation would have "a degree of analogy to yours." He hoped "the chance of better crops and prices, with the prospect of a more leisurely disposal of . . . property," would save him from the ruin facing Jefferson—perhaps implying, though, that he could not help his nearly bankrupt friend?

Third, and probably most distressing of all to Jefferson, was the accumulation of crises and tragedies among the large and complicated family living under his roof at Monticello. This family, ever since the Madisons' own marriage and that of Jefferson's daughter Martha in the early 1790s, had been in close and congenial connection with the Montpelier one. Martha Jefferson Randolph (1772–1836) was only four years younger than Dolley. For more than thirty years the two women served as "matrons of the family" for their complicated homesteads. Martha's daughter Septimia, age twelve when her grandfather died, remembered visits to Montpelier before James Madison's death, when her mother and Dolley sat over tea in the dining room for hours laughing and reminiscing as James listened and kibitzed from his sitting room. Before dinner they would gather in the drawing room for "the old Va. Custom [of] wine and cake . . . to give an appetite." Septimia's last visit to the Madison family came after James's death and shortly before that of her mother less than four months later. Septimia found Montpelier then a "great desolate house" where Dolley "sought comfort in the close friendship of her old and much-loved friend Mrs. Randolph."

Jefferson's extended family included Martha's large family of five boys and six girls, born between 1791 and 1818, ten of whom survived to maturity and seven of whom lived until after the Civil War. Her younger sister, Maria Jefferson Eppes (1778–1804) bore three children, but only one son survived infancy. All generally lived at Monticello, where Jefferson attended to and was concerned about their education, illnesses, travel, marital blessings and woes, and their children—his great-grandchildren. This attention and concern were deeply shared at Montpelier as the frequent exchange of visits continued during Jefferson's lifetime, and even after Monticello was lost.

The most personally troubling problem had to do with Martha's husband, Thomas Mann Randolph (1768–1828), the same age as Dolley Madison. Tom was an active and congenial political colleague of his father-in-

Martha Jefferson Randolph, by Thomas Sully. (Thomas Jefferson
Foundation / Monticello)

law for many years, but when he retired as governor of Virginia in 1822,
he faced financial ruin. His desperate efforts to save his property near
Monticello soon, in devious ways, encumbered both his father-in-law and
his son Jeff, Thomas Jefferson Randolph (1792–1875), already his grandfather's favorite, right hand, and literary legatee. In self-pity and humiliation Tom Randolph tried to mask his almost certain bankruptcy from
both his wife and his father-in law, as it also embroiled him with his son.
After frantic, embarrassing, undisclosed, and finally failed efforts to get
financial relief from a banker friend of Jefferson's in New York and to
receive an appointment as postmaster at Richmond from President Monroe, Tom Randolph then secured further notes cosigned by his son or his
father-in-law.

  At the same time, as a member of the Virginia Assembly, he quarreled
bitterly with University of Virginia supporter Joseph C. Cabell, a close

friend of both Jefferson and Madison. As a result Randolph was decisively defeated for reelection. Finally forced to give up (temporarily) his nearby Edgehill plantation in bitter quarrels with his son, Tom Randolph took to absenting himself from Monticello from before breakfast until after dark, returning only late at night to sleep. While awaiting the 1825 return visit of Lafayette along with Madison and Monroe, Jefferson, denying any animosity toward his son-in-law, wrote movingly for him to return to his family and to resume his place in its society. Tom Randolph did so briefly but withdrew again in humiliation and resentment. He wrote one time that he left again to avoid the supercilious glances of his father-in-law's guests. When finally forced to sell his last property, he dragged his son and father-in-law further into the morass of his affairs. Jefferson was distressed and housebound over the summer of 1825. Dr. Dunglison raised Jefferson's laudanum prescription to fifty drops at night to relieve the increasing pain. He was unable to accompany Lafayette and Madison to a banquet given by the students at the university. James and Dolley felt deeply the pain, anguish, and despair of this beloved lifelong friend and his troubled family.

At the very moment Jefferson poured out his heart to Madison, though, he had suffered yet one more heart-wrenching family tragedy. His eldest granddaughter, Anne Randolph Bankhead, a favorite companion (and also a favorite of Dolley Madison's) who from her childhood had shared her grandfather's love of gardening, had returned unexpectedly to Albemarle County in January 1826, sickly and on the verge of giving birth to her fourth child. The child, Jefferson's sixth great-grandchild, was born on January 30 at Jeff Randolph's house, but the mother, ill and exhausted, was soon moved to Monticello. Her poor condition was kept from Jefferson at first because of his own illnesses, but when Anne was clearly near death, Jefferson was "present in the adjoining apartment." Dr. Dunglison finally told him of Anne's desperate condition. Jefferson went to his granddaughter and was, the doctor reported, "speechless and insensible, . . .[and] abandoned himself to every evidence of intense grief." Anne Randolph Bankhead died a few hours later. Jefferson wrote Jeff Randolph: "Bad news . . . as to your sister. She expired about half an hour ago. . . . Heaven seems to be overwhelming us with every form of misfortune."

The anguish and distress, though, were not over. Anne's husband, Charles Bankhead, a notorious drunkard, brawler, and wife abuser, who had already caused the family immense woe, came for his wife's funeral. He was apparently "abstaining from the vices which have caused so much unhappiness in the family," a worried Martha Randolph observed, but she expected "frequent relapses." She knew that she herself would have to look after Anne's "poor little infant" and her other three children. When Jeff Randolph reached Monticello a few days later, he not only renewed his long-standing, near violent quarrel with Bankhead but experienced the wrath of his father, Tom Randolph, "gone more like a demon than ever," his niece wrote. Tom was furious at his son for having, he thought, virtually stolen his Edgehill plantation from him in Jeff's desperate efforts to save himself and his grandfather from his father's now certain ruin. Tom railed at his other children and forbade them from ever visiting Jeff's family or plantation. At the same time Jeff supported his mother's desire to keep Charles Bankhead away from his newborn son. Also, Jeff's news from his recent trip further upset Jefferson. He "turned quite white," a niece reported, when he heard that Jeff Randolph had put Monticello, lock, stock, and barrel, up for auction (luckily the auction was called off) and that one of the proposals for a public lottery to relieve Jefferson's financial distress had been stalled in the legislature, creating what Jeff later termed "a perfect hell of trouble." The Madisons received almost daily reports of these unhappy events but were forced to stand by helplessly as the misfortunes accumulated.

Writing Madison four days after his granddaughter's funeral and the bitter, sometimes violent quarrels of his son-in-law, grandson, and grandson-in-law, Jefferson concluded his farewell letter to Madison with a question: "Why afflict you with these details? I cannot tell, indeed, unless pains are lessened by communication with a friend." The ill and despondent sage of Monticello then moved to warm and principled recollection of his long association with the sage of Montpelier. "The friendship which has subsisted between us, now half a century, and the harmony of our political principles and pursuits . . . [have been] sources of happiness to me through that long period." If ever there was a government "conducted with a single and steadfast eye to the general interest and happiness of those committed to it," Jefferson continued, "one which, protected by truth, can never know reproach, it is that to which our lives have been devoted." He pronounced Madison his "pillar of support through life" and asked that Madison "take care of me when dead, and be assured that

I leave with you my last affections." Madison replied: "You cannot look back to the long period of our private friendship and political harmony, with more affecting recollections than I do. If they are sources of pleasure to you, what ought they not be to me? We cannot be deprived of the happy consciousness of the pure devotion to the public good with which we discharged the trusts committed to us. Wishing and hoping that you may yet live to increase the debt which our country owes to you, and to witness the increasing gratitude, which alone can repay it, I offer you the fullest return of affectionate assurances."

Jefferson's Death and Eulogies

Even the mood of somber yet affectionate and principled farewell, though, could not long distract Jefferson from his almost frantic anxiety over things being left in disarray as his strength diminished. At the University of Virginia much was unsettled and problematic. The law professor had not been chosen, uneasiness remained after the riots of the summer of 1825, and admissions and residences were unfilled as classes resumed. Jefferson implored Madison that "yourself or some other will mark out the track to be pursued by us. If I remove beyond the reach of attentions to the University, or beyond the bourne of life itself, as soon I must, it is a comfort to leave that institution under your care." Madison responded with his usual deference and support: "You do not overrate the interest I feel in the University, . . . but you entirely do my aptitude to be your successor in watching over its prosperity. . . . The best hope is the continuance of your cares." "Little reliance can be put even on the fellowship of my services," the seventy-five-year-old Madison noted. In fact, moving to share his friend's foreboding mood, he confessed that "the past year has given me sufficient intimation of the infirmities in wait for me. In calculating the probabilities of survivorship, the inferiority of my constitution forms an equation at least with the seniority of yours."

Though neither man seems to have expected it, they did see each other again at a Board of Visitors meeting in Charlottesville on April 3 and 4, 1826. The board still faced difficult problems of enrollment, lack of funds, student behavior, and recruitment of faculty. Jefferson hoped that the preeminent choice for the law professorship, United States attorney general William Wirt, a lawyer and writer, would accept the post if sweetened with a pay raise and the title of president as well, an office giving him substantial power over the affairs of the university. In his last official act, though, Jefferson finally opposed the additional title because creating such an office would encroach upon authority intended for the board and the faculty, countering Jefferson's ideal of a collegial institution managed by the faculty and students. The matter became moot when Wirt turned down the post, and the new title was not attached to the successful appointment of John Tayloe Lomax to the law professorship. Madison seems to have gone along with the idea, in Wirt's case, of creating a presidency for the university but agreed heartily to the appointment of Lomax. Jefferson's "favorite system" of faculty control along with board oversight continued during Madison's rectorship and until 1904.

A final exchange of letters, May 3 and 6, was made possible when, as Jefferson reported with relief to Madison, "in comparison to my sufferings of the last year, my health, although not restored, is greatly better." If he could simply enjoy "the passive occupation of reading," he said, "I should probably wear on in tolerable ease and tranquility." Instead, the "unceasing drudgery" of letter writing kept him in "unceasing pain and peevishness." He wished people would realize his circumstances and stop pestering him. He hastily added to Madison, though, that "the correspondence of my bosom-friends is still very dear, and welcome and consolatory, yours among the most." Madison responded with unusual sharpness: "The epistolary taxation with which you are still persecuted is a cruelty not to be borne." He proposed that Jefferson frame a general letter to be copied by one of his family, to be sent to imposing correspondents, merely offering thanks for their letter but explaining that Jefferson's health and age made his reply impossible. Only that, Madison insisted, perhaps thinking of his own impending circumstances, could provide relief from "the afflicting burden."

But Jefferson's days were nonetheless clearly numbered. He did muster strength on June 6 to go for the last time to the university, apparently on horseback by himself, to watch and doubtless supervise the installation of one of the columns of the Rotunda. His anxiety over his finances and his inability to provide for his large family after his death continued. His grandson Jeff returned from a trip to Boston in early June without good news about public efforts to relieve Jefferson of his financial woes. Dr. Dunglison made more and more frequent visits to Monticello. The

Madisons, along with other friends and relatives too distant or infirm to be at Monticello, awaited frequent messages from Jeff, Nicholas Trist, or Dr. Dunglison. On June 24, troubled with diarrhea and sure death was near, Jefferson summoned Dr. Dunglison, who stayed from then on near his patient. That same day Jefferson wrote his last letter, declining an invitation to be present in Washington for a celebration of the fiftieth anniversary of the Declaration of Independence. Madison and Monroe had declined invitations to the same event, with less "poetry" than Jefferson's; Madison had replied, "ever honored will be the day which gives birth to a nation, and a system of self-government, making it a new epoch in the history of man." But Jefferson used the ringing rhetoric that so generally distinguished his writing, as he summarized the republican faith they shared: "All eyes are opened, or opening, to the rights of man. The general spread of the light of science has already laid open to every view the palpable truth, that the mass of mankind has not been born with saddles on their backs, nor a favored few booted and spurred to ride them legitimately, by the grace of God."

Jefferson remained lucid though very weak until the last two or three days of his life, Martha at his bedside during the day, Jeff Randolph or Nicholas Trist at night, and Dr. Dunglison nearby. Jefferson's personal servant, more attentive to his physical needs than the others, slept on a pallet at his master's side. When eight-year-old grandson George Wythe Randolph seemed confused at the scene, Jefferson smiled weakly and said, "George does not understand what all this means." On July 1 Dr. Dunglison wrote the Madisons, postponing a visit to Montpelier because, he said, "my worst apprehensions must soon be realized." Jefferson's "serious indisposition" led the doctor to fear "the result of the struggle" to stay alive. On the evening of July 3, in a husky, indistinct voice, his last utterance, Jefferson asked Dunglison, "Ah, doctor are you still there? Is it the 4th?" The doctor replied, "It soon will be." Jefferson then lapsed into a coma and died about noon on the Fourth of July. He was buried in the graveyard at Monticello the next day.

Nicholas Trist wrote a brief note at once informing Madison of Jefferson's death, and in a few days Dr. Dunglison came to Montpelier to deliver to Madison, at Jefferson's bequest in his will, the latter's favorite "gold-mounted walking staff of animal horn." Madison accepted it, he wrote Jeff Randolph, as "a token of the place I held in the friendship of one whom I so much revered and loved when living, and whose memory can never cease to be dear to me." In a longer response to Trist's note, Madison eulogized his friend: "He lives and will live in the memory and gratitude of the wise and good as a luminary of science, as a votary of liberty, as a model of patriotism, and as a benefactor of human kind. In these characters I have known him, and not less in the virtues and charms of social life, for a period of fifty years, during which there has not been an interruption or diminution of mutual confidence and cordial friendship for a single moment, in a single instance. What I feel, therefore, now, need not, I should say, cannot, be expressed."

Dolley Madison's only known response to Jefferson's death was in a brief note to Payne Todd, in New York: "A few lines my dear son (if they reach you) will inform you that Mr. Jefferson died on the 4th—about 12 or 1 o'clock. Mr. M. feels his departure deeply, as no doubt his family must." James offered to help the Monticello family in any way he could, though all knew its fate was dire given the patriarch's insolvency, his son-in-law's bankruptcy and instability, his daughter's ill health, despondency, and grief, and the mixed prospects for her children and grandchildren. Martha Randolph, with her oldest son Jeff and two youngest children (ages twelve and eight), stopped at Montpelier in November 1826 in a stressful visit on their way to Boston. They would live for a while with daughter Ellen and her husband, Joseph Coolidge, the most settled and well-off branch of Jefferson's large progeny. "A change of scene," Madison wrote Lafayette after her departure, was "essential to her health, as well as to her feelings." For the rest of Martha's life, her struggles to find a place to live after the forced sale of Monticello and to continue the care of her large family so long shared with her father were much on the minds of the Madisons, and occasioned many visits, often under stress, to Montpelier. Martha wrote her Boston daughter three years before James Madison's death that "Virginia is no longer a home for the family of Thomas Jefferson." She herself died three months after Madison.

In the months following Jefferson's death, his friend at Montpelier had many occasions to further eulogize him and comment on his services to the nation. In September, Madison wrote his old friend and colleague from Philadelphia, Richard Peters (seven years older than Madison), that although "we cannot associate our names with the two luminaries [Jefferson and John Adams] who have just sunk below the horizon leaving inextinguishable traces behind, . . . we both have had the happiness of passing through a period glorious to our country, and more than any preceding one, likely to improve the social condition of man." "We have at least a place in the galaxy of faithful citizens," Madison concluded, "who did their best for their country when it most needed their services." Madison had saluted Peters as "my dear friend" and recalled their service together in the "Old Congress," 1781–83, when Peters had worked with Jefferson and Madison to defend Benjamin Franklin, the alliance with France, and a stronger union of the states.

Another eulogy came in response to a request for a "Memoir of Mr. Jefferson" from Washington newspaper editor Samuel Smith. Madison offered some comments on his friend's character, especially his devotion to study, books, and education. He learned French when very young, Madison pointed out, and knew well the "literary treasure which it contained." He also read and spoke Italian, had "a competent knowledge of Spanish," and knew "Anglo-Saxon as a root of the English and an element in legal philology." (Madison did not need to mention, of course, that Jefferson also knew Latin and Greek, the basis of all formal education in his day.) In architecture he "made himself adept . . . in its useful and in its ornamental characters, . . . exemplified in the buildings of the University" and, he might have added, in the design of both their houses. He never lost "his relish for books, . . . never letting the sun rise before him," and was altogether "one of the most learned men of the age." "He was a walking library," Madison concluded, "and, that can be said but of a few of such prodigies, that the genius of philosophy ever walked hand and hand with him." Thus, the University of Virginia, "the object nearest his heart . . . in retirement, . . . bears the stamp of his genius, and will be a noble monument to his fame, . . . a nursery of Republican patriots, as well as genuine scholars." In so describing Jefferson, Madison, of course, revealed something of his own intellectual aspirations and outlined the elements of perhaps the most fruitful meeting of minds in American history.

To Lafayette, also in November 1826, Madison wrote poignantly, but he felt obliged to add that there was "one affecting exception" to the scene of loving departure and concern for the grieving family at the "irreparable . . . loss . . . we have lately sustained at Monticello." "His family, so long in the lap of the best enjoyments of life, is threatened with the contrast of pinching poverty. The expenses of his numerous household, his extensive hospitalities, and a series of short crops and low markets, to which are to be added old debts contracted in public service abroad, and new ones for which private friendship have made him responsible . . . had produced [an] . . . impossibility of satisfying them without a complete sacrifice of his property, perhaps not even by that, at such a crisis. . . . A forced sale, under existing circumstances," Madison concluded, seemed inevitable. Worst of all, in a circumstance Madison seemed embarrassed to report to the fervently antislavery Lafayette, "the sale of the whole estate (negroes included), would not perhaps reach" all the demands of Jefferson's creditors.

Madison cannot have been unaware, of course, as he had intimated to Jefferson some months earlier, that his own situation, though perhaps not quite so extreme as Jefferson's, was also severe. The large expenses to cover Payne Todd's gambling and dissipation debts were much like the financial drain of Jefferson's ill-advised cosigning of notes for his friends. Madison told Lafayette of hopes that Jefferson's letters and papers, being taken to Boston by Jeff Randolph, would find "Northern printers" and provide a "pecuniary resource" for his family. He also thanked Lafayette for his offer to share with Jefferson's family some of the hoped-for proceeds of his lands in East Florida, but he thought they were "a resource perfectly dormant." As Madison had done so often, he recalled to Lafayette the efforts of the three men on behalf of many efforts to extend human liberty: The American Revolution and then the French Revolution, whose moderate beginnings Jefferson had helped Lafayette with in Paris and Madison had welcomed in Congress; the campaign for religious freedom in Virginia; the establishment of constitutional government in the United States; the unfulfilled hopes for the end of slavery; the reforming aspirations of Fanny Wright; and the on-going struggles for liberty in Greece and South America. In recurring to these events, Madison reviewed the actions, purposes, and sentiments that had guided, with Jefferson, the most useful political friendship in American history as well as one of the great collaborations of all time. But after July 4, 1826, Madison sensed more and more that for him and his generation, time was running out.

Old Friends Pass: James Monroe and Others

Besides Mother Madison's death in 1829, James and Dolley lost other long-time friends and relatives in the years following Jefferson's death. Near at home was his cousin Catlett Conway (whose father was Nelly Madison's brother), the same age as James and his playmate as a young child at his mother's ancestral home on the Rappahannock River below Fredericksburg. He had moved with his family to Orange County, perhaps as early as the 1750s, where he grew up and was probably James Madison's closest family companion until he died in 1827. He had a farm in Orange, the same Greenwood conveyed to Sarah Madison Macon's daughter, Lucie, who was married to Catlett's son, Reuben, in turn a pallbearer at James's funeral. Madison's youngest sister, Frances Madison Rose, had died in 1823. In 1828 James's ward and favorite nephew, Robert Madison, who more than any other relative had succeeded his uncle as the family politician, died of tuberculosis, leaving a young wife and three children who were in some way under care at Montpelier. Other grown children of William Madison died in the 1820s; and his wife, in 1832. Dolley's brother-in-law Justice Thomas Todd died in 1826, as well as two of her nephews, children of Lucy Payne Washington Todd, in 1831. Brother-in-law John G. Jackson, long a political colleague of James, died in 1825, and the favorite and beloved Anna Cutts suffered deteriorating health before her death in 1832. The correspondence of both James and Dolley Madison is filled with grief and then eulogies of the deaths of longtime and valued friends, public and private, local and far afield.

The deaths of friends from the Madisons' political life were especially poignant, because one of the satisfactions of the early retirement years at Montpelier was time to savor these old friendships, apart now from the public spotlight. After Jefferson's passing, the most difficult of this kind for the Madisons was the death of James Monroe. Even during Monroe's presidency from 1817 to 1825, he, and sometimes his wife and family, usually stopped at Montpelier for summer visits, though their plans were occasionally altered for official or political reasons. The Monroes canceled a visit in the summer of 1817, for example, because they did not want to overlap with the visit of the French minister for fear it would signal official favoritism of France. Visits of the president to Montpelier, as well as correspondence about public affairs, had to be coordinated with political leaders—John Quincy Adams, John C. Calhoun, Henry Clay, William H. Crawford, Andrew Jackson, and others—in order to avoid implying unintended alliances, especially as the bitterly contested presidential campaign of 1824 approached. Though Madison and Monroe had been present together at the celebration in October 1819 of the laying of the cornerstone of the first building at the University of Virginia, Monroe then withdrew as a board member while in office in Washington. He and Madison, though, kept in close touch by mail and through Monroe's annual or semiannual stops at Montpelier on his way to or from his seat, then called Highlands, near Monticello. The sense of the warmth, strength, and longevity of their colleagueship and friendship grew as both men became legends of the Founding: Madison, the father of the Constitution, and Monroe, "the last of the cocked hats," the last president to have been a battlefield hero of the Revolution who had fought with Lafayette and Washington.

The acquaintance was fraught with some difficulty, however. The problem was not Monroe himself; he was unfailingly good-natured, devoted to public duty, and loyal, if a bit stiff and uneasy at being in the shade of his presidential predecessors. It was his wife, Elizabeth, and especially their older daughter, Eliza Monroe Hay. Mother and daughter were beautiful and elegantly dressed women with courtly manners; but compared to Dolley Madison, who "was much more popular," according to Louisa Adams, they cast a pall over the Washington social scene. The lively, informal events, mixing cabinet officials, members of Congress, foreign diplomats, military officers, notable visitors to the capital, and local socialites, that Dolley conducted with such charm and graciousness to complement the republican style of the government were no more. Many of the wives in the capital who had remained Dolley's close friends were aghast. The two Elizas refused to make or even return calls, and the Monroes attended only ceremonial occasions. Their orchestrated fortnightly "drawing rooms," open to anyone "decently dressed," were stiff occasions where guests could formally meet the President and his ladies, but two staples of Washington parties in Dolley's day, dancing and cards, did not happen. Dolley's letters from Washington friends were full of complaints and unfavorable comparisons with better times in the past.

By 1824 Phoebe Morris wrote archly to Dolley of "Mrs. Hay's personal elegance of deportment and costume," and Dolley wrote Anna Cutts, knowingly and snippily, after being in Richmond with the Monroes during the Virginia Convention of 1829–30, "that Mrs. Hay was just the same minded person that she used to be." During her father's indisposition there she had refused admission of all visitors to see him, except Dolley once. Apparently the trouble was that during her years as a teenager in Paris when her father was American minister there and during the Napoleonic years when she had gone to school with none other than the empress Josephine's daughter, Hortense de Beauharnais, Eliza had acquired the haughty, aristocratic airs of that court. She even named her only daughter Hortensia. Seeming displaced in republican America, she held everyone except her immediate family in snobbish disdain. Before her marriage she seems to have jilted Edward Coles, to Dolley's dismay. After the deaths of Eliza's parents and husband in 1830–31, she moved back to Washington for a while as Dolley worried about her unsuitability there. Finally, probably to Dolley's relief, she moved to Paris where she converted to Roman Catholicism and entered a convent until her death in 1840. Anna Cutts and Dolley gossiped incessantly about where she was and what she was doing and never ceased to worry, wonder, and put down this woman perceived as so cold and haughty—that is, unrepublican. Her visits, with those of her mother, to Montpelier were uneasily anticipated: James and Dolley would warn each other of their approach.

After Monroe retired, the relations between the two former presidents themselves, though, became more relaxed and cordial. Monroe rejoined the University of Virginia Board of Visitors just as Jefferson died and Madison became rector. After that, from October 1825 until the rapid decline in Monroe's health in the summer of 1830, the two sometimes met four times a year, for Board of Visitors meetings in the spring and fall and then to conduct examinations in July and December. Monroe (frequently unaccompanied by his wife or daughter) usually stopped at Montpelier on his way to or from Charlottesville and his estate, Oak Hill, near Washington in Loudoun County. The aged statesmen, each up and down with bouts of illness, enjoyed as much as they could rides together back and forth from Montpelier to Charlottesville and rambles around Montpelier. In Albemarle County during an "interesting" walk around Monticello, Madison once lost a pair of shoe buckles that Monroe promised to replace for him when he got back to Oak Hill. Forgetfulnesses sometimes occurred: Monroe had to ask his even older companion (Madison was seventy-seven; Monroe seventy-one) to send him a copy of a board document he had lost track of and to remind him of "the precise day" of its next meeting. Monroe reported to his fellow plantation owner that though it had rained some in Loudoun, it was "not enough to secure the corn," but luckily the wheat rust had done less damage than he had observed in Orange. He had been "so much overcome by the heat and fatigue of the journey" home, Monroe added, that "in consequence of it, . . . I have been incapable of any exertion since."

Besides the pleasant visits of Monroe to Montpelier (James and Dolley seem not to have visited the Monroes, either at Highlands or at Oak Hill) and the companionship on many meetings in Charlottesville and one in Richmond for the Virginia Convention of 1829–30, Madison also supported Monroe in the quarrels left over from the increasingly acrimonious last years of his presidency. As the election of 1828 approached, Madison helped refute charges that Monroe had improperly directed or inadequately supported Andrew Jackson's campaigns at Pensacola and New Orleans, or that he had not been evenhanded in his cabinet to Secretary of the Treasury William H. Crawford, or that he had too much or too little favored internal improvements or too much or too little backed a protective tariff, or that he had too much supported John Quincy Adams in the coming election. Both Monroe and Madison withdrew as Virginia presidential electors in 1828 after their unauthorized nominations. All these controversies or issues somehow involved Madison, so he was drawn in reluctantly to lend his vast prestige and insider knowledge to refute charges against Monroe. The correspondence of each man is filled with long, unwillingly written letters regretful at being drawn into current political controversy, with each author insisting on his own desire to remain above partisanship and attentive to the public good and the survival of the Union.

Madison also shared Monroe's desperate efforts to rescue his finances, perhaps not so severe as Jefferson's situation had been but, at least in the 1820s, worse than Madison's. Monroe had accumulated at least $75,000 in debt over more than thirty years of public service, much of it abroad, where he had lived beyond his means and seldom received adequate reimbursement from the government. His salaries as a cabinet officer under Madison and then as president did not allow him to cover his expenses then or enable him to recoup his foreign arrears. His farms were no more productive than those of other Virginians. He hoped to regain solvency by selling lands, especially Highlands, his estate in Albemarle, and then persuading Congress to repay the arrears he had accumulated overseas, itemized in a laboriously gathered statement. He managed to sell the Albemarle land in 1825 or 1826, but the pleas to Congress stalled. Jacksonians apparently resented what they perceived as Monroe's unfair, partisan, and neglectful response while president to their leader. Monroe enlisted Madison earnestly in this effort; both men insisted vehemently on their constant support of and admiration for the hero of New Orleans, news of whose triumph James and Dolley had greeted so gloriously in Washington almost fifteen years earlier.

Madison anguished over the distress of one whose public services and private virtues he so much respected. He had to stand by helplessly, though, as Monroe's efforts and indeed his whole world collapsed in 1830. It seemed he would have to sell Oak Hill, his last property and home in Virginia; his wife and son-in-law George Hay died within two days of each other; his own health failed; and he himself could only find care and comfort in his final months by moving, with the widowed Eliza Hay, to New York to be with his younger daughter and her family. A friend at Oak Hill on the morning Mrs. Monroe died remembered "the touching grief manifested by the old man." "With trembling frame and streaming eye," Monroe "spoke of the long years they had spent happily together, and expressed his conviction that he would soon follow her" to the grave.

In New York, bedridden in his daughter's house, Monroe wrote in the same mood to Madison:

> My ill state of health continuing, consisting of a cough, which annoys me by night and by day into considerable expectoration, . . . renders the restoration of my health very uncertain. In such a state I could not reside on my farm. . . . My daughters [wish] that I should remain here. . . . I do not wish to burthen them. . . . I could make no establishment here without the sale of my property in Loudoun. . . . The accounting officers [in Congress] have made no decision on my claims & have given me much trouble. . . . I deeply regret that there is no prospect of our ever meeting again, since so long have we been connected, and in the most friendly intercourse, in public & private life, that a final separation is among the most distressing incidents that could occur. I shall resign my seat at the Board [of Visitors] in due

time. . . . I beg to assure Mrs. Madison that I never can forget the friendly
relation which has existed between her and my family.

His closing message to Dolley was an example of Monroe's remarkable
ability, even at desperate times, to see the bright and ignore the dark side
of things.

Madison tried earnestly in reply to bolster and cheer up his failing and
discouraged friend. He began with New York's cold, gloomy climate: was
it not "unsuited to your period of life and the state of your health?" If, as
Madison perhaps too optimistically hoped, the "vexations . . . of the accounting process at Washington" might fade, could not Monroe, "with
an encouraging improvement of your health, . . . reconsider" his move
from Virginia? The journey back "at a rate of your own choice, might
co-operate in the re-establishment of your health, . . . and perhaps enable
you to join your colleagues at the University once more at least." Madison
hoped further that "your cough and weakness [might] give way to the
influence of the season and the innate strength of your constitution" and
enable you "to keep up your connexion with Virginia." Madison, nearly
eighty and "in comfortable health," and "notwithstanding the short period
I could enjoy" Monroe's company, still hoped he might return to his native
land and the scenes of their many common labors. Responding to his
friend's somber, heartfelt farewell, though, Madison assured him that "the
pain I feel at the idea, associated as it is with a recollection of the long,
close, and uninterrupted friendship which united us, amounts to a pang I
cannot well express. . . . Whatever may be the turn of things, be assured
of the unchangeable interest felt by Mrs. M., as well as myself, in your
welfare, and in that of all who are dearest to you." (Did Madison deliberately omit specific mention of Eliza Hay?) He added a postscript on his
own condition: "In explanation of my microscopic writing, I must remark
that the older I grow the more my stiffening fingers make smaller letters,
as my feet take shorter steps; the progress of both cases being, at the same
time, much more fatiguing as well as more slow."

After Monroe died on July 4, 1831, Madison responded to notice of that
event by the former's great-grandson with his fulsome eulogy on Monroe. Madison was grateful, he said, for the kind attentions given "our
excellent friend" by his family "in his last days." "I need not say to you,"
Madison continued, "who so well knows how highly I rated the compre-

hensiveness and character of his mind; the purity and nobleness of his principles; the importance of his patriotic services; and the many private virtues of which his whole life was a model; nor how deeply, therefore, I must sympathize, on his loss, with those who feel it most. A close friendship, continued through so long a period and such diversified scenes has grown into an affection very imperfectly expressed by that term."

Thus closing the book on the life of the last of his close colleagues in the long half century of the founding of the new nation, Madison would have agreed with the view John Quincy Adams expressed in his two-hour eulogy of Monroe in Boston that his public service had been devoted to building the nation and its Union and establishing it securely on republican principles. "Thus strengthening and consolidating the federal edifice of his country's Union," Adams concluded, left Monroe "entitled to say, like Augustus Caesar of his imperial city, that he had found her built of brick and left her constructed of marble."

Madison's mood and principled, patriotic nostalgia had been shared and eloquently captured six years earlier in a note sent to Monroe by Chief Justice John Marshall three days after he had administered the oath of office to John Quincy Adams, Monroe's successor as president. This tenth inauguration was the last time all three participants in that ceremony had been heroes of the American Revolution. "You have filled," Marshall wrote the retiring president, "a large place in the common mind, and have been conspicuously instrumental in effecting objects of great interest to our common country." "Affectionate resolutions [were] excited in my bosom," Marshall exclaimed, as he "looked back to times long since gone by" when he and Monroe had fought together in Washington's army. Faded were the differences over ratification of the Constitution, when Marshall was Federal, Monroe Antifederal, and over the bitter quarrels with France in the 1790s. In reply, Monroe expressed his "highest gratification" for Marshall's praise for his conduct of the "arduous" office he had just relinquished and recalled nostalgically that "we began our career together in early youth." Moreover, Monroe added, "the whole course of my public conduct has been under your observation," so he held the venerable justice's "approbation" (and willingness to set aside differences) in "the highest estimation." Monroe and Marshall, along with Madison, had all extended their careers and active attention to public affairs well past the biblical three score and ten, as would John Quincy

Adams. They all felt great affection for and appreciation of their honored and able colleagues in the founding, articulation, defense, and fulfillment of the Union that each saw as embodying their ideal of republican self-government. Disagreements and quarrels faded; shared understanding and commitment remained.

The Founding Era Passes

Writing to Jared Sparks about associations with other now dying "argonauts" of the Revolutionary and founding eras, and anticipating Monroe's death, Madison observed sadly that "having outlived so many of my contemporaries, I ought not to forget that I may be thought to have outlived myself." This bemused state led Madison to respond to a request from James K. Paulding, a frequent visitor to Montpelier, who sought again to pick his brain for information about a work of American history he contemplated. Madison offered a summary commentary:

> Of Doctor Franklin I had no personal knowledge till we served together in the Convention of 1787: and the part he took there has found its way to the public; with the exception of a few anecdotes which belong to the unveiled proceedings of that assembly. He has written his own life: and no man had a finer one to write, or a better title to be himself the writer. There is eno' of blank left however for a succeeding pen.
>
> With Mr. Jefferson I was not acquainted till we met as members of the first Revolutionary Legislature of Virginia. I had of course no personal knowledge of his early life. Of his public career, the records of his Country give ample information. And of the general features of his character, with much of his private habits, and of his peculiar opinions, his writings before the world, to which additions are not improbable, are equally explanatory. The Obituary Eulogiums, multiplied by the Epoch and other coincidences of his death, are a field where some things not unworthy of notice may perhaps be gleaned. It may on the whole be truly said of him, that he was greatly eminent for the comprehensiveness and fertility of his Genius; the vast extent and rich variety of his acquirements; and particularly distinguished by the philosophic impress left on every subject which he touched. Nor was he less distinguished for an early and uniform devotion to the cause of liberty, and for a systematic preference of a Form of Government

squared in the strictest degree, to the equal rights of Man. In the social and domestic spheres he was a model of the virtues and manners which most adorn them.

In relation to Mr. John Adams I had no personal knowledge till he became Vice President of the U.S.; and then saw no side of his private character which was not visible to all; whilst my chief knowledge of his public character and career was acquired by means now accessible or becoming so to all. His private papers are said to be voluminous; and when opened to public view will doubtless be of much avail to a biographer. His official correspondence during the Revolutionary period just published, will be found interesting, both in a historical and a biographical view. That he had a mind rich in ideas of its own, as well as in its learned store; with an ardent love of Country, and the merit of being a Colossal Champion of its Independence, must be allowed by those most offended by the alloy in his Republicanism, and the fervors and flights originating in his moral temperament.

Of Mr. Hamilton I ought perhaps to speak with some restraint, tho' my feelings assure me that no recollection of political collisions could controul the justice due to his memory. That he possessed intellectual powers of the first order, and the moral qualities of integrity and honor in a captivating degree, has been decreed to him by a suffrage now universal. If his Theory of Govt. deviated from the Republican standard, he had the candor to avow it, and the greater merit of co-operating faithfully in maturing and supporting a System which was not his choice. The criticism to which his share in the administration of it, was most liable was that it had the aspect of an effort to give to the Instrument a constructive and practical bearing not warranted by its true and intended character.

We do not have Madison's own summary comments about Washington, universally regarded as the preeminent founder in a class by himself, but there is little doubt Madison would have agreed with Jefferson's eloquent view of their common chieftain:

His mind was great and powerful, without being of the very first order; . . . as far as he saw, no judgment was ever sounder. It was slow in operation, being little aided by invention or imagination, but sure in conclusion. . . . He was incapable of fear, meeting personal dangers with the calmest unconcern. Perhaps the strongest feature in his character was prudence, never acting until every circumstance, every consideration, was maturely weighed, refraining if he saw a doubt, but, when once decided, going through with his purpose, whatever obstacles opposed. His integrity was most pure, his justice the most inflexible. . . . His temper was naturally irritable and high-toned, but reflection and resolution had obtained a firm and habitual ascendency over it. . . . His person was fine, his stature exactly what one would wish, his deportment easy, erect, and noble; the best horseman of his age. . . . Although in a circle of his friends, . . . he took a free share in conversation, his colloquial talents were not above mediocrity, possessing neither copiousness of ideas, nor fluency of words. . . . He wrote readily, rather diffusely, in an easy and correct style. . . . His was the singular destiny and merit, of leading the armies of his country successfully through an arduous war, for the establishment of its independence; of conducting its councils through the birth of a government, new in its forms and principles, until it had settled down into a quiet and orderly train; and of scrupulously obeying the laws through the whole of his career, civil and military, of which the history of the world furnishes no other example.

In writing to Paulding, in preparing his uniquely valuable notes on the convention of 1787 for publication, and in coming to the fateful understanding that he had outlived all his colleagues in revolution and nation building, Madison became even more aware of his mythic existence at Montpelier: he and Dolley, who had sustained him and had created a suitable social style for the republic, were the living embodiment of the nation declared independent more than half a century earlier. "The father of the Constitution" and "the first First Lady" were, after the passing of the aged former presidents Adams, Jefferson, and Monroe, the living "national treasures."

Thus surrounded with death and aware that his own could not be far distant, Madison recalled his earlier comment to a friend who had lost two children: "Afflictions of every kind are the onerous conditions charged on the tenure of life; and it is a silencing if not a satisfactory vindication of the ways of Heaven to man that there are but few who do not prefer an acquiescence in them to a surrender of the tenure itself." Madison may have recalled, too, his response in 1825 to questions about the nature of the deity. "Belief in a God All Powerful wise and good," Madison noted, "is so essential to the moral order of the World and to the happiness of man, that arguments which enforce it cannot be drawn from too many sources." Always an empiricist, Madison thought reasoning from effect to cause, "from Nature to Nature's God," would be "more persuasive" than theological abstractions. As for his own views, he noted:

> The finiteness of the human understanding betrays itself on all subjects, but more especially when it contemplates such as involve infinity. . . . The infinity of time and space forces itself on our conception, a limitation of either being inconceivable; that the mind prefers at once the idea of a self-existing cause to that of an infinite series of cause and effect, which augments, instead of avoiding the difficulty; and that it finds more facility in assenting to the self-existence of an invisible cause possessing infinite power, wisdom and goodness, than to the self-existence of the universe, visibly destitute of those attributes, and which may be the effect of them. In this comparative facility of conception and belief, all philosophical Reasoning on the subject must perhaps terminate.

Though not inclined to religious speculations, Madison adhered to a calm faith in a moral, orderly universe presided over by a God beyond the limited capacity of man to fully conceive or understand.

Next-Generation Madisonians

As Madison's life drew to a close, however, he looked not only backward over his life and the lives and contributions of his fellow founders but forward to new generations that might carry on the principles of his public life. Four young men especially were Madison's legatees. Richard Rush (1780–1859) as a diplomat and cabinet officer nourished plans of national growth long urged by Madison. As minister to England during Monroe's presidency, he helped fashion the "alliance" of Great Britain and the United States to resist European efforts to reverse the revolutions against Spain in South America, formalized in the Monroe Doctrine, and to resist tyranny and nourish the peaceful expansion of world trade that has generally held ever since. Madison continued to counsel Rush when he joined John Quincy Adams's cabinet, fostering broad national plans Madison had foreshadowed in his pathbreaking State of the Union message of December 1815.

Edward Coles (1786–1868) mingled Virginia courtliness with a moral fervor that resulted in a lifetime of effective opposition to slavery. Dolley's cousin and James's private secretary and emissary abroad from 1811 to 1818, Coles had lived with the Madisons in Washington and often visited Montpelier. Widely acknowledged as the person best acquainted with their lives, he frequently explained and defended their acts and careers. He was earnestly antislavery, freeing his slaves in 1819 by settling them on their own farms in Illinois. His youngest son, though, became a Confederate officer and killed in battle in 1862.

William Cabell Rives (1793–1868), a piedmont neighbor, sustained Madison's principles in Virginia public life until the Civil War and then preserved Madison's record by writing a three-volume biography of him and editing four volumes of his letters and other writings. In a long public career, Rives quite self-consciously invoked Madison, especially in his early fervent opposition to nullification and secession and even in holding slavery a moral evil and repugnant to his Madisonian vision of the Union. In the end, though, Rives succumbed to Southern and Virginia loyalty, joined in secession, and was a member of the Confederate Congress. He surely departed, though, from Madison's Lincolnian understanding of the Union in accepting his son's description of the Great Emancipator: "a hideous half civilized creature, of great length of figure—in color like a rotten pumpkin or Mississippi sediment—and of a certain smartish grotesque obscenity of mind shut off from all light"—this from one who as a boy had probably visited the Madisons at Montpelier.

Nicholas Trist (1800–1874), half a century Madison's junior, great-grandson of Madison's Philadelphia landlady Mary House, and married to Jefferson's granddaughter Virginia, by nourishing the University of Virginia, by fighting nullification and secession, and by negotiating honestly yet realistically to end the Mexican War, was thus a lifelong Madisonian. In the years before and after Jefferson's death, Trist and his wife were often the Madisons' guests at Montpelier. Then Trist, as President Jackson's private secretary, worked to bring Madisonian doctrines to bear on Jackson's firm Unionist response to the nullification crisis.

Each of these four men, young and unformed when Madison first knew them, declared unequivocally that Madison was for him the pre-eminent guide, in principles and conduct, for his every public act. Each labored often, in the generation or more he survived Madison, to vindicate his memory and to defend his career against a host of detractors. They had learned from the master himself an understanding of the character and virtues of "the extended republic," which he had expounded and sustained throughout his own public life. Each thus stood out in some way against the divisive sectional tendencies so strong and catastrophic in the thirty years following Madison's death. The course of events, from their arrival on the public stage at about the time of Madison's retirement, did not always conform either to their hopes or to Madison's. In fact, the triumph of an often merely rapacious Jacksonian democracy, the growth of an often merely crass Northern industrialism, the arrogance of an often merely defensive Southern slavocracy, and the secession and civil war that ensued would have been as unwelcome to Madison as they were to his young associates. The careers of all four were in some sense failures, engulfed by aggressive partisanship and civil war. Insofar as Madison's wisdom had relevance for the future, however, they gave it some effect and projected his wisdom meaningfully into the middle of the nineteenth century and beyond. They thus also played a part in the growth of the purposeful, people-empowering Union that Madison had envisioned and helped make constitutional in 1787 and that John Marshall, John Quincy Adams, Daniel Webster, and then Abraham Lincoln helped to assure would "long endure" in the next centuries. No legacy would have pleased Madison more.

"The Last of the Great Lights of the Revolution Has Sunk below the Horizon"

HROUGH 1835 AND 1836, IN MADISON'S OWN METAPHOR, THE CAN-
dle of life in the old man at Montpelier sputtered toward its socket.
Dolley Madison wrote that "my days are devoted to nursing and comforting my sick patient," while a visitor observed that "her devotion to Mr.
Madison is incessant, and he needs all her constant attention." In February
1835, in a visit that found both James and Dolley in a period of better
health and experiencing a winter respite from the sometimes burdensome
parade of company, Harriet Martineau, the English novelist and writer
already well-known at Montpelier, came for three days, much enjoyed by
all. Martineau was on the carefully planned visit to the United States that
resulted in her three-volume *Retrospect of Western Travel,* published in
London and New York in 1838. Excepting only Alexis de Tocqueville's
Democracy in America, it is the fullest and best known of the many accounts
by Europeans of what they saw as a perhaps hopeful and beckoning, perhaps less civilized and retrograde new society unlike any other in the
world. After a beautiful fall trip across New York State on the Erie Canal
to Niagara Falls, she went via Pennsylvania to Washington where she
spent a month observing Congress, meeting President Jackson, and so-
cializing with government officials and their wives, many of whom, of
course, were friends of the Madisons, through whom she received an invitation to Montpelier.

Before leaving Washington, Martineau had visits not only with Clay,
Calhoun, Webster, and other Jackson-era leaders, but also with former
president and now congressman John Quincy Adams and Chief Justice
John Marshall, each a veteran of half a century or more in public life and,

like Madison, stalwart but embattled defenders of the Constitution and the Union against the forces of nullification, secession, sectionalism, party strife, and slavocracy. She heard and saw Calhoun and others defend these forces in Congress and in Washington newspapers and drawing rooms, all of which had reverberated at Montpelier through the reports of visitors and the packets of papers and pamphlets Madison received regularly through the post. Martineau found Adams embodied "the subordination of glory to goodness, of showy objects to moral ones," and "the pure, simple morals which are assumed to prevail in the thriving young republic." She fully grasped, as Adams had noted in his eulogy of James Monroe, that "the Declaration of Independence . . . [was] a proclamation of Union already formed, by *the whole people* of the United States," to which Chief Justice Marshall agreed, asserting to Adams that "the independence of the states is a graft on the stock of . . . a previously existing Union." Eighty years old and in office as chief justice for thirty-four years when Martineau met him in Washington, Marshall struck her as "a tall, majestic, bright-eyed old man" zealous in his defense of the moral and indivisible Union to which he and Adams (and Madison) were devoted. She also found him possessed of a "reverence for woman" that left him "convinced of their intellectual equality with men, . . . [and with] a deep sense of their social injuries." She was pleased at Marshall's contempt for religious establishment, "so monstrous in principle, and so injurious to true religion in practice, that he could not imagine it could be upheld for anything but political purposes."

Martineau also talked with the two old Revolutionary veterans about Adams's *Oration on the Life and Character of Gilbert Motier de Lafayette,* delivered to both houses of Congress a month before. When Marshall received his copy of the oration a day or two before his visit with Martineau, he commended the Frenchman for "the worth and services of one of the most extraordinary personages of the extraordinary and eventful age in which he lived." If Martineau then delivered a copy of the oration to the Madisons, she would have heard further agreement. With these fervent endorsements from veterans with Madison of the founding of the American republic, Martineau's parting comment could have been no surprise: "The most animated moment of our conversation was when I told him [Marshall] I was going to visit Mr. Madison on leaving Washington. He instantly sat upright in his chair, and with beaming eyes began to praise

Montpelier, engraving by John Francis Eugene Prud'homme, 1833. (Courtesy of The Library of Virginia)

Mr. Madison. Madison received the mention of Marshall's name in just the same manner." This is Marshall's last known comment about Madison, affirming after earlier decades of often sharp political disagreement their fundamental agreement on the nature of the Union and the American republic. The chief justice died in office five months later, age eighty. The stage was set for one of the last visits to James and Dolley Madison at Montpelier, and perhaps the most insightful and interesting of all. Martineau recorded:

> At six o'clock in the morning of the 18th of February [1835], my party arrived at Orange Courthouse, five miles from Montpelier; and while two proceeded to Charlottesville, where we were to join them in three or four

days, a friend [Louisa Jeffreys] and I stopped, first to rest for a few hours, and then to proceed to Mr. Madison's. After some sleep, and breakfast at noon, we took a carriage for the five miles of extremely bad road we had to travel. The people of the inn overcharged us for this carriage, and did not mention that Mr. Madison had desired that a messenger should be sent over for his carriage as soon as we should arrive. . . .

It was a sweet day of early spring. The patches of snow that were left under the fences and on the rising grounds were melting fast. The road was one continued slough up to the very portico of the house. The dwelling stands on a gentle eminence, and is neat and even handsome in its exterior, with a flight of steps leading up to the portico. A lawn and wood, which must be pleasant in summer, stretch behind; and from the front there is a noble object on the horizon, the mountain-chain which traverses the state, and makes it eminent for its scenery. The shifting lights upon these blue mountains were a delightful refreshment to the eye after so many weeks of city life as we had passed.

We were warmly welcomed by Mrs. Madison and a niece, a young lady who was on a visit to her; and when I left my room I was conducted to the apartment of Mr. Madison. He had, the preceding season, suffered so severely from rheumatism, that, during this winter, he confined himself to one room, rising after breakfast, before nine o'clock, and sitting in his easy-chair till ten at night. He appeared perfectly well during my visit, and was a wonderful man of eighty-three. He complained of one ear being deaf, and that his sight, which had never been perfect, prevented his reading much, so that his studies "lay in a nutshell;" but he could hear Mrs. Madison read, and I did not perceive that he lost any part of the conversation. He was in his chair, with a pillow behind him, when I first saw him; his little person wrapped in a black silk gown; a warm gray and white cap upon his head, which his lady took care should always sit becomingly; and gray worsted gloves, his hands having been rheumatic. His voice was clear and strong, and his manner of speaking particularly lively, often playful. Except that the face was smaller, and, of course, older, the likeness to the common engraving of him was perfect. He seemed not to have lost any teeth, and the form of the face was therefore preserved, without any striking marks of age. It was an uncommonly pleasant countenance.

His relish for conversation could never have been keener. I was in perpetual fear of his being exhausted; and at the end of every few hours I left

my seat by the arm of his chair, and went to the sofa by Mrs. Madison on
the other side of the room; but he was sure to follow and sit down between
us; so that, when I found the only effect of my moving was to deprive him
of the comfort of his chair, I returned to my station, and never left it but for
food and sleep, glad enough to make the most of my means of intercourse
with one whose political philosophy I deeply venerated.

Martineau revealed the essence of the political philosophy she shared
with Madison with the quotation with which she headed the chapter
that followed her account of the visit to Montpelier: "That the legislator
should especially occupy himself with the education of youth, no one
can dispute; for when this is not done in states, it is a cause of damage to
the polity. For a state must be administered with reference to its polity;
and that which is the peculiar characteristic of each polity is that which
preserves and originally constitutes it; as, for instance, the democratical
principle in a democracy, and the oligarchical in an oligarchy; and that
which is the best principle always constitutes the best polity. Aristotle,
Politik., book viii."

Her description of her visit continued:

There is no need to add another to the many eulogies of Madison; I will
only mention that the finest of his characteristics appeared to me to be his
inexhaustible faith; faith that a well-founded commonwealth may, as our
motto declares, be immortal; not only because the people, its constituency,
never die, but because the principles of justice in which such a commonwealth originates never die out of the people's heart and mind. This faith
shone brightly through the whole of Mr. Madison's conversation except on
one subject. With regard to slavery he owned himself almost to be in
despair. . . .

He talked more on the subject of slavery than on any other, acknowledging, without limitation or hesitation, all the evils with which it has ever
been charged. He told me that the black population in Virginia increases far
faster than the white; and that the licentiousness only stops short of the
destruction of the race; every slave girl being expected to be a mother by
the time she is fifteen. He assumed from this, I could not make out why,
that the negroes must go somewhere, and pointed out how the free states
discourage the settlement of blacks; how Canada disagrees with them; how

Hayti shuts them out; so that Africa is their only refuge. He did not assign any reason why they should not remain where they are when freed. He found, by the last returns from his estates, that one third of his own slaves were under five years of age. He had parted with some of his best land to feed the increasing numbers, and had yet been obliged to sell a dozen of his slaves the preceding week. He observed that the whole Bible is against negro slavery; but that the clergy do not preach this, and the people do not see it. He became animated in describing what I have elsewhere related of the eagerness of the clergy of the four denominations to catch converts among the slaves, and the effect of religious teaching of this kind upon those who, having no rights, can have no duties. He thought the condition of slaves much improved in his time, and, of course, their intellects. This remark was, I think, intended to apply to Virginia alone, for it is certainly not applicable to the southwestern states. He accounted for his selling his slaves by mentioning their horror of going to Liberia, a horror which he admitted to be prevalent among the blacks, and which appears to me decisive as to the unnaturalness of the scheme. . . . Mr. Madison admitted the great and various difficulties attending the scheme, and recurred to the expression that he was only "less in despair than formerly about slavery." He spoke with deep feeling of the sufferings of ladies under the system, declaring that he pitied them even more than their negroes, and that the saddest slavery of all was that of conscientious Southern women. They cannot trust their slaves in the smallest particulars, and have to superintend the execution of all their own orders; and they know that their estates are surrounded by vicious free blacks, who induce thievery among the negroes, and keep the minds of the owners in a state of perpetual suspicion, fear, and anger.

Mr. Madison spoke strongly of the helplessness of all countries cursed with a servile population in a conflict with a people wholly free; ridiculed the idea of the Southern States being able to maintain a rising against the North; and wondered that all thinkers were not agreed in a thing so plain. He believed that Congress has power to prohibit the internal slave trade. . . .

Mrs. Madison's son by a former marriage joined us before dinner. We dined in the next room to Mr. Madison, and found him eager for conversation again as soon as we had risen from table. Mrs. M. is celebrated throughout the country for the grace and dignity with which she discharged the arduous duties which devolve upon the president's lady. For a term of eight years she administered the hospitalities of the White House with such discretion, impartiality, and kindliness, that it is believed she gratified every one and offended nobody. She is a strong-minded woman, fully capable of entering into her husband's occupations and cares; and there is little doubt that he owed much to her intellectual companionship, as well as to her ability in sustaining the outward dignity of his office. When I was her guest she was in excellent health and lively spirits; and I trust that though she has since lost the great object of her life, she may yet find interests enough to occupy and cheer many years of an honoured old age.

Mr. Madison expressed his regret at the death of Mr. Malthus, whose works he had studied with close attention. He mentioned that Franklin and two others had anticipated Malthus in comparing the rates of increase of population and food; but that Malthus had been the first to draw out the doctrine, with an attempt at too much precision, however, in determining the ratio of the increase of food. He laughed at [William] Godwin's methods of accounting for the enormous increase of population in America by referring it to emigration, and having recourse to any supposition rather than the obvious one of an abundance of food. He declared himself very curious on the subject of the size of the Roman farms, and that he had asked many friends where the mistake lies in the accounts which have come down to us. Some Roman farms are represented as consisting of an acre and a quarter, the produce of which would be eaten up by a pair of oxen. The estate of Cincinnatus being three times this size, he could scarcely plough after having lost half of it by being surety. Either there must be some great mistake about our notion of the measurement of Roman farms, or there must have been commons for grazing and woods for fuel, the importation of grain from Sicily and other places not having taken place till long after. He asked by what influence our corn-laws, so injurious to all, and so obviously so to the many, were kept up, and whether it was possible that they should continue long. He declared himself in favour of free trade, though believing that the freedom cannot be complete in any one country till universal peace shall afford opportunity for universal agreement.

He expressed himself strongly in favour of arrangements for the security of literary property all over the world, and wished that English authors should be protected from piracy in the United States without delay. He believed that the utterance of the national mind in America would be through small literature rather than large, enduring works. After the schools and pulpits of the Union are all supplied, there will remain an immense number of educated sons of men of small property who will have things to say; and all who can write, will. He thought it of the utmost importance to the country, and to human beings everywhere, that the brain and the hands should be trained together; and that no distinction in this respect should be made between men and women. He remembered an interesting conversation on this subject with Mr. [Robert] Owen, from whom he learned with satisfaction that well-educated women in his settlement turned with ease and pleasure from playing the harp to milking the cows.

The active old man, who declared himself crippled with rheumatism, had breakfasted, risen, and was dressed before we sat down to breakfast. He talked a good deal about the American presidents and some living politicians for two hours, when his letters and newspapers were brought in. He gaily threw them aside, saying he could read the newspapers every day, and must make the most of his time with us, if we would go away as soon as we talked of. He asked me, smiling, if I thought it too vast and anti-republican a privilege for the ex-presidents to have their letters and newspapers free, considering that this was the only earthly benefit they carried away from their office.

I will not repeat his luminous history of the nullification struggle; nor yet his exposition, simple and full, of the intricate questions involved in the anomalous institution of the American Senate, about its power of sanctioning appointments to office, and whether its weight should be increased by making its sanction necessary to removal from office; to which increase of power he was decidedly opposed.

In fact, Madison, in one of his first efforts to explain the Constitution, had led the fight in Congress in 1789 to uphold executive power by denying the Senate this sanction.

He declared himself perfectly satisfied that there is in the United States a far more ample and equal provision for pastors, and of religious instruction for the people, than could have been secured by a religious establishment of any kind; and that one of the greatest services which his country will be hereafter perceived to have rendered to the world, will be the having proved that religion is the more cared for the more unreservedly it is committed to the affections of the people. He quoted the remark of Voltaire, that if there were only one religion in a country, it would be a pure despotism; if two, they would be deadly enemies; but half a hundred subsist in fine harmony. He observed that this was the case in America, and that so true and pregnant a remark as this ought to be accepted as an atonement for many that would die of untruth. He went on to notice the remarkable fact that creeds which oppose each other, and which, in concatenation, would seem to be most demoralizing, do, by virtue of some one common principle, agree in causing the moral elevation of those who hold them. He instanced Philosophical Necessity, as held by Hume, Kaimes, Edwards, and Priestley. He told me how he had once been prejudiced against Priestley, and how surprised he was, when he first met the philosopher at Philadelphia, to find him absolutely mild and candid.

The whole of this day was spent like the last, except that we went over the house looking at the busts and prints, which gave an English air to the dwelling, otherwise wholly Virginian. During all our conversations, one or another slave was perpetually coming to Mrs. Madison for the great bunch of keys; two or three more lounged about in the room, leaning against the doorposts or the corner of the sofa; and the attendance of others was no less indefatigable in my own apartment. . . .

I glanced at the newspapers when they came in, and found them full of the subject of the quarrel with France [over commercial treaty obligations], the great topic of the day. Mr. Madison gave me an account of the relations of the two countries, and of the grounds of his apprehensions that this quarrel might, in spite of its absurdity, issue in a war. This is all over now, but some of his observations remain. He said it would be an afflicting sight if the two representative governments which are in the van of the world should go to war; it would squint towards a confirmation of what is said of the restlessness of popular governments. If the people, who pay for war, are eager for it, it is quite a different thing from potentates being so who are at no cost. He mentioned that George the Fourth, as prince regent, was a large gainer in the last war, from his share of the Droits of the Admiralty, amounting to 1,000,000l. per annum; a pretty premium, Mr. Madison observed, to pay a king for going to war. He told me about the formation of the philosophical and humane agreement between Franklin and Frederic of Prussia, that merchant ships, unarmed, should go about their business as freely in the war as in peace. The Salem merchants, who were formerly in favour of war, and who suffered from captures in the course of it, were, on the present occasion, petitioning against war and for reprisals.

Franklin was near seventy when Mr. Madison first knew him. He went to the Hall of Congress in a sedan, and sat all the time, writing what he had to say, and getting it read, because he could not stand. He was soon afterward bedridden, when Madison was his frequent visitor. He had much self-command; and, when seized by severe pain, soon roused himself to converse almost as if it did not exist. One of the most striking points about him was his dislike of argument. He would listen to his adversary, and then overthrow him with an anecdote.

After avowing a very unfashionable admiration of [Erasmus] Darwin's poetry, and declaring that the splendour of the diction put his imagination into a very gay state, Mr. Madison went into a speculation about what would eventually become of all existing languages and their literature; declaring that he had little hope of the stability of languages when terms of even classical derivation are perpetually changing their meanings with time. Then, by some channel, now forgotten, we got round to the less agreeable subject of national debts and taxation, when, as might be expected, Mr. Madison expressed his horror of the machinery necessary under a system of indirect levy, and his attachment to a plan of moderate expenditure, provided for by direct taxation. He remarked upon Pitt's success in obtaining revenue when every other man would rather have surrendered his plans than used the means he employed. He observed that king, lords, and commons might constitute a government which would work a long while in a kingdom no bigger than Great Britain, but that it would soon become an absolute government in a country as large as Russia, from the magnitude of its executive power; and that it was a common but serious mistake to suppose that a country must be small to be a republic, since a republican form, with a federal head, can be extended almost without limits, without losing its proportions, becoming all the while less, instead of more, subject to change. In a small republic there is much noise from the fury of parties; while in a spreading but simply working republic, like that of the Union, the silent influence of the federal head keeps down more quarrels than ever appear. . . .

I have written of him under a strong desire to say nothing that he would have objected to have repeated, suppressing whatever he dropped relating to private persons or to public men yet living, while attempting to afford what gratification I could to the strong interest felt in England about this virtuous statesman. It is something that, living under institutions framed by the few for the subordination of the many, the English feel the interest they do about such men as Jefferson and Madison; men inspired by the true religion of statesmanship, faith in men, and in the principles on which they combine in an agreement to do as they would be done by. This political religion resembles personal piety in its effect of sustaining the spirit through difficulty and change, and leaving no cause for repentance, or even solicitude, when, at the close of life, all things reveal their values to the meditative sage. Madison reposed cheerfully, gayly, to the last, on his faith in the people's power of wise self-government.

Advising the Younger Generation

Dolley Madison wrote her niece Mary Cutts two weeks after Martineau left Montpelier of "how much we were pleased with her enlightened conversation and unassuming manners." A few weeks later, though, she wrote another niece, Dolley Cutts, that "*my days* are devoted to nursing and comforting my *patient,* who walks only from the bed in which he breakfasts, to the one in the little chamber. . . . Anna [Payne, Dolley's then sixteen-year-old niece] who is a sterling girl stays much at home with me and sleeps beside my bed ever since the illness of Mr. Madison in April. . . . He is better now but not yet well enough to walk across the two rooms or decide on entering a carriage to go to any springs or even to the road." Expressing what she knew was an almost surely forlorn hope, Dolley wished he might sometime be well enough so she and nieces Dolley and Mary might "meet 'at Phillippi.' "

At the same time, as James approached the last year of his life, most of his letters, when he was able to get to them, closed with comments on his extreme age and debility. To an Ohio committee seeking his presence at a celebration of its earliest settlement, James replied, "Having now reached my 85th year, and being otherwise enfeebled by much indisposition, . . . I am necessarily deprived of the pleasure of accepting the invitation." James had been in the Congress that passed the Northwest Ordinance in the 1780s, authorizing statehood for Ohio. Then in 1803 he was secretary of state presiding over the formalities of its admission to the Union, and finally, as president during the War of 1812, he defended the state against

British-led intrusions. He saw Ohio, perhaps with some sense of personal satisfaction, "as a monument of the happy agency of the free institutions which characterize the political system of the United States."

In correspondence with friend and cousin Hubbard Taylor, he spoke of "the infirmities belonging to [his advanced age] . . . to which are added inroads on my health, which among other effects, have so crippled my fingers as to oblige me to avail myself of borrowed ones." This letter was in John C. Payne's hand, signed by James. He was thankful, though, to be occasionally "freed from the most painful stages of the rheumatic cause." Acknowledging to Andrew Jackson the hoped-for good effect from their shared public endorsement that "ardent spirits be everywhere banished from the list of drinks" (apparently not including, though, the wines he, Dolley, and her sister Lucy had imbibed so merrily in Washington), Madison also reported to the current president that his health "has been for a considerable time much broken by chronic complaints, which, added to my great age, have reduced me to a state of much debility, particularly in my limbs." To an eighteen-year-old nephew, Richard D. Cutts, who had "request[ed] my advice on the choice of a profession," James apologized that his brief answer had had to be "dictated in the crippled state of my health." Madison approved young Cutts's inclination to practice law, despite the crowded field, as long as he continued as well to study "philosophy and literature," including the "oracular . . . Cicero."

Dolley's reports of her own health were up and down; trouble with her eyes, fatigue caused by household management and tending to her husband, and a bout of influenza in the winter of 1835 that left her worse off than her husband. As they both improved, she hoped "to make him much more so when the season advances, for exercise abroad, [for neither] he nor I could ever be quite well again if we remained stationary, as we have been for many years past." Dolley's other worries and concerns were for her son, brother, nieces, and nephews and for the young people in Jefferson's family, now mostly living rather precariously in Washington: could the young men find livelihood and advancement in depressed Virginia, and could the young women find good and interesting husbands? Son Payne Todd continued wandering, drinking, and gambling in between ineffective efforts to be useful at Montpelier. Though he was forty-three years old, Dolley continued to hope that he would woo and win one of the eligible young women she fantasized might look seriously upon him.

Her brother John, by now fifty-three, at Montpelier daily and usefully occupied helping Madison deal with his papers and correspondence, was still unable to support his family on his Orange County farm or overcome his alcoholism amid local distractions. Nephew James Madison Cutts asked, "Will Uncle John go westward?"

When Cutts's brother Richard decided he would have to go that route, Dolley wrote sister Lucy, well established in Frankfurt, Kentucky, to "shew him the kindness of an affectionate aunt." Dolley was "melancholy," she wrote the young man going west, "at the idea of your departure for a country as far from us as Kety [Kentucky]!" Nonetheless she approved; "so does your Uncle, believing that you can push your fortunes, in that quarter more surely & with more expedition than in this." He stopped at Montpelier in October 1835, eighteen years old, on his way to Kentucky where he hoped his Aunt Lucy could help him find a promising career in the expanding and prosperous West. This young man, much a favorite of his aunt and uncle, eventually returned east, married a relative of Thomas Jefferson, became a distinguished engineer, and was Dolley's most reliable support during her last, widowed years in Washington. He was later a Union officer in the Civil War.

James Madison Cutts himself, who had come to Montpelier on his wedding journey in 1834 and had been toasted with his bride by the former president at a party on the lawn there, was a year later despondent and discouraged when he wrote his aunt. He was so "closely confined to my office" that he was unable to properly look after his wife and infant child; she had been unwell and the baby so sick the doctor had feared for its life. The "mobocratic spirit" of public life was such that "of politicks I hear & meddle in little or none." (Translate: there was little hope for a leftover Madisonian in the Jacksonian era.) "I am often disheartened— here having sacrificed years of my life [and] . . . am not one iota advanced toward independence. . . . young and old, it almost seems we cannot get a start." He sent Aunt Dolley and cousin Anna Payne a copy of *Richard of York: or The White Rose of England* and intended to send other books from his library, all part of an informal book club circulating volumes between Washington and Montpelier to keep the country folks up on the modern literary world. But he could not suppress his anxiety and in fact was pleading for help and direction: *"We are barely vegetating,"* he exclaimed.

Dolley only occasionally revealed her real state of mind when she wrote. In one of her last known letters to the Cutts children before her husband's death, she had ordered "now burn this & all like it." She pleaded urgently "to know everything of the [Martha Jefferson] Randolph family." Had Nicholas Trist, she asked, given up his post as President Jackson's private secretary, an important job but with a low salary, to accept a more remunerative consulship in Cuba? Trist had written James that such a post would be "of infinite service to my constitution as well as pocket." His need for money was "as much for Mrs. Randolph as myself." She was living dependently in Washington with her still unmarried children, about whom Dolley was much concerned. Was Meriwether Lewis Randolph, age twenty-five, to be married, she asked? (He had been, on April 9, but died two years later.) Benjamin Franklin Randolph, age twenty-seven, had finally married the year before. James Madison Randolph had died, unmarried, in 1834, at age twenty-eight, about the same age at which so many of William Madison's children had died, mostly of consumption.

The circumstances of the Randolph daughters was even more on Dolley's mind; she had entertained them, visited them, and seen them grow up before and after their grandfather's death. Ellen, a favorite at both Monticello and Montpelier, had married well but lived in Boston with her admired and wealthy husband, Joseph Coolidge. The Madisons tried hard to keep up with this couple, and they were attentive to life at Montpelier. Ellen's letters home to Virginia, though, were hardly comforting. She spoke of how much better off New England was without slavery, how a public system providing education for all was largely paid for by taxes on the wealthy, how much opportunity there was in its expanding commercial economy, how large stacks of split firewood easily lasted through the winter, and how keeping warm, despite the cold winters, was easier than in drafty Virginia because houses were tight with double doors. Women dressed in warm garments that were not confining or bulky. Two other older Randolph daughters, Cornelia, age thirty-six, and Mary, age thirty-two, were single and still dependent on their mother. Dolley was concerned about them, and especially about the younger Septimia, age twenty-one, who did marry Dr. David Scott Meikleham three years later. Clearly, "knowing everything" about this family was a taxing and poignant enterprise, keeping Dolley and James in close touch with connections heartfelt and cherished since their own marriage forty years earlier, and it also must have sharpened their sense of Virginia's decline and social pathology.

Dolley's deepest concern and responsibility, though, were the coming of age of her virtual daughters, Dolley Madison Cutts and Mary Estelle Elizabeth Cutts, age twenty-one and eighteen, respectively, when Dolley's beloved sister-daughter, Anna Payne Cutts, had died in 1832. Small children when the Madisons retired to Montpelier, they had spent months at a time there every summer with their mother before she died. In the poignant letter written the day of Anna's death, Dolley had begged her sister to "strive to be happy and well . . . for my sake and for your childrens! What should we do without you!" When she learned that Anna was gone, Dolley felt she had to be mother to the young women, just as she had to their own mother, a teenager in Philadelphia in the 1790s when her family had been ravaged by disease and hard times. Dolley often began her letters to the girls with general sentiments, sometimes in poetic form (a style she practiced increasingly in her later years), or with epigrams of the kind put in the autograph books then in vogue. A favorite was "Habit and hope are the crutches which support us through the vicissitudes of life." She advised Mary that "we have all, a great hand in the formation of our own destiny. We must press on that intricate path leading to perfection and happiness by doing all that is good and handsome, before we can be taken under the silver wing of our rewarding angel. . . . I need not recapitulate all the virtues necessary to render us worthy and deserving of good fortune," she concluded.

More specifically, she urged Dolley Cutts to always "appear in feminine and more congenial character, . . . *always entertaining* a sweet and gentle character." Warning her nieces of the ways of Washington, Dolley noted that she did "not admire contention in any form, either political or civil." Getting down to cases, though, Dolley snooped and advised, especially about the young men possibly available for the Cutts girls. They were decidedly eligible, eager to flourish in the Washington social life once dominated by their aunt, but somewhat out of sync with a "mobocratic" (their brother's term) Jacksonian scene torn by the Peggy Eaton imbroglio.

In March 1833, getting over a winter cold and occupied copying letters and papers for her husband, Dolley tried to warn Mary about a "Mrs.

—— . . . [who has] it in her power to be kind and useful to you, but if she is ever offended in any way she is *bitter*." Dolley also coached her about a "Mr. ——, an elegant and accomplished person, but—be perfectly respectful to him and ready to receive the instruction which lurks forever in his conversation." After gossiping about some of her old Washington friends—Mrs. Lear, Mrs. Decatur, Mrs. Bomford, etc.—Dolley got to the point. The Madisons had heard that the Russian minister to the United States, Baron Paul von Krüdener, had just returned to Washington. "Suppose," she told Mary, "you sett your Cap or Curls, at him. . . . I see no objection to your becoming Baroness de ——." Dolley perhaps had in mind Sally McKean, her friend and one of the belles who, along with Dolley, Anna, and Lucy Payne, had charmed Philadelphia society in the 1790s. Sally married Carlos Martínez de Yrujo y Tacón, marquis de Casa Yrujo, the Spanish minister to the United States, in 1798 and spent the rest of her life in Spanish palaces and embassies all over Europe.

Turning to Dolley Cutts's prospects, the mistress of Montpelier was glad her niece had "too much sense to encourage any man [a 'Mr. A.'] to her disadvantage." The aunt was sure that Mary, "a kind sister who is a looker on," would "be able to give the best advise, and I *will* help her." No doubt. Dolley Madison warned that "a good hearted *ignoramus*," W. Willis, an Orange County connection and University of Virginia student who had been stabbed in a brawl, would "anoy" her nieces. She did not "know his family, but hear they are good and respectable"; clearly Dolley hoped her nieces would steer clear of him. She also reported about "my dear Payne," sick at Montpelier with "an alarming cough, which makes me melancholy to hear." She had heard a "young lady . . . more of his likeing . . . whom report gave him for a wife" was apparently no longer in the picture. "I'm sorry for it," his mother said. Dolley had already experienced twenty years of such dashed and unrealistic hopes and would experience sixteen more before her death in 1849.

Dolley wrote her nieces' widowed father in August that she thought it would "be an advantage to them to see other characters. . . . You know it expands the minds of men and women to look into the varieties of this world. . . . If my prayers for them may have effect, they will be happy in their Husbands & fortune & make their Father so." Richard Cutts lived despondently in Washington, looking after his children as best he could, but he was not the active political and social colleague he had been before two financial catastrophes linked to his devotion to the Madisons: the loss of his shipping fortune as a result of War of 1812 restrictions and depredations and then loss of the government job Madison had subsequently arranged for him, when Andrew Jackson fired the Jefferson-Madison-era appointees in his "to the victors belong the spoils" effort of 1829. Three months later Dolley was back to social advice she hoped would advance the cause of good husbands. "I feel quite sorry," she wrote "dearest Mary," "that *you* have *not* called on Madame Serurier [Dolley's close friend, the wife of the former French minister to the United States]." "As I lived sixteen years in the midst of *ceremonies* in Washington," she scolded further, "I can tell you, that you and Dolley as young ladies—are to visit our own ministers and Foreign Ministers ladies first, if you desire their acquaintance. I was also four years in Philadelphia, where Mrs. Washington presided, and intimate with the heads of Departments and Ministers from Europe, and I never knew their ladies to visit young girls first—indeed! I know they made a point of *not doing so,* and in my humble opinion they were in the right." Do not, Dolley admonished her nieces, let foolish social lapses deprive you of "the acquaintance and friendship of Madame Serurier." Go visit her "immediately," she said. "May heaven help you both," she concluded, "the children of my most beloved sister!"

Dolley continued social instructions in a March 1835 letter to Mary. She had "no idea of the new dance or its motions but approve of your declining to learn it, if it is disapproved of by society—*Our sex* are ever losers, when they stem the torrent of public opinion." She was glad to hear of Baron von Krüdener's parties (no advances from him, apparently) and those of the English minister, Sir Charles Vaughn, too, but again fretted over her nieces' social lapses. Harriet Martineau had said that she "had not been favored with your attentions": why had her nieces not called on such an important and interesting visitor? During their visit at Montpelier, Dolley reported, the "English ladies" had mentioned "Mr. Pitt Adams," a British diplomat soon to leave Washington. They noted that he "would be greatly missed in the city, and that he was a fine fellow." This presumably was the "Mr. A" previously discouraged by Dolley Cutts. Two months later, in a letter to that niece, Dolley Madison remarked merely that she had seen "the compliment to Mr. Adams in the Globe and other papers." Dolley Madison was encouraged nonetheless that "your interesting friend Mr. Hodgson . . . with his two cousins" had been at Montpelier. He told of a pleasant party with the Cutts girls and "how much he admired and regarded you both."

This seems to have been less than Dolley wished and hoped to hear, and in the surviving correspondence with her nieces there is nothing further about Adams, Hodgson, his cousins, or other potential suitors. Dolley Cutts died unwed three years later. Mary, also unwed, spent the last twenty years of her life (she died in 1856) first looking after her aunt at Montpelier or in Washington and then attending to her papers and affairs after her death. Instead of becoming social triumphs and finders of fortune and good husbands, as Dolley so ardently hoped and prayed, these beloved nieces seem to have shared much of the unfulfillment in their lives that plagued their young male counterparts. Accounts of those who went west, male and female, were generally more upbeat.

As the lives of these two women reveal, the young people entertained and guided so faithfully from Montpelier by James and Dolley Madison—and in many ways by Thomas Jefferson from Monticello—were caught, ironically, in the decline of the Virginian part of the new and hopeful republic presided over by Jefferson, Madison, and Monroe for twenty-four years, from 1801 until 1825. The system of elite leadership and administration they installed, sometimes turned stagnant and inbred, fell prey to the robust commercial egalitarianism of the Jacksonian era. When Richard Cutts lost his sinecure federal job in Washington, it was because government office was no longer a "species of property" to be held by allegedly well-qualified and experienced civil servants, as Jackson proclaimed in his inaugural address. It was rather a place of "plain and simple" tasks almost anyone could perform, and positions there were properly filled, as Jackson's ally, Senator William L. Marcy of New York, famously asserted, under "the rule, that to the victor belong the spoils of the enemy." When Jefferson and Monroe faced bankruptcy, in part because their Virginia farms had become unprofitable, they and their families were saved in some measure from ruin and even homelessness by next-generation members who moved away. Monroe's younger daughter, Maria Hester Monroe, married to her cousin Samuel L. Gouverneur and comfortably settled in New York City, was able to take him in during his terminal illness. Jefferson's granddaughter Ellen Randolph had married a well-off Boston man of commerce, Joseph Coolidge, and could provide support and even temporary domicile for her mother and numerous siblings.

Northern commerce, rather than Southern agrarianism, seemed the wave of the future and even the path to survival. Madison's second cousin, Zachary Taylor, was born on an Orange County farm not ten miles from Montpelier on land first patented, as was Montpelier, by their common great-grandfather, Colonel James Taylor. Dolley Madison may have been present at his inauguration as the twelfth president of the United States in 1849, and he attended her funeral that year. By then he was a Louisianan, a Kentuckian, a western hero of the Mexican War, no longer a Virginian, as was true for many of James Madison's Taylor relatives.

Thus the hope and expansiveness of the frontier in piedmont Virginia experienced by James Madison as he grew up—and by Dolley's family as well, in Virginia and North Carolina, before they moved to Philadelphia— increasingly unraveled. The prosperity, growth, and sense of optimism experienced at Montpelier by three and even four generations of Madisons, from the 1740s and 1750s until after the War of 1812, had by the 1820s and 1830s become problematic. Nostalgia replaced hope. James Madison Cutts's plaintive cry was "we are barely vegetating." Many economic and social causes affected the decline, but perhaps most baneful of all was what Ellen Randolph Coolidge called "the canker of slavery. . . . [It] eats into [Southern] hearts, and diseases the whole body by this ulcer at its core." It prevented, she thought, the "great gifts of Nature" possessed by Virginia from yielding the "wealth and improvement" of New England. Northerners were "at least a century in advance of us in all the arts and embellishments of life," she declared. Whether to the fertile lands of the West or to the free and burgeoning economy of the North, the young people of the Virginia piedmont often turned outward and away for their fulfillment.

The Last Visit to James Madison's Montpelier

When Madison drew his will in April 1835, he left generous bequests to Princeton, the University of Virginia, and the American Colonization Society and to his nieces and nephews. The residue of his estate was to go to his widow. A series of illnesses, including a painful, itching eruption over his whole body, so sapped his strength that his valet, Paul Jennings, recalled that "for six months before his death, he was unable to walk, and spent most of his time reclining on a couch." His mind, though, Jennings continued, "was bright and with his numerous visitors he talked with as much animation and strength of voice as I ever heard him in his best days." Madison told one of his invited guests that of the uninvited ones, "some were taxes and other bounties." Sad family news continued: Mary Willis Lee, daughter of favorite niece Nelly Conway Willis, died in March 1836, and James probably heard a month or two before he died that his youngest nephew, twenty-year-old James Madison Rose, had been killed in the Alamo on March 6. Fever and fatigue so filled the winter of 1835–36 that by the spring a shortness of breath affected Madison's speech. The last visitor to record full impressions of him was Charles J. Ingersoll of Philadelphia, who came in May 1836. He had been another young colleague and supporter of Madison during the War of 1812, who had continued to uphold what he regarded as Madisonian principles in his writing career. Ten years earlier he had been the first to toast Madison as "the Father of the Constitution." He was warned by Dolley to talk a great deal himself to keep James from overexerting himself in trying to speak. Ingersoll wrote an account of his visit, published in a Washington newspaper two months after Madison's death.

> I had long promised myself a visit to Mr. Madison, whom I had not seen for twenty odd years: and on Monday, the 2d of May, 1836, after sleeping the night before at the village of Orange Court House, six miles from Montpelier, we got there before breakfast, and were most hospitably received. The ride is rough, the road not good, and the country not much cultivated. . . . The woods were in foliage, the white-thorn and red-bud trees in greater number than I had ever seen them, giving a pleasant coloring to what was otherwise rather a wild, poor, and uninteresting region. Nearer Mr. Madison's, the country is more improved, and the mountain scenery is very agreeable. You enter his outer gate from the woods, and at once get into something like a park, with his well-looking house about half a mile off; the whole cleared and improved, with trees in clumps, and other signs of ornamental agriculture. The house is a two story brick mansion, with wings and colonnades front and back, in good design, but decayed and in need of considerable repairs, which, at a trifling expense would make a great difference in favor of the first impression of his residence. The house was built by his father; the wings and colonnades by himself. The rooms are good, furnished with French carpets, large mirrors, and a good many paintings, and

James Madison, by Asher Brown Durand, 1833. (Collection of The New-York Historical Society)

Dolley Madison, by Eastman Johnson, 1846. (Harvard Art Museum, Fogg Art Museum, Bequest of Grenville L. Winthrop, 1943.572; Photo by David Mathews © President and Fellows of Harvard College)

some statuary—altogether without any fashionable or very elegant equipment, yet in a gentleman-like style of rural propriety. The table not only
abundantly, but handsomely provided; good soups, flesh, fish, and vegetables, well cooked—dessert and excellent wines of different kinds; and when
Mrs. Madison was prevailing on me to eat hot bread at breakfast, she said,
"You city people think it unwholesome, but we eat heartily like the French,
and never find ourselves worse for it." She looks just the same as she did
twenty years ago, and dresses in the same manner, with her turban and cra-
vat; rises early, is very active, but seldom leaves the house, as her devotion
to Mr. Madison is incessant, and he needs all her constant attention. The
view from the front of the house is very picturesque, bounded by the blue
ridge, which being about eighteen miles off, seeming to be close by; and
though the thermometer marked 88 degrees in the colonnade, yet the
mountain air kept the house cool enough. The estate consists of near two
thousand acres of good land—the red soil, John Randolph said, in which
Presidents grow—with about one hundred slaves, not one of whom, I was
told by Mr. Payne Tod, had been flogged for several years.

They raise about a thousand bushels of corn; but the principal crop for
sale is tobacco, productive of income for the time being, though injurious
to the ground. There were some horned cattle of the superior breeds; the
horses, equipages, and stabling, however, the whole equestrian department,
in a useful state, but by no means elegant. Mr. Madison told me that ever
since his Presidency he has been obliged to live beyond his means selling off
some of his capital continually, and that he is now in debt. He spoke often
and anxiously of slave property as the worst possible for profit, unless
employed in manufactures, as he is sure it will be to advantage; and when I
mentioned Mr. Rush's farm of ten acres, near Philadelphia, he said he had
no doubt it was more productive than his with two thousand.

Among the deplorable effects of the abolition excitement, he considers,
first, that in teaching southern people to imagine that slavery is right and
useful, a change of opinion suddenly arises, . . . secondly, deteriorating the
condition of the poor savage whose bondage is embittered by laws and
measures intended to counteract the ill-timed efforts to put an end to it. Mr.
Madison said he always told the southern people that the tariff was not
their chief grievance; . . . yet in his apprehension the inexhaustible new
lands of the southwest brought into competition with the worn soils of Virginia and the Carolinas, were the principal cause of their sufferings. Nearly

two-thirds of his slaves are too young or too old to work much, while the support of so many is very expensive. It takes nearly all he makes to feed, clothe, and preserve them; and when a handsome column or other ornamental part of his mansion falls into decay, he wants the means of conveniently repairing it, without encroaching on necessary expenditures. . . . "There will be troubles and explosions, I predict," said he, "though it is perilous to be a prophet;" and it seemed to me that he did not believe that the cotton plantations would continue to be very productive any more than those of rice or grain. There was a considerable failure of the wheat crop last year, (he said,) and he spoke with uneasiness of its prospects this year.

Soon after our arrival, Mrs. Madison took us into the room he occupies during the day, and from that time I passed the greater part of three days at his side, listening to his conversation. He is very infirm—eighty five years old last March—never was strong, and is now extremely emaciated and feeble. Longacre's picture [an engraving based on the Durand portrait] gives a perfect likeness of his whole appearance; much better, I should say, than Stewart's [Gilbert Stuart] ever did, which is the best portrait of him as he was formerly. He cannot sit up, except a little while now and then to rest from reclining on a sofa; and at first, when I saw him, he wore gloves, which were laid aside, however, as the weather became warm. We found him more unwell than usual, and with a difficulty of breathing, which affects his speech; so that Mrs. Madison told me I must talk, and not let him. But as I wanted to listen, and he appeared to grow better every day, our conversation animated without fatiguing him. . . .

Mr. Madison is a man of medium, the middle way—avoiding all extremes, and perhaps fond of checks and balances; but he is in grain a genuine republican. You perceive directly that Mr. Jefferson is the god of his idolatry; and while he acknowledges the talents, services, and merits of his first great antagonist, Alexander Hamilton, yet when I told him that Prince Talleyrand [was] eulogized as the Hamilton of France, "Yes," said Mr. M., "Talleyrand was a great dabbler in stocks." Not that he disparages General Hamilton, to whose abilities he does justice; and, indeed he speaks ill of no one, being fastidiously measured in his language and abstemious from personalities; but he has no idea that Hamilton, the author of the funding system, is to be classed with those country gentlemen, like Washington, Jefferson and himself, whose foundations were in the mother earth, and who held stocks, scrip, and such ephemeral and delusive things, in great dises-

teem. Mr. Jefferson's portraits, by Stewart, by Kosciuscu, and others, his rel-
ics and his recollections are all about Mr. Madison's apartments. When he
mentioned Mr. Monroe, he called him *Monroe,* as was natural, Mr. Monroe
having served under him; but when he spoke of Mr. Jefferson, he called him
Mr. Jefferson, as one he looked up to. He spoke also, with obviously natural
respect and affection, of Washington. . . . He supposed there was nothing
that General Washington would not have given him if he chose it, as they
[worked] very well together. . . . General Washington was a very remarkable man, and singularly endowed, not only with the powers of judgment,
but of suspending his judgment till he had heard all that could be said *pro*
and *con,* and then inflexibly determining. . . . He said, too, (which I had
never heard,) that he was a very eloquent man, and that some one he mentioned, (I forgot his name,) who was a member, with Washington, of a
Church Vestry, used to say that in a discussion on the affairs of the church,
in which Washington took an active part, he never heard more eloquent
speaking than from him.

He mentioned, that in the worst stage of the war [of 1812], just after the
capture of Washington while the British frigates were lying before Alexan-
dria, and an attack on Georgetown was continually apprehended, . . . Mr.
Hanson, then editor of the Federal Republican newspaper, afterwards Senator, offered confidential caution against designs said to be in agitation
against Mr. Madison's person. I have heard Governor Coles say, who was his
Secretary, when he was every day called tyrant, murderer, despot, &c., that
he was never known to speak harshly of those who vilified him. His
patience and forbearance were inexhaustible. . . . I have heard Rufus King
tell of John Jay's taking offence at what he considered disrespect to him by
the Queen of England, at her drawing-room, and his abruptly leaving it,
refusing to return till assured by proper mediation that no offence was
intended. Mr. Madison said it was like Mr. Jay.

Mr. Madison's temper is perfectly amiable, and the best word I know of
to describe his love of the country, is to call it beautiful or lovely patriotism,
such natural, profound, and pure republicanism, untainted by the least par-
ticle of European preference—never having been out of his own country,
and being thoroughly imbued with the faith, the religion, that Democratic
Government is not only relatively, but positively, the best in the world.
Infirm as his body is, his understanding is as bright as ever; his intelligence,
recollections, discriminations, and philosophy, all delightfully instructive.

He loves to talk freely on all subjects of political, and historical interest, which do not involve the mere politics of the day. From nullification up to the Congress of the Revolution, he speaks unreservedly as to measures, but with almost prudish reserve as to persons, including himself.

He intimidated a pleasing, but it may be rather fanciful anticipation, of the effect of our laws against primogeniture, and entails, viz: that in process of time there will be no large fortunes, but that a state of mediocrity will be the common condition. With strong impressions of the indispensable advantages of education, he appeared to be as thoroughly impressed with the dangerous tendencies of merely lascivious life: the middle ground is obviously his predilection.

There was one topic of our national policy on which he spoke with enthusiasm, as the greatest and best means of the United States taking a lead in the inculcation of a principle calculated to prevent war; that is, the principle that free ships make free goods. . . . He repeated many and striking reasons for the wisdom of our advancing, and [Great Britain] conceding this rule now, because in twenty years, according to his calculation, our commerce will be greater than hers: all the rest of the civilized world will second us. We shall put ourselves at their head, establishing a principle which England must concede—and that principle is the pledge of permanent maritime peace, and unlimited commercial prosperity.

His circumspection and reserve—in fact, silence, whenever he deemed it indiscreet to speak, contrast curiously with General Jackson's bold, open, and unhesitating conversation on most of the topics introduced by or to him. Dining with him a few days before I was at Mr. Madison's, I was struck with the entire freedom with which he discussed subjects of public controversy. . . . Mr. Madison could never talk in this way. I think the strongest approach I heard to it from him was when speaking of his dismissal of Mr. Granger, the Postmaster General he mentioned his *rupture* with him. . . . I mention their total difference in this particular, only that I may better sketch the moral portrait here attempted. Mr. Madison's abhorrence of war is as remarkable as that it was his destiny to be President during the war. His politics are as simple and lovely as his patriotism, peace and union. They are the whole system—to avoid war at almost any price, and to preserve the Union at all events. . . .

He spoke very freely of nullification, which he altogether condemned. . . . He asserted the power of the President to send foreign ministers without the advice of the Senate at all, arguing that they were mere agents of the Executive, whom he might charge as he pleased with foreign relations. He mentioned the treaty making power, observing that though it might be in theory confined to the President and Senate, yet, that when a grant of money was to follow, it was the right of the House of Representatives to participate in the measure. . . . He spoke of the Post Office Department as a dangerous incongruity in our system [because of] . . . the improper influence which Postmasters General have over members of Congress. He was clearly of opinion that this state of things ought to be changed. The Postmaster General, (said he,) can take a Senator, if he chooses, and by giving him a lucrative post office, change the majority of the Senate. . . . He mentioned a long letter from Mr. Jefferson to him [September 6, 1789], with an argument to prove that legislatures cannot blind succeeding legislatures after a certain period, the ordinary term of a man's life. But Mr. Madison said that he had written an answer to that letter of Mr. Jefferson, very considerably qualifying his doctrine. . . . He mentioned, with obvious acquiescence, the right of the Judiciary to settle questions of constitutional law. He condemned all monopolies and perpetuities as inconsistent with republican institutions; though, he said, some corporations seemed to be indispensable to public improvements; but he thought that every legislature should have power to view the by-laws and other proceedings of corporations, as they pass from time to time, and to affirm, alter, or disaffirm them, as they pleased. . . .

Shortly after my visit, the spirit of this just man was made perfect, as I trust, by his death. A purer, brighter, juster spirit, has seldom existed. . . . I ought, perhaps, to add that, several times, on my expressing hopes of his health improving, he said, with perfect composure and resignation, that he believed he had a proper sense of his situation; that he felt he was on the descending, not the ascending line; that, weak and emaciated as I saw him, I had still no idea how extremely feeble he was, but that he viewed his decline with serenity.

Death and Eulogies of James Madison

The stimulation proved too much for Madison. Dolley wrote "dearest sister" Lucy Todd the day Ingersoll left that "I am grieved to tell you that my dear Husband has been unusually sick for some days, and is at present unable to write or even to exert his thoughts without excessive fatigue." Annie Payne reported that Dolley was "incessantly engaged as Uncle's deputy morning, noon, and night." He begged his wife "to be composed if not cheerful" as the end approached. Dr. Robley Dunglison, moved to Baltimore from Charlottesville by the demands of his growing practice, was called to Montpelier in late May to attend the failing former president, as he had been summoned to Monticello ten years earlier to attend Jefferson. Madison shared some recently arrived sherry with the doctor, regretting his own palate was too vitiated for him to pass proper judgment on it. Dunglison pronounced the sherry "to be of the first chop," as he saw the ravages of old age had left his patient beyond help. Madison used his last strength looking at the manuscript of Professor George Tucker's life of Jefferson. On June 27 Madison spent several hours painfully dictating to John C. Payne his thanks for Tucker's dedication of the book to him. He managed a final summary of his friendship with Jefferson: "A sincere and steadfast co-operation in promoting such a reconstruction of our political system as would provide for the permanent liberty and happiness of the United States" had been their undeviating goal. His trembling signature, barely legible and tumbling off the side of the page, was the last mark of Madison's pen, made, Tucker noted, "about thirteen hours before his decease." He was ready to die at his appointed hour, having rejected suggestions that he take stimulants to extend his life a few days so he could die on July 4, 1836, the sixtieth anniversary of the Declaration of Independence, just as Adams and Jefferson had died on its fiftieth anniversary and Monroe on its fifty-fifth.

The morning of June 28 Jennings joined his master as usual, about six o'clock, and shaved him as he had every other day for sixteen years. Sukey, Dolley's favored household servant, brought James his breakfast. These two faithful slaves, since their service in the White House at the time of its destruction in 1814, had long been intimate parts of life at Montpelier. Nelly Willis, always at Montpelier at times of need, came to the sickroom to visit with her uncle as he ate. When he seemed to have difficulty swallowing, Mrs. Willis asked him what the trouble was. Jennings recalled that Madison replied, "Nothing more than a change of *mind*, my dear," and then "his head instantly dropped, and he ceased breathing as quietly as the snuff of a candle goes out."

Madison was carried the next day to his grave in the family plot by his neighbors, James and Philip Barbour, Charles Howard, and Reuben Conway. This yard still exists, containing the graves of his mother and father as well as dozens of other members of the family. It is half a mile south of the Montpelier mansion, near the site of the Mount Pleasant house where James had lived as a child. Following Dolley Madison, the family, and friends from all over Orange County were one hundred Montpelier slaves, "decently attired," James Barbour recalled, who remained silent until they heard the words "dust to dust" in the Episcopal service, when they "gave vent to their lamentations in one violent burst that rent the air." As words of Madison's death spread, eulogies poured into Montpelier, and memorial services were held all around the country. The *National Intelligencer* reported that "the last of the great lights of the Revolution . . . has sunk below the horizon . . . [and] left a radiance in the firmament." At an Orange County memorial service in August, Barbour made the common judgment that Madison's contributions to the nation had been exceeded only by those of Washington. He asked his listeners to compare Madison's useful labors and lamented death, when "every hill and every valley of this vast republic resound with benedictions on his name," with the bloody ambition and wretched end of Napoleon.

President Jackson informed Congress on June 30 that James Madison "departed this life at half past six o'clock, on the morning of the 28th inst., full of years and full of honours." John Patton, the congressman from Madison's district, responded that "his appropriate and enduring eulogium is to be found in those pages of his country's history which are identified with her honor and glory." Representative John Quincy Adams added, "Is it not in a pre-eminent degree by emanations from his mind, that we are assembled here as the representatives of the people, and the states of the Union? Is it not transcendently by his exertions that we address each other here by the endearing appellation of countrymen and fellow-citizens?" Madison and Adams had known of each other's contributions to the nation for sixty years, since Adams had heard of Madison's service in the Continental Congress, 1780–83 and Madison had supported the mission to France of John Adams and his ten-year-old son (traveling as his father's private secretary) across the Royal Navy–infested Atlantic Ocean. Madison, as president, had sent the younger Adams to Europe on another peace mission, this time as its head, to end the War of 1812.

In Quincy, Massachusetts, Adams labored for two months on a much longer eulogy of Madison, which he delivered to a crowded audience at the old Federal Street Theatre in Boston in late September. To prepare the two-and-one-half-hour oration, Adams wrote Dolley Madison for information on Madison's early life and pored over Jefferson's recently published letters. Noting privately in his diary that Madison was "a greater and far more estimable man" than Jefferson, "Old Man Eloquent" turned his stirring phrases on the figure he had come to regard with the deepest veneration. Madison, Adams proclaimed, had "improved his own condition by improving that of his country and his kind." The orator summarized the triumphs of Madison's career, such as that at the Virginia ratifying convention of 1788, during which "the all but irresistible power of his eloquence, and the inexhaustible resources of his gigantic mind [had overcome] . . . the dazzling but then beclouded genius . . . of Patrick Henry." After noting that Madison's death removed the last of the nation builders who had drafted and signed the great founding documents, Adams asked his listeners to shun the whirlwind of discord, the earthquake of war, and the fires of nullification and civil dissension to listen to "the still small voice . . . that spoke the words of peace—of harmony—of union. And for that voice . . . fix your eyes upon the memory, and listen with your ears to the life of James Madison."

Senator Henry Clay wrote Dolley, "And yet why should we be grieved? Mr. Madison . . . after having rendered more important services to his country than any other man, Washington only excepted, has sunk down into the grave as tranquilly as he lived. . . . . His was not a case of death but of transition." A few years earlier, when Clay had been asked to compare the administrations of Jefferson and Madison, he had made a more subtle point. Jefferson, Clay thought, "had most genius—Madison most judgment and common sense." Jefferson's enthusiasms often led him into "rash and imprudent and impracticable measures, [while] Madison [was] cool, dispassionate, practical, safe." When a companion declared that Jefferson's "power and energy," superior to Madison's, had better carried the nation through difficulties and dangers, Clay responded that "prudence and caution would have produced the same results." He pronounced Madison "after Washington our greatest statesman and first political writer," but he agreed finally that Madison and Jefferson "both were *great* and *good,* and though *different*—yet equal." Madison did lack the dramatic and even reckless qualities sometimes useful in public life, but within his own chosen style of statesmanship, valuing prudence, wisdom, and judgment, he was without peer.

In the fall of 1834, at a moment of both revived health and foreboding for the future, Madison had written down for posthumous disclosure his own final "Advice to My Country":

> As this advice, if it ever see the light will not do it till I am no more, it
> may be considered as issuing from the tomb, where truth alone can be
> respected, and the happiness of man alone consulted. It will be entitled
> therefore to whatever weight can be derived from good intentions, and
> from the experience of one who has served his country in various stations
> through a period of forty years, who espoused in his youth and adhered
> through his life to the cause of its liberty, and who has borne a part in most
> of the great transactions which will constitute epochs of its destiny. The
> advice nearest to my heart and deepest in my convictions is that the Union
> of the States be cherished and perpetuated. Let the open enemy to it be
> regarded as a Pandora with her box opened; and the disguised one, as the
> Serpent creeping with his deadly wiles into Paradise.

A year later Madison had regretfully declined an invitation to be present at a commemorative dinner in Orange because of "a continuance, and of late increase in the causes which have long confined me to my home, and at this time confines me for the most part to a sick chamber." For those who would be there, he did, however, summarize more fully

> the great and fundamental principles of Republicanism; . . . the dependence
> of our prosperity on those principles, and of the ultimate connexion of
> both with the preservation of the Union in its integrity, and of the Constitu-
> tion in its purity. The value of the Union will be most felt by those who
> look with most forecast into the consequences of disunion. Nor will the
> Constitution, with its wise provisions for its improvement under the lights
> of experience, be undervalued by any who compare the distracted and omi-
> nous condition from which it rescued the country, with the security and
> prosperity so long enjoyed under it, with the bright prospects which it has
> opened on the civilized world. It is a proud reflection for the people of the
> United States, proud for the cause of liberty, that history furnishes no exam-
> ple of a Government producing like blessings in an equal degree, and for

the same period, as the modification of political power in the compound Government of the U. States, of which the vital principle pervading the whole and all its parts is the elective and responsible principle of Republicanism. May not *esto perpetua* [So be it in perpetuity] express the hopes as well as the prayer of every citizen who loves liberty and loves his country?

James Madison's life reveals that he cherished the Union because only the positive power it released could bring the justice necessary to fulfill the legal and moral equality of humankind. He further cherished liberty because only it could open to humans the opportunities due their limitless potential and their capacity for self-government. Dolley Madison, in creating the role of "First Lady," had fashioned a style and civility for American public life that provided a social basis for the republicanism she shared with her husband. Together in retirement at Montpelier they lived lives that kept the nation mindful of its principled origins, and through their connections and visitors, especially the young people, they pointed hopefully toward a fulfilling future in the Union.

POSTSCRIPT
Dolley Madison, 1836–1849

DOLLEY MADISON SPENT THE SUMMER AFTER HER HUSBAND'S DEATH at Montpelier, responding to visits and letters of condolence and pursuing publication of the already gathered and edited volumes of James's papers. She made an unfortunate decision to put this publication largely in the hands of undependable Payne Todd, who failed to negotiate a contract with any commercial publishers, despite spending months traveling to Philadelphia, New York, and Boston seeking one. Hoping to realize $100,000 from the publication, a royalty no publisher seemed willing to guarantee or even discuss, Dolley instead sold three volumes of papers—including the Notes on the Debates of the Constitutional Convention—to Congress in 1837 for $30,000. She was thus able to honor the bequests of her husband's will but was left with only $9,000 for her livelihood. With Payne Todd as disinclined and ill-suited as ever to manage or even live at Montpelier, which was in decline anyhow as a prosperous plantation, and most of her friends and close relatives living in Washington, Dolley decided in November 1837 to move there, at least for the cooler months each year when Congress was normally in session—"the season."

She moved into the house on Lafayette Square the Madisons had owned for nearly twenty years, in which the Cuttses had lived. It was Dolley's home for the rest of her life. She resumed at once her role as "First Lady Emeritus," receiving a host of visitors and more invitations than she could possibly accept. She was present at every important Washington social occasion. Financial worries, including the continued mismanagement of the Montpelier estate, though, compelled Dolley to move back there for the summer of 1838, and again in the summer of 1839 where she stayed, this time, through the summer of 1841. But all was in disarray. Dolley Cutts had died, and brother John C. Payne had moved to Kentucky with his family, leaving his twenty-year-old daughter Annie to live with Dolley Madison as her adopted daughter. Payne Todd, as dissipated, unreliable, but emotionally dependent on his mother as ever, was often at Montpelier. He spent most of his time building and enlarging his eccentric quarters, Toddsberth (designed to suit his mother, Payne said) over the Southwest Mountains behind Montpelier, and hoping to strike it rich with a gold mine or a marble quarry; neither materialized. Some of Toddsberth, including valuable furnishings, artworks, and papers from Montpelier, burned in 1841. Meanwhile, Montpelier, ill managed by a series of incompetent and dishonest overseers, became more and more a financial burden. Dolley was forced to continue her husband's practice of selling off parts of it, sometimes including slaves, to neighbors or speculators to raise cash. She spent the 1841–42 winter in Washington negotiating with friends, relatives, and officials and visiting Edward Coles in Philadelphia and John Jacob Astor in New York in desperate efforts to rescue her sinking finances.

Dolley returned to Montpelier in September 1842 for the last time. She began negotiations with Henry Moncure, a merchant from Richmond, for the sale of the estate, many slaves included. Quarrels and legal battles with Payne Todd and heirs of William Madison, who had died in 1843, prolonged negotiations, but Dolley, certain she could no longer afford to keep Montpelier and anxious to resume her life in Washington, left for good in December 1843. Nearly bankrupt, she settled in Washington as the new year began. The sale of Montpelier to Moncure was completed in August 1844. Payne Todd remained at partially ruined Toddsberth, attempting to maintain solvency by managing, ineptly, a few hundred acres and about thirty slaves left him after the final sale of Montpelier. More furnishings, books, and works of art had been carted to Toddsberth as Moncure took possession of the Montpelier mansion. The books were stored on shelves and the papers in a wooden desk or flat chest, supposedly to be safe for Dolley's examination and disposal, but she probably never saw them again.

Dolley was pleased to be again living in Washington, more or less comfortably, but still in desperate financial straits. Disheartened again with efforts at commercial publication of her husband's remaining papers, which included dozens of important letters from Washington himself, as well as other items of immense historical value, she took up again a long and frustrating effort to sell them to Congress. This was finally completed in 1848, for $25,000, much less than she had hoped for. It provided $5,000 in immediate cash to meet Dolley's most pressing debts—her total indebtedness exceeded $10,000—and then $20,000 in an inalienable trust to be managed by Secretary of State James Buchanan and two other Washington friends of Dolley's, the income of which would go to her during her lifetime and then to be divided between son Payne Todd and adopted daughter Annie Payne. The point of the trust was to prevent Todd from raiding it for his own purposes and thus depriving his mother of her livelihood.

Still, Dolley's life in Washington was day-to-day a social triumph. Mary Cutts, a few years after her aunt's death, in effusive recollection exclaimed:

> Her return to Washington was hailed by all—those who formerly knew her and those who desired to know this First Lady of the Land. Her house was filled morning and evening with the most distinguished of all parties. . . . It had been twenty years since she had left the city, the favorite of Society, yet she came [back] without influence or power and the citizens welcomed her return and gladly gave her the position she had left. . . . She with her gracious smile and warm heart made friends with all. . . . She had infinite tact, and always saw the good and not the evil, which exists in all. Her memory was excellent. She was noted for never forgetting a name or face.

Her next-door neighbor for two years was the British minister, Lord Ashburton, who "at the twilight hours when [Dolley] was most apt to be alone, . . . would come over and enjoy youthful reminiscences with her." When he was a young, single British diplomat in Philadelphia in the 1790s, he had married the daughter of the strikingly beautiful Anne Willing Bingham, one of the belles who, along with the Payne sisters, had brightened society in those days. Writing sentimental poems also entertained Dolley, as she took part in the popular custom of exchanging autograph epigrams.

A resolution of the House of Representatives in 1844 granted her "a seat within the Hall" whenever she chose to visit. Close friends with whom she shared official and unofficial occasions included Elizabeth Hamilton, the aged widow of Alexander, with whom Dolley renewed "the old association of their honored husbands," and Louisa Catherine Adams, whose husband, John Quincy, served in Congress throughout Dolley's residence in Washington. Dolley had known Elizabeth Hamilton fifty years earlier in Philadelphia "at Lady Washington's drawing rooms." (Martha Washington, a not-too-distant relative of Dolley's, had approved her marriage in 1794 to James Madison.) Through these old friendships, the friends and families of her husband's colleagues, and her acquaintance with younger members of Congress and current administrations, Dolley knew and enjoyed social relations with every president from Washington to Lincoln, who was a young Whig representative in Congress during the last two years of Dolley's life. She knew as well distinguished diplomats from overseas and senatorial notables from Webster, Clay, and Calhoun on down. Indeed, she created and lived out for more than half a century the style and model of "republican lady" suitable to the form of government her husband had had such a prominent role in bringing into existence.

Crisis and tragedy, though, also continued to darken her last years in Washington. In 1844, along with two hundred other dignitaries, she was the guest of President John Tyler on board a dinner cruise of the steamer *Princeton* when a misfired cannon explosion killed eight people, including two members of Tyler's cabinet. Dolley was not hurt and assisted in the care and comfort of the injured and grieving. In May 1848 an arsonist's fire broke out in her house. At four in the morning she and Annie were roused and taken downstairs and out of the house "thro' a crackling fire" by trusted slave servant Ralph Taylor. He then returned upstairs in the burning house, Dolley wrote, to rescue "trunks of papers," presumably the very ones Congress bought in a bill passed a week later.

The care and disposition of her remaining slaves remained troublesome. Some were included in the sale of Montpelier to Henry Moncure; others were deeded to Payne Todd, who freed those he had not already sold upon his death in 1852; and a few were kept as household servants in Washington. In the month before Dolley's fire, one slave, Ellen Stewart, had taken part in the attempt of seventy-six African Americans, mostly slaves in Washington and Georgetown households, to flee aboard the schooner *Pearl*, "freighted for the North by Abolitionists," Dolley explained. Paul Jennings likely also took part in the *Pearl* incident, though Dolley apparently did not know that. The attempt failed, and Ellen was jailed along with the other fugitives. Hearing "a bad account of her morals and conduct," Dolley decided to let her be "kept quietly in jail until she recovers from her six months of dissipation." Then Dolley sold Ellen for $400, money sent at once to Payne Todd in Virginia, who was desperate as always for funds to hold off his creditors. Dolley was caught pathetically in the dilemma of owning trusted slaves dependent on her, but for whom she could provide only with the money she could gain by their sale. Dolley's sale of Paul Jennings to Daniel Webster, doubtless with the proviso that Jennings would be freed soon after the sale, as was done, was one way to handle the problem. Bankruptcy or sale into continued slavery often seemed the only other alternatives.

By the spring of 1849, Dolley's strength and health began to ebb. She withdrew from social events and spent much of her time in bed, cared for by Annie and visited regularly by friends and relatives. Soothed with opium, she lapsed into semiconsciousness on July 8 and died four days later surrounded by lifelong friends and her nieces and nephews, "at peace with her maker, and with all the world, and it with her," her nephew James Madison Cutts reported. Her funeral at St. John's Episcopal Church four days later was a state occasion with all government business canceled. President Zachary Taylor, the cabinet, Supreme Court justices, and members of Congress, as well as throngs of Washington residents, attended. Her will, dividing her trust and what remained of her property after payment of her debts between her son and adopted daughter, was promptly contested by Payne Todd. It remained in dispute until both died in 1852. Payne sought desperately to sell or auction off papers, books, and anything else of value before he died. Only remnants of Dolley's possessions and papers were saved, some going to her niece Mary and other Cutts relatives and others to Annie's descendants through the husband she had recently married, Dr. James Causten. Much more was scattered through auctions in Washington and Virginia in the last settlements of the affairs of Payne Todd and Annie Payne Causten. After their deaths in 1852, the sale of Montpelier and Dolley's house on Lafayette Square, and the decay and abandonment of Toddsberth, the tangible legacies of James and Dolley Madison were no more. At last with the opening of the restored mansion in 2008, Montpelier can carry on their stories once again.

Source Notes

Sources for each section are listed together, in general in the order in which they appear in the text.

Return to "Books and Farm, to Tranquility and Independence" (pp. 1–4)
Addresses to the Madisons in the *National Intelligencer,* Mar. 4, 5, 10, 1817; TJ to JM, Apr. 15, 1817, John Adams to TJ, May 16, 1817, in Brant, *JM* 6:418–20, and Ketcham, *JM,* 611; Eliza Collins Lee to DPM, Mar. 4, 1817, W. Johnson to DPM, Mar. 16, 1817, *LDPM,* 216, 225–26.

Montpelier: The Mansion in 1817 (pp. 4–9)
Cutts, "Life and Times of DPTM"; Green and Miller, *Building a President's House;* Allgor, *DPM,* 239, 345.

John Payne Todd (pp. 9–14)
Allgor, *DPM,* 112, 145, 352, 400–405; DPM to Anna Cutts, May 5, 1812, Sally M. Yrujo to DPM, June 20, 1812, *LDPM,* 165–67, and passim; Ketcham, *JM,* 614–16; Cutts, "Life and Times of DPTM"; Moore, *The Madisons,* 349–66.

Madison Family Visitors (pp. 14–17)
Chapman, "Descendants of Ambrose Madison"; Miller, *Antebellum Orange;* "Madison Family Tree," in Hutchinson, *Papers of JM* 1:212; Ketcham, *JM,* 370–72, 375–76.

Payne and Cutts Family Visitors (pp. 17–21)
DPM to Anna Cutts, Apr. 8, 1812, to Mary Allen, Feb. 25, 1834, Lucy Todd to DPM, Apr. 18, 1812, *LDPM,* 160–63, 303, and passim; Ketcham, *JM,* 377–83, 617–19; JM to Richard D. Cutts, Jan. 4, 1829, *Letters of JM* 4:1–2; Roberts, *Ladies of Liberty,* 148; Allgor, *DPM;* Cutts, "Life and Times of DPTM."

James K. Paulding's Impressions (pp. 21–24)
Ketcham, "An Unpublished Sketch of James Madison by James K. Paulding," 432–37.

Daily Life at Montpelier (pp. 24–30)
DPM to Anna Cutts, Apr. 3, July 23, 1818, *LDPM,* 228–32; Cutts, "Life and Times of DPTM"; M. B. Smith to Mrs. Boyd, Aug. 17, 1828, and diary, Aug. 4, 1809, in Smith, *First Forty Years of Washington Society,* 232–37, 81–83; Ketcham, *JM,* 620–21; JM to J. K. Paulding, Mar. 10, 1827, to Jared Sparks, May 5, 1827, *Letters of JM* 3:567–69, 582–83.

Dolley's Preoccupations (pp. 30–32)
DPM to Anna Cutts, Apr. 3, 1818, JM to DPM, July 30, 1818, *LDPM,* 228, 232; JM to Robert Walsh, Dec. 22, 1827, *Letters of JM* 3:603–5; Ketcham, *JM,* 621.

Virginia Agriculture in Decline (pp. 33–35)
Hyland, *Montpelier and the Madisons,* 79–84; JM to Richard Peters, May 15, 1811, in Rutland, *Papers of JM, Presidential Ser.* 3:222; JM, "Address to the Agricultural Society of Albemarle," May 12, 1818, *Letters of JM* 3:63–95.

Further Challenges to the Virginia Economy (pp. 36–38)
Dunn, *Dominion of Memories;* JM to James Monroe, May 5, 1821, *Letters of JM* 3:97–98; JM to TJ, Feb. 24, 1826, to Frances Wright, Sept. 1, 1825, to N. P. Trist, Jan. 29, 1828, *Selected Writings of JM,* 313, 322–26.

Slavery, That "Dreadful Calamity" (pp. 38–47)
JM to Robert Evans, June 15, 1819, to Thomas R. Dew, Feb. 23, 1833, *Selected Writings of JM,* 314–21; Ketcham, *JM,* 625–30; JM to Monroe, Feb. 10 and 23, 1820, to Frances Wright, Sept. 1, 1825, *Letters of JM* 3:164–69, 188–90, 224–29; Ketcham, "The Dictates of Conscience: Edward Coles and Slavery," 46–72; Martineau, *Retrospect of Western Travel* 2:191; Chambers, *Murder at Montpelier,* 200–201; JM to Edward Coles, Oct. 3, 1834, in McCoy, *Last of the Fathers,* 258–59; Allgor, *DPM,* 183–84.

Continuing Public Involvement (pp. 48–57)
Ketcham, *JM,* 630–36; JM to Monroe, Oct. 2 and 28, 1818, Feb. 13 and 18, 1818, Oct. 30, 1818, Aug. 5, 1824, to Richard Rush, Nov. 13, 1823, to Lafayette, Nov. 25, 1820, *Writings of JM* 8:414–23, 9:157–66, 197–98, 35–36; Notes ca. 1820, JM to J. Q. Adams, Dec. 23, 1817, to Spencer Roane, Sept. 2, 1819, May 6, June 29, 1821, ibid., 8:447–53, 399–401, 9:56–68, 137–44; TJ to Roane, Mar. 9, June 27, 1821, Roane to JM, Apr. 27, June 6, 1821, in Brant, *JM* 6:433–34; TJ to J. Morse, Mar. 6, 1822, to JM, Feb. 25, 1822, in Ketcham, *JM,* 634–35; JM to TJ, Mar. 5, 1822, to Morse, Feb. 16, 1822, to T. McKenney, May 2 and 14, 1825, Feb. 26, Mar. 27, 1826, *Letters of JM* 3:159–61, 487, 490, 515–16, 522; DPM to Phoebe Morris, Aug. 16, 1812, *LDPM,* 171; JM, "Talk to the Indians," Aug. 9, 1812, in Rutland, *Papers of JM, Presidential Ser.* 4:437–8; JM to T. Cooper, Mar. 23, 1824, to Clay, Mar. 22, Apr. 24, 1832, to J. Cabell, Sept. 18, Oct. 30, 1828, to N. P. Trist, May 29, 1832, *Writings of JM* 9:177–87, 316–40, 472–82; Brant, *JM* 6:473–74.

Virginia Convention of 1829 (pp. 58–66)
Ketcham, *JM,* 636–40; Brant, *JM* 6:461–67; McCoy, *Last of the Fathers,* 240–52; Dunn, *Dominion of Memories,* 155–70; DPM to John C. Payne, Dec. 4, 1829, to Anna Cutts, June 6, Dec. 28, 1829, Jan. 1, 1830, to Dolley Cutts, Mar. 10, 1830, *LDPM,* 278–85; JM, speech, Dec. 2, 1829, and Notes on Suffrage and Majority Governments, 1829? and 1833, *Selected Writings of JM,* 349–60; JM to C. J. Ingersoll, Jan. 8, 1830, to Lafayette, Feb. 2, 1830, *Letters of JM* 4:57–61.

Nullification, "a Deadly Poison" (pp. 66–73)
Ketcham, *JM,* 640–46; Brant, *JM* 6:468–500; McCoy, *Last of the Fathers,* 130–70; JM to R. Hayne, Apr. 4, 1830, to M. I. Hurlbut, May 30, 1830, to Edward Everett, Aug. 28, 1830 (published in the *North American Review,* Oct. 1830), *Writings of JM* 9:370–403; Marshall to Joseph

Story, Oct. 15, 1830, in Johnson, *Papers of Marshall* 11:420; JM to Andrew Stevenson, Nov. 27, 1830, to Reynolds Chapman, Jan. 6, 1831, to N. P. Trist, Dec. 31, 1831, May and Dec. 23, 1832, to Clay, Mar. 1, Apr. 2, June 1833, to W. C. Rives, Mar. 12, 1833, *Writings of JM* 9:411–37, 471–91, 511–18, and *Letters of JM* 4:567.

Fears and Sorrows at Montpelier (pp. 73–78)
DPM to Payne Todd, Apr. 27, 1828, July 7, 1832, to Dolley Cutts, Mar. 10, 1830, to Mary Cutts, Jan. 5, Sept. 16, 1831, to Elizabeth Coles, Apr. 8, 1831, to Frances Lear, Mar. 1832, to Anna Cutts, May 15, Aug. 4, 1832, to Richard Cutts, Aug. 6, 1832, *LDPM*, 174–75, 184–85, 290–97; "Estate of Nelly Conway Madison," 1829, Montpelier Foundation; John Marshall to James K. Marshall, Sept. 15, Oct. 3, 1832, in Johnson, *Papers of Marshall* 12:235–39; Allgor, *DPM*, 373–76.

Establishing the University of Virginia (pp. 78–98)
Bruce, *History of the University of Virginia*, vols. 1, 2; Adams, *TJ and the University of Virginia;* Ketcham, *JM*, 646–58; Brant, *JM* 6:450–67; Malone, *TJ: Sage*, 233–82, 365–443; Minutes of the Board of Visitors, May 5, July 28, Oct. 28, 1817, Central College subscription list, Feb. 21, 1818, and TJ, JM, and others to Va. House of Delegates, Jan. 6, 1818, *TJ-Cabell Letters*, 393–411; JM to DPM, July 30, 1818, Nov. 30, 1821, Dec. 4 and 8, 1826, *LDPM*, 232, 245–46, 265–68; Cabell to TJ, Dec. 19, 1817, Jan. 12, Mar. 15, 1818, Feb. 22, Mar. 2 and 8, Apr. 17, 1819, TJ to Cabell, Feb. 26, 1818, and Report of the Commissioners, Aug. 4, 1818, Minutes of Central College Board, Feb. 26, 1819, and of Board of Visitors, Oct. 4, 1819, Oct. 3, 1820, *TJ-Cabell Letters*, 89–132, 165–76, 432–47, 451–55; JM to TJ, Mar. 6, 1819, to F. Beasley, Dec. 22, 1824, to E. Everett, Mar. 19, 1823, to TJ, Sept. 1824, *Letters of JM* 3:126, 306–7, and *Writings of JM* 9:202–7, 212; JM to TJ, Sept. 10, Oct. 9, 1824, Jan. 15, Feb. 8, 1825, TJ to JM, Feb. 1, 1825, Feb. 17, 1826, in Smith, *Corres. TJ and JM* 3:1898–1901, 1904–5, 1921–26, 1964–68; TJ to Ellen Coolidge, Nov. 14, 1825, to T. J. Randolph, Feb. 8 and 11, 1826, in Betts and Bear, *Family Letters of TJ*, 460, 469–70; Cabell to TJ, Mar. 16, 1825, TJ to Cabell, Apr. 15, 1825, and Rector's Report, Oct. 7, 1825, *TJ-Cabell Letters*, 343, 350, 484–85; University of Virginia, Minutes of Board of Visitors, UVa Library; JM to DPM, Dec. 4, 8, and 14, 1826, DPM to JM, Dec. 5, 1826, July 16, 1827, *LDPM*, 265–72; JM to W. T. Barry, Aug. 14, 1822, *Selected Writings of JM*, 307–11.

"I May Be Thought to Have Outlived Myself" (pp. 99–101)
JM to E. Coles, Aug. 27, 1834, to N. P. Trist, May 29, 1832, to Andrew Stevenson, Nov. 20, 1832, *Writings of JM* 9:542, 480–81; JM to J. Cabell, Sept. 18, Oct. 15, 1828, *Letters of JM* 3:636–37, 647–48; DPM to Mary Cutts, Sept. 16, 1831, to Anna Cutts, May 15, 1832, to Mary and Dolley Cutts, Aug. 1, Sept. 9, July 20, 1833, Dec. 2, 1834, to J. P. Todd, July 20, 1833, *LDPM*, 293, 295, 299, and Shulman, *Dolley Madison Digital Edition;* Brant, *JM* 6:489–90.

Living and Making History (pp. 101–105)
JM to Jacob Gideon, Jan. 28, Feb. 20, Aug. 20, 1818, to Jared Sparks, Oct. 30, 1830, to J. Q. Adams, Oct. 2, 1818, June 7, 1819, June 19, 1820, to Joseph Gales, Aug. 26, 1821, to E. Everett, Mar. 19, 1823, to Jared Elliot, Feb. 14 and Nov. 1827, to J. K. Paulding, Apr. 1831, *Writings of JM* 8:408–17, 438–39, 9:25–29, 128–29, 270–71, 291–92, 451–54; E. Everett to JM, June 9, 1835,

in Everett Papers, Mass. Hist. Soc.; Proctor, "After Dinner Anecdotes of James Madison," 553–55; Hutchinson, *Papers of JM* 1:xv–xxiv.

Lafayette Comes to Virginia (pp. 105–113)
Brandon, *Lafayette Guest of the Nation* 3:128–36; Levasseur, *Lafayette in America;* JM to DPM, Nov. 5, 1824, *LDPM,* 255–56; TJ to Lafayette, Oct. 9, 1824, Lafayette to TJ, Oct. 1, 1824, in Chinard, *Letters of Lafayette and Jefferson,* 421–27; Eckhardt, *Fanny Wright,* 74–84; Brant, *JM* 6:442–44; JM to TJ, Oct. 17, 1784, in Hutchison, *Papers of JM* 8:120–21; Brant, *JM* 6:442–44; JM to Frances Wright, Sept. 1, 1825, to Lafayette, Nov. 26, 1825, *Letters of JM* 3:498, 543.

Farewell to Thomas Jefferson (pp. 114–127)
Crawford, *Twilight at Monticello,* 210–33; Malone, *TJ: Sage,* 447–62; Smith, *Corres. TJ and JM* 3:1943–51; Ketcham, "A Letter of John Quincy Adams," 172–82; JM to TJ, Oct. 14, 1825, Feb. 24, 1826, TJ to JM, Oct. 18, 1825, Feb. 17, 1826, in Smith, *Corres. TJ and JM* 3:1941–42, 1964–68; Lafayette to TJ, Feb. 24, 1826, in Chinard, *Letters of Lafayette and Jefferson,* 437; Septimia Randolph, recollections, Montpelier Foundation, 2008; JM to Washington Comm., June 20, 1826, *Letters of JM* 4:565.

Jefferson's Death and Eulogies (pp. 127–132)
Crawford, *Twilight at Monticello,* 236–46; Malone, *TJ: Sage,* 495–99; TJ to JM, Feb. 17, May 3, 1826, to Board of Visitors, Apr. 3 and 21, 1826, JM to TJ, Feb. 24, May 6, 1826, R. Dunglison to JM, July 1, 1826, N. P. Trist to JM, July 4, 1826, JM to Trist, July 6, 1826, in Smith, *Corres. TJ and JM* 3:1966–73; DPM to J. P. Todd, July 6, 1826, *LDPM,* 264–65; JM to Richard Peters, Sept. 8, 1826, to S. H. Smith, Nov. 4, 1826, to Lafayette, Nov. 1826, *Letters of JM* 3:527–40.

Old Friends Pass: James Monroe and Others (pp. 133–140)
Chapman, "Descendants of Ambrose Madison"; Ammon, *James Monroe,* 405–6 and passim; Phoebe Morris to DPM, Jan. 19, 1824, DPM to Anna Cutts, Jan. 25, 1830, *LDPM,* 251, 284; Monroe to JM, June 16, 1826, May 18, 1830, Apr. 11, 1831, in Hamilton, *Writings of Monroe* 7:85, 177–78, 231–34; JM to Monroe, May 18, 1830, Apr. 21, 1831, to Tench Ringgold, July 12, 1831, *Letters of JM* 4:82–83, 178–79, 189–90; Marshall to Monroe, Mar. 7, 1825, Monroe to Marshall, Mar. 10, 1825, in Hamilton, *Writings of Monroe* 7:55–56.

The Founding Era Passes (pp. 140–143)
JM to J. K. Paulding, Apr. 1831, *Letters of JM* 4:173–77; TJ to Walter Jones, Jan. 2, 1814, in Koch and Peden, *Life and Selected Writings of Jefferson,* 163–64; JM to J. G. Jackson, Dec. 27, 1821, to F. Beasley, Nov. 10, 1825, *Writings of JM* 9:77, 229–31.

Next-Generation Madisonians (pp. 143–145)
Richard Rush Papers, Hist. Soc. Pa.; Ketcham, "The Dictates of Conscience: Edward Coles and Slavery," 46–72; McCoy, *Last of the Fathers,* 308–69; Kersh, *Dreams of a More Perfect Union,* esp. 23–197.

"The Last of the Great Lights of the Revolution Has Sunk below the Horizon" (pp. 146–156)
Martineau, *Retrospect of Western Travel* 1:150–51, 189–99; Marshall to J. Q. Adams, Aug. 9, 1831, Adams to Marshall, Sept. 17, 1831, in Johnson, *Papers of Marshall* 12:96–99.

Advising the Younger Generation (pp. 156–164)
DPM to Mary Cutts, Mar. 10 and Oct. 1835, J. M. Cutts to DPM, Sept. 4, 1835, DPM to Dolley Cutts, Aug. 11, 1833, Feb. 10, May 11, and Oct. 1835, to R. D. Cutts, Oct. 23, 1835, to Lucy Todd, Oct. 23, 1835, *LDPM,* 309–16; JM to Ohio Comm., Mar. 25, 1835, to Hubbard Taylor, Aug. 15, 1835, to R. D. Cutts, Sept. 12, 1835, to Andrew Jackson, Oct. 11, 1835, *Letters of JM* 4:377–84; DPM to Anna Cutts, Aug. 4, 1832, to Mary Cutts, Mar. 13, Aug. 1, Nov. 4, 1833, Dec. 2, 1834, to Richard Cutts, Aug. 11, 1833, *LDPM,* 296–308; Ellen Coolidge to TJ, Aug. 1, 1825, in Betts and Bear, *Family Letters of TJ,* 454–55; Malone, *TJ: Sage,* 502–3; Dunn, *Dominion of Memories,* 31–84.

The Last Visit to James Madison's Montpelier (pp. 164–171)
Chapman, "Descendants of Ambrose Madison"; Ingersoll, "A Visit to Mr. Madison at Montpelier, May 2, 1836."

Death and Eulogies of James Madison (pp. 171–176)
DPM to Lucy Todd, May 5, 1836, Annie Payne note, May 1836, in Shulman, *Dolley Madison Digital Edition;* JM to G. Tucker, June 27, 1836, in Library of Congress "American Memory" Web site; Jennings, *A Colored Man's Reminiscences of JM,* 18–20; Ketcham, *JM,* 668–71; Brant, *JM* 6:518 52; Adams, *Lives of Madison and Monroe,* 101–4; JM, "Advice to My Country," 1834, facsimile copy, Brant, *JM* 6:530; JM to Orange County Comm., 1835, *Letters of JM* 4:389–90.

Postscript: Dolley Madison, 1836–1849 (pp. 177–181)
LDPM, 317–27; Allgor, *DPM,* 377–408; Cutts, "Life and Times of DPTM," 73–84; Coté, *Strength and Honor;* Moore, *The Madisons;* letters from and to DPM, 1836–49, *LDPM,* 327–91.

Bibliography

ABBREVIATIONS

JM   James Madison   VMHB   Virginia Magazine of History and Biography
DPM   Dolley Madison   VQR   Virginia Quarterly Review
TJ   Thomas Jefferson

PRIMARY SOURCES

Betts, E. M., and J. A. Bear, eds. *The Family Letters of Thomas Jefferson*. Columbia, MO, 1966.

Chinard, Gilbert, ed. *The Letters of Lafayette and Jefferson*. Baltimore, 1929.

Cutts, "Life and Times of DPTM"   Mary E. E. Cutts. "The Life and Times of Dolley Payne Todd Madison," ca. 1850. Transcribed by Lee Langston-Harrison, Montpelier, VA, 2002–5.

"Estate of Nelly Conway Madison," 1829. Montpelier Foundation.

Everett, Edward. Papers. Massachusetts Historical Society, Boston.

Hamilton, Stanislaus M., ed. *The Writings of James Monroe*. Vol. 7. New York, 1903.

Hutchinson, W. T., et al., eds. *The Papers of James Madison*. 17 vols. (Chicago and Charlottesville, VA, 1962–91).

Ingersoll, Charles J. "A Visit to Mr. Madison at Montpelier, May 2, 1836." *Washington Globe*, Aug. 6, 1836. In Peter Force Scrapbook, UVa Special Collections, MSS9911.

Johnson, Herbert A., et al., eds. *The Papers of John Marshall*. 12 vols. Chapel Hill, NC, 1974–2006.

Ketcham, Ralph, ed. "A Letter of John Quincy Adams." *VMHB* 66 (1958): 172–82.

———. "An Unpublished Sketch of James Madison by James K. Paulding." *VMHB* 67 (1959):432–37.

Koch, Adrienne, and William Peden, eds. *The Life and Selected Writings of Thomas Jefferson*. New York, 1993.

LDPM   David B. Mattern and Holly C. Shulman, eds. *The Selected Letters of Dolley Payne Madison*. Charlottesville, VA, 2003.

Letters of JM   William C. Rives and Philip R. Fendall, eds. *Letters and Other Writings of James Madison*. 4 vols. Philadelphia, 1865.

Levasseur, Auguste. *Lafayette in America in 1824 and 1825*. Trans. J. D. Goodman. Philadelphia, 1825.

Madison, James. Papers. Library of Congress, "American Memory" Web site.

Martineau, Harriet. *Retrospect of Western Travel.* 2 vols. New York, 1838.

Proctor, C. C., ed. "After Dinner Anecdotes of James Madison: Excerpts from Jared Sparks' Journal for 1829–1831." *VMHB* 60 (1952): 255–65.

Randolph, Septimia. Recollections. Montpelier Foundation, 2008.

Rush, Richard. Papers. Historical Society of Pennsylvania, Philadelphia.

Rutland, Robert A., et al., eds. *The Papers of James Madison, Presidential Series.* Charlottesville, VA, 1984–.

Selected Writings of JM   Ralph Ketcham, ed. *The Selected Writings of James Madison.* Indianapolis, 2006.

Shulman, Holly C., ed. *Dolley Madison Digital Edition.* Charlottesville, VA, 2006.

Smith, *Corres. TJ and JM*   James M. Smith, ed. *The Republic of Letters: The Correspondence between Thomas Jefferson and James Madison.* 3 vols. New York, 1995.

University of Virginia. Minutes of Board of Visitors. UVa Library, Charlottesville.

Writings of JM   Gaillard Hunt, ed. *The Writings of James Madison.* 9 vols. New York, 1900–1910.

SECONDARY SOURCES

Adams, Herbert B. *Thomas Jefferson and the University of Virginia.* Washington, DC, 1888.

Adams, J. Q. *The Lives of James Madison and James Monroe.* Boston, 1850.

Allgor, *DPM*   Allgor, Catherine. *A Perfect Union: Dolley Payne Madison and the Creation of the American Nation.* New York, 2006.

Ammon, Harry. *James Monroe: The Quest for National Identity.* New York, 1971.

Brandon, Edgar E. *Lafayette Guest of the Nation.* Vol. 3. Oxford, Ohio, 1957.

Brant, *JM*   Brant, Irving. *James Madison: Commander-in-Chief, 1812–1836.* Indianapolis, 1961.

Bruce, Philip A. *History of the University of Virginia, 1819–1919: The Lengthened Shadow of One Man.* Vols. 1, 2. New York, 1920.

Chambers, Douglas B. *Murder at Montpelier: Igbo Africans in Virginia.* Jackson, MS, 2005.

Chapman, C. Thomas. "Descendants of Ambrose Madison, Grandfather of President James Madison, Jr." Montpelier Foundation, 2005.

Coté, Richard. *Strength and Honor: The Life of Dolley Madison.* Mount Pleasant, SC, 2005.

Crawford, Alan Pell. *Twilight at Monticello: The Final Years of Thomas Jefferson.* New York, 2008.

Dunn, Susan. *Dominion of Memories: Jefferson, Madison, and the Decline of Virginia.* New York, 2007.

Eckhardt, Celia. *Fanny Wright, Rebel in America.* Cambridge, MA, 1984.

Green, Bryan Clark, and Ann L. Miller, with Conover Hunt. *Building a President's House: The Construction of James Madison's Montpelier.* Montpelier Foundation, 2007.

Howe, Daniel Walker. *What Hath God Wrought: The Transformation of America, 1815–1848.* New York, 2007.

Hyland, Matthew G. *Montpelier and the Madisons: House, Home, and American Heritage.* Charleston, SC, 2007.

Jennings, Paul. *A Colored Man's Reminiscences of James Madison*. Brooklyn, NY, 1865.

Kersh, Rogan. *Dreams of a More Perfect Union*. Ithaca, NY, 2001.

Ketcham, *JM*   Ketcham, Ralph. *James Madison: A Biography*. New York, 1971; rept. Charlottesville, VA, 1990.

Ketcham, Ralph. "The Dictates of Conscience: Edward Coles and Slavery." *VQR* 36 (1960):46–72.

Malone, *TJ: Sage*   Malone, Dumas. *The Sage of Monticello*. Vol. 6 of *Jefferson and His Time*. Boston 1981.

McCoy, Drew R. *The Last of the Fathers: James Madison and the Republican Legacy*. Cambridge, MA, 1989

Miller, Ann. *Antebellum Orange: The Pre-Civil War Homes, Public Buildings, and Historic Sites of Orange County, Virginia*. Orange County Historical Society, Inc., 1988.

Moore, Virginia. *The Madisons, a Biography*. New York, 1979.

Roberts, Cokie. *Ladies of Liberty: The Women Who Shaped Our Nation*. New York, 2008.

Smith, Margaret B. *The First Forty Years of Washington Society*. Ed. Gaillard Hunt. New York, 1906.

TJ-Cabell Letters   *Early History of the University of Virginia as Contained in the Letters of Thomas Jefferson and Joseph C. Cabell*. Richmond, 1856.

Wilentz, Sean. *The Rise of Democracy: Jefferson to Lincoln*. New York, 2005.

Index